THE DOCTRINE OF ASSURANCE

THE DOCTRINE OF ASSURANCE

With Special Reference to John Wesley

by

ARTHUR S. YATES
B.A., B.D. (LOND.), PH.D. (LEEDS)

WIPF & STOCK · Eugene, Oregon

Wipf and Stock Publishers
199 W 8th Ave, Suite 3
Eugene, OR 97401

The Doctrine of Assurance
With Special Reference to John Wesley
By Yates, Arthur S.
Copyright©1952 Methodist Publishing - Epworth Press
ISBN 13: 978-1-4982-0504-7
Publication date 1/15/2015
Previously published by Epworth Press, 1952

Every effort has been made to trace the current copyright owner of this publication but without success. If you have any information or interest in the copyright, please contact the publishers.

TO
EDNA, MY WIFE
AND TO
MAUREEN, SHEILA,
DAVID AND KENNETH

CONTENTS

PREFACE ix
FOREWORD: By Rev. Dr C. Ryder Smith . . . xi
SUMMARY xiii

Part One
Assurance in the Experience of the Eighteenth Century

1. THE ESSENCE OF WESLEY'S ALDERSGATE EXPERIENCE . 3
2. 24th MAY 1738—AN END AND A BEGINNING . . . 12
3. THE EARLY INFLUENCE OF THE MORAVIANS . . . 20
4. A VISIT TO GERMANY 31
5. THE TESTIMONY OF THE EARLY METHODISTS . . . 39

Part Two
Assurance in its Theological Setting

1. 'A NEW GOSPEL'? 53
2. HOW THE DOCTRINE GREW 61
3. THE MAIN FEATURES OF WESLEY'S TEACHING . . 72
4. THE DOCTRINE EXPRESSED IN SONG 82
5. THE SPIRIT'S WITNESS IN CHARLES WESLEY'S HYMNS . 91

Part Three
Assurance in the New Testament

1. THE BIBLE AND THE WESLEYS 105
2. THE DIRECT WITNESS 111
3. THE INDIRECT WITNESS 121
4. DEGREES OF ASSURANCE 128
5. WAS WESLEY'S EXPOSITION ADEQUATE? . . . 133
6. THE APOSTOLIC CHURCH 139

Part Four
Assurance in the History of the Church

1. THE EARLY FATHERS 149
2. THE MEDIEVAL CHURCH 157
3. THE REFORMERS 163
4. THE SEVENTEENTH CENTURY 171

Part Five
Assurance and its Validity

1. THE CHARGE OF 'ENTHUSIASM' 179
2. THE INDICTMENT OF 'HERESY' 185
3. WAS WESLEY'S DOCTRINE ORTHODOX? . . . 189
4. THE DANGERS OF 'STILLNESS' 198
5. THE RELEVANCE OF MYSTICISM 204
6. THE VALIDITY OF AN INNER SENSE OF CERTAINTY . . 210

POSTSCRIPT 219
BIBLIOGRAPHY 223
INDEX OF NAMES 229
INDEX OF SUBJECTS 233
INDEX OF BIBLICAL REFERENCES 241

PREFACE

THIS is the first book, as far as I know, to offer a comprehensive survey of the Doctrine of Assurance. When I began this study, I inquired on both sides of the Atlantic for literature on the subject. The answer was that Assurance had been briefly treated in some books of theology and in pamphlets. That was all! Yet Assurance, or the 'Witness of the Spirit', is one of the distinctive doctrines of Methodism—a doctrine which, as Dr H. B. Workman says, is 'the fundamental contribution of Methodism to the life and thought of the Church'.

I did not realize at the beginning how rich and rewarding this research was going to be. It soon became clear that the doctrine had ramifications that went far and wide in the realm of religion. My chief difficulty was to decide what to leave out. Many interesting bypaths have tempted me to wander from the highway fixed by the purpose and scope of this book. As far as Assurance is concerned, however, I have tried to leave out nothing that is vital to its understanding or its exposition. I have attempted to write a book which, I trust, will prove to be not only sound in the treatment of its subject, but also interesting to read. This twofold aim has determined the arrangement of these pages.

The 'jumping-off' ground, so to speak, is the eighteenth century—the age which offers the clearest evidence, in practice and in theory, for the Doctrine of Assurance. Part One presents Assurance in the experience of 'living witnesses'; while Part Two expresses this experience in terms of theology. Wesley defended the doctrine by reference to the Bible and to the Christian tradition. Part Three, therefore, deals with the biblical foundation of Wesley's teaching; while Part Four briefly traces the Spirit's witness in the history of the Church. Difficulties still remain; and these are tackled in Part Five.

This book owes much to many scholars. The footnotes themselves are evidence of that. But I must also mention here indebtedness of a more personal nature. I am grateful for the encouragement given by Professor L. E. Brown and Dr D. E. Easson, of Leeds University, where my research was rewarded by the Degree of Doctor of Philosophy. During the initial stages of this study, I had helpful conversations or correspondence with Dr Wilbert F. Howard, then Principal of Handsworth

College, Dr W. Edwin Sangster, and Dr Alfred C. Lamb.

I had the privilege of access to many libraries, including those at most of the Methodist Theological Colleges. The Rev. J. T. Wilkinson, M.A., B.D., kindly introduced me to the collection of early Methodist documents at Hartley-Victoria College, Manchester. The typescript was ably criticized by my friend and former Principal, Dr C. Ryder Smith, who has since increased my indebtedness by writing the Foreword. The typescript was also examined in some detail by Dr Sydney Cave, Principal of New College, London, Dr Henry Bett, Dr W. F. Lofthouse, Dr J. E. Rattenbury, and the Rev. J. Baines Atkinson, B.D.

On Parts One and Two, I had the benefit of many valuable comments from Dr Sydney G. Dimond, the Rev. Frank Baker, B.A., B.D., Secretary of the Methodist Historical Society, and the Rev. John C. Bowmer, M.A., B.D. Part Three was read by Dr J. A. Findlay and by the Rev. C. E. B. Cranfield, M.A., of Durham University, whose criticism enriched the work of revision. Comments made by the Rev. E. H. Robertson, M.A., B.Sc., Assistant Head of Religious Broadcasting, helped me in re-writing the chapter on the 'Early Fathers'. The Rev. E. Gordon Rupp, M.A., B.D., of Richmond College, gave advice on the chapter dealing with the 'Reformers'. For relevant data in the medieval period, I am grateful to Professor H. Francis Davis, the Vice-Rector of Oscott Roman Catholic College, Birmingham, though he does not accept my general interpretation. Dr. R Scott Frayn, Dr W. Lawson Jones and the Rev. W. L. Doughty, B.A., B.D., carefully read Part Five and offered many useful suggestions.

Much time and thought have been given by Miss Joyce M. Nye, B.A., in drawing up the excellent indexes. For most careful proof-reading and for much valuable help, I am indebted to the Rev. H. Guy Sanders, M.A., B.D., and the Rev. R. H. Copestake. Assistance in typing has been kindly given by Miss G. M. Martin and Miss M. F. Fordham.

I owe more than I can say here to Mr A. S. Davidson, of Liverpool, and to Mr W. H. Cattmull, of St Neots, whose kindness over the years has helped to make this book possible. My wife's literary gifts have always been at my disposal. In the interests of this study, she and my family have made many personal sacrifices for which I am more than grateful.

ARTHUR S. YATES

FOREWORD

By the Rev. Dr C Ryder Smith
Formerly Principal of Richmond College
and
Professor of Theology in the University of London

'The Spirit Himself beareth witness with our spirit that we are children of God.' This is the classic text for the Methodist doctrine of 'Assurance'. Of course, during the many centuries between Paul and Wesley there were those who knew what it was to live in fellowship with Christ through the Spirit, but the doctrine never took its right place in theology. When Wesley preached it, Bishop Butler, speaking for the eighteenth century, called it a 'very horrid' doctrine. Now, however, it has become more than respectable. Indeed, the 'I—Thou' theology, in its Christian form, is just its exposition. In particular, this vindicates the early Methodists' claim that their experience of fellowship with God in Christ was self-authenticating. In reply to the challenge, 'How *can* a sinner *know* his sins on earth forgiven?', all they could say was, 'What *we* have felt and seen, with confidence *we* tell'. But our 'I—Thou' theologians tell us that this answer was just right. Of course, difficulties still attend the doctrine, but this is so with all truths.

It was high time that somebody gave us an up-to-date study of the doctrine of 'Assurance' in its various aspects, and this is what Dr Yates does in his excellent book. It is a special pleasure to commend this volume, for it is written by a friend whom it was once my privilege to teach.

C. Ryder Smith

SUMMARY

PART ONE

ASSURANCE IN THE EXPERIENCE OF THE EIGHTEENTH CENTURY

Chapter 1. *The Essence of Wesley's Aldersgate Experience*

Is Wesley's religious crisis on 24th May 1738 rightly termed 'Conversion'? After considering the views of certain scholars, the question is answered in the negative. The Aldersgate experience was *not*: (1) an initial resolve to lead a holy life; (2) a dedication to the service of God; (3) the dawning of compassion for his fellows; (4) a marked intellectual change. Further evidence shows that on 24th May Wesley experienced the 'Witness of the Spirit', on which he based his Doctrine of Assurance.

Chapter 2. *24th May, 1738—An End and a Beginning*

Wesley's Aldersgate experience was the end of his search for certainty. His writings reveal that assurance had been his quest for many years—in England and in Georgia. A weighing of the diverse evidence leads to the view that Wesley's spiritual crisis remained a powerful factor in his later life and thought.

Chapter 3. *The Early Influence of the Moravians*

The Moravians—on the *Simmonds*, in Georgia and in England—wielded a powerful influence over Wesley. The reality of their simple faith and Spangenberg's teaching on the 'Witness of the Spirit' helped to prepare him for his Aldersgate experience. Peter Böhler also stressed this need of Christian certainty. Wesley demanded, and received, biblical and experimental proof. Wesley, at last convinced, waited and prayed for assurance.

Chapter 4. *A Visit to Germany*

Wesley's visit to Germany both confirmed and corrected his ideas of Assurance. He gleaned valuable information from 'living proofs'. In assessing this visit, we observe that: (1) Wesley's esteem for the Moravians inclined him to credulity; (2) Böhler had over-simplified Moravian theology; (3) Assurance was not essential to salvation; (4) the Spirit's witness was variously experienced and estimated.

Chapter 5. The Testimony of the Early Methodists

Assurance is first traced in the experience of George Whitefield and Charles Wesley. The 'testimonies' of other early Methodists, some of which reflect the Wesleys' influence, reveal various aspects of Christian certainty. Subjective tendencies are usually checked by lives of virtue and service.

PART TWO
ASSURANCE IN ITS THEOLOGICAL SETTING

Chapter 1. 'A New Gospel'?

In what sense was Peter Böhler's teaching 'a new gospel'? Some answers are considered and dismissed. Features of Böhler's theology, which were new to Wesley, include: (1) its simplicity; (2) Justification by faith *alone*; (3) *instantaneous* conversion; (4) a personal faith in a crucified Christ.

Chapter 2. How the Doctrine Grew

In Wesley's earlier writings, Assurance is essential to salvation. Later modifications allow 'exempt cases', 'infinite degrees of seeing God', until in 1768 a 'consciousness of acceptance' is not deemed essential. The Spirit's witness distinguishes a 'son' from a 'servant'. Assurance remains, however, 'a common privilege' to be sought by all.

Chapter 3. The Main Features of Wesley's Teaching

Wesley's sermons of 1746 and 1767 on Romans 8[16] outline his doctrine of Assurance. Certain inconsistencies in his writings are noted. The main aspects of his teaching include: (1) degrees of Assurance; (2) the Direct Witness; (3) the Indirect Witness; (4) its availability for all.

Chapter 4. The Doctrine Expressed in Song

Much theology is expressed in Methodist hymns. John Wesley's role as editor is assessed and Assurance is traced in his translations. Special attention is given to the 'conversion hymns' or to those closely linked to the Wesleys' transformation in May 1738.

Chapter 5. The Spirit's Witness in Charles Wesley's Hymns

Other hymns by Charles Wesley bearing on Assurance are studied under various theological heads. Assurance is shown to be no isolated tenet, but based on Scripture and linked to the cardinal doctrines of the universal Church.

SUMMARY

PART THREE

ASSURANCE IN THE NEW TESTAMENT

Chapter 1. The Bible and the Wesleys

For the Wesleys, the Bible was the supreme authority. They practised 'Bible dipping', however; and, of course, had only slight apprecatiion of 'progressive revelation'. The original was infallible. Yet, Wesley's New Testament translation and *Notes* improve on the Authorized Version (1611) and anticipate in parts the Revised Version (1881). A list is given of the New Testament Greek words bearing on Assurance.

Chapter 2. The Direct Witness

We consider the main texts on which Wesley based the Direct Witness of the Spirit. The chief passage is Romans 8^{16}, with which is linked Galatians 4^6. These and other texts are examined in the light of modern scholarship, and are generally approved as providing a sound biblical foundation.

Chapter 3. The Indirect Witness

This aspect of assurance is 'laid in those numerous texts ... which describe the marks of the children of God'. Wesley's sermon on 'The Witness of our own spirit' is based on an unsuitable text. Consideration is given to Wesley's use of 2 Corinthians 13^5 and Galatians 5^{22}. Is the underlying thought of 1 John 2$^{3, 5, 29}$ a synthesis of Gnosticism and of Hebrew 'God-consciousness'? 1 John 3$^{4, 19}$ are also studied.

Chapter 4. Degrees of Assurance

'Assurance' in Hebrews 11^1 refers only to faith in general. Wesley's use of 'the full assurance of faith' (Hebrews 10^{22}) is examined. 'The full assurance of hope' (Hebrews 6^{11}) refers to future glory. We consider the use of 'full assurance' with the word 'understanding' in Colossians 2^2 and its absolute use in 1 Thessalonians 1^5. The difference between 'saving faith' and these uses of 'full assurance' is only one of degree.

Chapter 5. Was Wesley's Exposition Adequate?

Criticism is levelled against: (1) Wesley's statement that he never used the word 'Assurance' because 'it was not Scriptural'; (2) his interpretation of the prefix 'συν' (Romans 8^{16}); (3) his confusing the two meanings of the word 'know' (1 John 4^{19}); (4) the narrowness of his Biblical foundation. Wesley did not sufficiently relate Assurance to: (a) Christ's life and work; (b) Paul's teaching and experience.

Chapter 6. The Apostolic Church

A study of the disciples' post-Resurrection experience and of the essence of Pentecost reveals how central Assurance was in the Primitive Society. Similarities are noted between Pentecost and Wesley's Aldersgate experience. The much used phrase 'in Christ' is related to the Risen Lord and to an inner sense of certainty.

PART FOUR

ASSURANCE IN THE HISTORY OF THE CHURCH

Chapter 1. The Early Fathers

Wesley held that Assurance could be traced in the Early Fathers. Clement of Rome speaks of those who have the 'full assurance of the Holy Ghost'. The Shepherd of Hermas refers to the Holy Spirit's bearing witness. Certainty shines out in the martyrs. For Ignatius the Spirit is 'the Author of saving knowledge'. Justin, Aristides and Tatian hold that Christians can be sure of their Divine inheritance. A sense of adoption appears in the writings of Irenaeus and of Clement of Alexandria. Tertullian stresses the Indirect Witness, while Origen writes about an 'inner Divine sense'. Hilary interprets passages from John 14 and Romans 8 in terms of Assurance. Basil speaks of spiritual sensitiveness and relates knowledge to belief. Gregory links 'full assurance' with the Trinity. In Ambrose, adoption and the Cross are the source of certainty. Assurance is found in Augustine's conversion.

Chapter 2. The Medieval Church

The emphasis of the Roman Church on the externals of religion tended to obscure the need for an individual experience of Assurance. Hence, years later, the doctrine was condemned by the Council of Trent. Aquinas regarded Christian certainty as very rare and then only by direct revelation. Assurance was also deprecated by the 'medieval Reformers', including Wyclif. The Spirit's indwelling, however, was recognized; and in the mystics there was an 'inner light' which could not be put out.

Chapter 3. The Teaching of the Reformers

At the Reformation the individual came into his own. In some quarters, however, the Pope's infallibility was matched, if not by biblical infallibility, by excessive claims to illumination. Did Luther teach Assurance? The '*Testimonium Spiritus Sancti*' is distinguished from Wesley's doctrine of the 'Witness of the Spirit'.

SUMMARY xvii

The later decline of certainty is traced to Luther's growing intellectualism. In Calvinism, Assurance was vitiated by Election. Yet, present salvation is related to future hope. Calvin's comments on Romans 8^{16}, Galatians 4^6, and Hebrews 6^{11} are significant. Assurance, in Calvinism, both falls short of and goes beyond the Bible.

Chapter 4. The Seventeenth Century

Reference is made to the 'Lambeth Articles' and to the views of Hooker and John Smith. Evidence is drawn from the 'Westminster Confession' (1688) and from the writings of John Owen, George Fox, Isaac Penington and Robert Barclay. The 'inner light' of Quakerism is distinguished from Wesley's teaching on the 'Witness of the Spirit'.

PART FIVE

ASSURANCE AND ITS VALIDITY

Chapter 1. The Charge of 'Enthusiasm'

Deism was the dominant creed of the eighteenth century—a creed mostly antagonistic to Assurance. 'Enthusiasm' is defined. Consideration is given to the evidence on which various charges of 'enthusiasm' were based. Wesley resisted the charges by stressing the rational and objective features of his doctrine.

Chapter 2. The Indictment of 'Heresy'

The claim to have the Spirit's inner witness was considered a 'heresy' because 'rationalism had penetrated the ranks of orthodoxy'. The reasons for the clergy's failure to appreciate Wesley defence include: (1) the ignorance of Doctrinal Standards; (2) the diversity of interpretations; and (3) the widespread opposition toward 'supernaturalism' in religion.

Chapter 3. Was Wesley's Doctrine Orthodox?

Wesley's quotations from the Anglican Standards are examined. Some make only a general reference to the Spirit, others refer more plainly to the inner witness. A much more explicit reference to Assurance is found in the writings of Anglican divines. Wesley's claim to orthodoxy is upheld.

Chapter 4. The Dangers of 'Stillness'

Attention is given to Wesley's struggle with Molther's 'Stillness'. This 'Moravian mysticism' deprecated the 'means of grace', the 'going to church' and 'good works'—thus leading to a dangerous

A*

individualism. Wesley resisted 'Stillness' by emphasizing the objective aspects of Assurance. Separation from Moravianism followed.

Chapter 5. The Relevance of Mysticism

The causes of Wesley's dislike of mysticism include: (1) extravagant individualism; (2) Antinomianism; (3) neglect of reason; and (4) anti-social tendencies. Mystical elements, however, are traceable in Wesley's life and thought. His maturer judgement was more appreciative of the mystics. Some Methodist hymns express mystical sentiments. Features common to Assurance and Mysticism are: (1) 'ineffability'; (2) 'noetic quality'; and (3) inner 'illumination'.

Chapter 6. The Validity of an Inner Sense of Certainty

Assurance by its very nature does not admit of 'proof'. The 'noetic element', being 'ineffable', cannot be communicated. The knowledge of another person's inner consciousness can only be inferred. The trend of eighteenth-century philosophy is outlined. Though Wesley was not strictly a philosopher, his doctrine both reflected and reacted against current philosophical thought. He revealed the importance of spiritual phenomena. Like the sciences, the Doctrine of Assurance is not without its 'mysteries'— and these do not admit of 'final explanation'.

Part One

Assurance in the Experience of the Eighteenth Century

CHAPTER ONE

THE ESSENCE OF WESLEY'S ALDERSGATE EXPERIENCE

WHAT is the place of assurance in John Wesley's religious life? We begin with this vital question because Methodist doctrine illustrates the fact that man lives first and thinks afterwards.[1] Methodist thought has its roots in experience. It follows that no inquiry into Wesley's doctrine of assurance can ignore the personal experience on which the doctrine is based.

We turn first, therefore, to Wesley's spiritual transformation on 24th May 1738, at the meeting in Aldersgate Street. The event is often mentioned in Methodist literature, but a thorough examination and interpretation of it are not easy to find. A clearer explanation of this important religious crisis is needed to replace a multitude of vague and misleading references.

Controversy has centred on the question whether 24th May 1738 was the day on which Wesley was converted. Dr Augustin Leger, a French writer, maintains that Wesley's conversion should be dated, not in 1738, but in 1725 when he took Holy Orders.[2] Dr Maximin Piette, a Franciscan Friar and Professor of History in Brussels, agrees with Dr Leger. He argues that Wesley underwent a far deeper spiritual change in 1725 than the 'gust of feeling' experienced in 1738. 'All the authors', writes Piette, 'who speak so glibly of the great conversion which took place in May 1738 . . . would they not be well advised to place . . . his true conversion fourteen[3] years before the time that the Wesleyan legend . . . wishes, with official approval, to place it?'[4]

Other writers have followed in the wake of Piette and Leger. The same view has been put forward on the other side of the Atlantic.[5] Dr Umphrey Lee holds that Wesley's experience of 24th May 1738 has been over-emphasized for the following reasons:

[1] Dr S. G. Dimond, *Psychology of the Methodist Revival* (1926), p. 224.
[2] *La Jeunesse de Wesley* (1910), pp. 77ff., 350, 364.
[3] Dr Piette obviously means '*thirteen* years before'.
[4] *John Wesley in the Evolution of Protestantism* (E. T., 1937), p, 306.
[5] Lee, *John Wesley and Modern Religions* (1936), pp. 89f., 100, 102.

(1) The doubts and uncertainty that later beset Wesley.⁶
(2) The meagre references to it in subsequent writings.
(3) The lack of faith expressed in a letter to his brother, Charles.⁷
(4) The absence of any reference to the Aldersgate experience at the opening of City Road chapel, when Wesley reviewed the development of Methodism.
(5) The later modifications made by Wesley in the original description of his religious experience prior to Aldersgate.
(6) It is not included in Wesley's *Short History of the People called Methodists*.⁸

On the other hand, many writers incline more to the traditional view that on 24th May 1738 Wesley was 'converted', and hold that the meeting in Aldersgate Street was 'an hour supremely important . . . without which Wesley's great work would never have been done'. They discountenance the view that Aldersgate was 'incidental both in his life, and in his own subsequent thought, and magnified into a legend only by the theological bias of those who came after him'.⁹

In refutation of the view that Wesley's real conversion was in 1725, Dr W. R. Cannon, Professor of Church History at Emory University, holds that the very same problems which harassed his existence and tormented his life prior to the year 1725 continued in full force up to the date of his conversion on 24th May 1738. In reference to Aldersgate, Dr Cannon continues: 'From an examination of Wesley's writings . . . one is convinced of the marked change which took place in his thought, of the new emphasis which emerged, and in very truth of the birth of his own system of theology.'¹⁰

In subsequent chapters of this book, it will be seen that Dr Cannon's assessment here of the Aldersgate experience is in part an over-statement.¹¹ The year 1725, for instance, solved the problem of Wesley's career in life,¹² and his intellectual perplexities ebbed prior to 24th May 1738, especially in March and April of that year.¹³

⁶ *Journal of John Wesley*, ed. Curnock, II.88–126. (Hereinafter referred to as *Journal*.)
⁷ *Letters of John Wesley*, ed. Telford, V.15f. 27th June 1766. (Hereinafter referred to as *Letters*.)
⁸ Published in 1781: *Works*, VIII.347–51.
⁹ Dr W. E. Sangster, *Path to Perfection* (1943), p. 93.
¹⁰ *Theology of John Wesley* (New York, 1946), p. 67.
¹¹ Part I, ch. 3 and 4; Part II, ch. 1. ¹² *Journal*, I.466. ¹³ ibid., pp. 442ff.

Dr G. C. Cell, Professor of Historical Theology at Boston University, argues that Piette's inability or failure to discover the objective significance of Wesley's 'conversion-experience' arises chiefly from two sources: First, he operates with a special definition of conversion that will not fit the case of Wesley. It is assumed that conversion can have a positive meaning only on a personal background of lurid sinfulness. Secondly, his analysis of the original sources was far from adequate, so that the decisive considerations have been entirely overlooked.[14]

Dr Cell makes a positive contribution to the subject in emphasizing the importance of 24th May 1738 by reference to:

(1) Wesley's increased effectiveness as a preacher.
(2) His 'offensiveness' to the religion of his day.[15]
(3) His use of the double system of chronology—'*anno domini*' and '*anno meae conversionis*'.[16]

It is not our intention, however, to generate further heat on this controversial question as to whether 24th May 1738 was the day of Wesley's 'conversion'. We believe that a better line of approach is an attempt to answer the query: What is the distinctive feature of Wesley's Aldersgate experience? This distinctive feature will the more easily emerge as we clear the ground by showing what Aldersgate was *not*.

(1) And, first, *Aldersgate was not marked by an initial resolve to lead a holy life*. 'All are agreed', says Dr W. E. Sangster, 'that Wesley made no *volte-face* on that day from a life of blatant sin to one of impressive goodness. Whatever happened, it was an event in the life of a man disciplined in virtue and constantly on the stretch for the highest.'[17] He had set uncertain feet on the path to perfection long before he came in sight of Aldersgate.

In Wesley's search for saintliness, the year 1725 was an important milestone. He was then twenty-two and had just taken his bachelor's degree at Oxford. Prompted by his father, the young Wesley entered the Anglican ministry.[18] While holding the traditional view regarding Wesley's 'conversion' on 24th May 1738 Dr Henry Bett says: 'No one doubts that there was a real experience in 1725; no one disputes that it may be

---

[14] *Rediscovery of John Wesley* (New York, 1935), p. 171.
[15] See Part V, ch. 1 and 2, pp. 179ff., 185ff., *infra*.
[16] Cell, op. cit., pp. 177, 183, 185; cf. Dr J. E. Rattenbury, *Conversion of the Wesleys* (1938), pp. 31ff.
[17] op. cit., p. 93.   [18] *Journal*, I.466.

regarded as the proper beginning of Wesley's religious life, in so far as any such thing can be dated at all.'[19]

And so it was that, some thirteen years before Aldersgate, Wesley was poring over Thomas à Kempis's *Christian Pattern*, Jeremy Taylor's *Holy Living*, and Scougal's *Life of God in the Soul of Man*. Assessing the religious value of these early days at Oxford, Wesley wrote in 1738: 'I began to alter the whole form of my conversation and to set in earnest upon a new life. I set apart an hour or two a day for religious retirement. I communicated every week. I began to aim at, and pray for, inward holiness. So that now, "doing so much and living a good life" I doubted not but that I was a good Christian.'[20]

Later in life, Wesley looked back over the years and traced the early stages in his pursuit of the holy. 'In the year 1725', he wrote, 'I met with Bishop Taylor's *Rules and Exercises of Holy Living and Dying*.[21] In reading several parts of this book I was exceedingly affected: that part in particular which relates to purity of intention.... In the year 1726, I met with Kempis's *Christian Pattern*.[22] The nature and extent of inward religion, the religion of the heart, now appeared to me in a stronger light than ever it had done before.... A year or two after, Mr Law's *Christian Perfection*[23] and *Serious Call*[24] were put into my hands. These convinced me more than ever of the absolute impossibility of being half a Christian.'[25]

At this distance from Aldersgate, the youthful Wesley had chosen the path of self-denial. From now on a firm self-discipline was to be a hall-mark of his life. Believing himself naturally drawn to indolence,[26] he treated this alleged trait as a sin and guarded himself against it by seldom rising later than 4 a.m. This young pilgrim of heaven, though compassed about by religious indifference and pleasure seeking, resolutely bade farewell to leisure and all 'trifling acquaintance'.[27] From henceforth, he rarely failed to devote the first hour of every

[19] *Spirit of Methodism* (1937), p. 34.   [20] *Journal*, I.467.
[21] This book is omitted in Wesley's account under 24th May 1738. See *Journal*, I.466f.
[22] The *Journal* record appears to place the reading of this book a year earlier. *Journal*, I.466.
[23] Published in 1726.   [24] Published in 1729.
[25] Wesley's *Plain Account of Christian Perfection*, pp. 5f.
[26] See Diaries written at Oxford and on the *Simmonds—Journal*, I.54f. Dr Johnson's only complaint against Wesley was his niggardly use of time. 'The dog enchants you, but he always has an appointment and must leave you'—Eayrs, *Wesley, Christian Philosopher and Church Founder* (1926), pp. 48f.
[27] *Journal*, I.467.

day to prayer and also aimed at setting aside five minutes of every other hour for this devotional exercise.

On 1st September 1778 Wesley referred to a sermon written in 1733: 'I know not that I can write a better on the Circumcision of the Heart than I did five-and-forty years ago.'[28] It is manifest that the significance of Aldersgate does not lie in Wesley's decision to seek the goal of Christian Perfection. We do not doubt that this high resolve was deepened and strengthened on 24th May 1738; but this end was already being pursued by Wesley at least thirteen years earlier.

(2) *Nor is the distinctive feature of the Aldersgate experience to be found in Wesley's dedication to the service of God.* Wesley's consciousness of being a man of destiny is clearly traceable prior to 24th May 1738. This is not to be ruled out as pure subjectivism or egoism, for it was shared by others and especially by his mother. This sense of destiny was accentuated by his miraculous escape from the Rectory fire on 9th February 1709.[29] John was then only six years old, but this perilous incident remained with him all his days.[30]

No sympathetic student of the Georgia *Journals* can read Wesley's account of his love affair with Miss Sophia Hopkey without being deeply moved. This young Anglican missionary, sensing a conflict he can scarce define between his pure love for this attractive girl and 'the high calling of God', wins our admiration. It is no part of our purpose to conjecture what Wesley's future would have been had he married her. Suffice it to say that on the blank outside leaf of the document, in which he recounts his contacts with Sophia Hopkey, he has inscribed the memorable words: 'Snatched as a brand out of the fire.'[31] While it may be true that Wesley's marriage prospects were spoilt by his thinking of any future wife in terms of his wonderful mother, there is more significance in Dr Leger's conclusion that 'God was after all the only lasting, absorbing passion of John Wesley'.[32]

In reference to these early years, Wesley could write: 'I resolved to dedicate all my life to God.'[33] After two years as his father's curate at Wroote, Wesley returned to Oxford in 1729 and assumed the leadership of the 'Holy Club', a group of

[28] *Journal*, VI.209.   [29] See Wesley's Diary for 9th March 1737.
[30] cf. *Journal*, III.453f., IV.90.   [31] ibid., I.288.
[32] Quoted by Dr J. E. Rattenbury, *Wesley's Legacy to the World*, p. 43. See also Maria Conway Oemler, *The Holy Lover*.
[33] Wesley's *Plain Account of Christian Perfection*, p. 5f.

university men who not only spent 'some evenings together in reading, chiefly the Greek Testament',[34] but who were ready to take the Christian message to the inmates at the Castle.[35]

Wesley appears to have replied harshly to his father's proposal that he should succeed him as Rector of Epworth. But Wesley's rejection of this arrangement must be viewed in the light of the fact that he regarded such a plan as conflicting with his divine vocation. Wesley wrote: 'I do not say the glory of God is to be my first or principal consideration, but my only one.'[36] We need only quote the date of this letter in order to show the significance of Wesley's words—10th December 1734—four years before Aldersgate.

(3) *Nor was Aldersgate the dawning of Wesley's compassion for men and women.* Writing in 1738 of his work as a member of the Holy Club, Wesley said: 'In 1730, I began visiting the prisons; assisting the poor and sick in town; and doing what other good I could, by my presence or my little fortune, to the bodies and souls of men. To this end I abridged myself of all superfluities and many that are called the necessaries of life.'[37]

Wesley gave away more than some not-ungenerous people would deem prudent. Though he uses the third person, the following statement about an Oxford Methodist can be taken as referring to himself: 'One of them had thirty pounds a year. He lived on twenty-eight and gave away forty shillings. The next year he had sixty pounds, he still lived on twenty-eight and gave away two and thirty. The third year he received ninety pounds and gave away sixty-two. The fourth year he received a hundred and twenty pounds. Still he lived on twenty-eight and gave to the poor ninety-two.'[38]

There is a fine Pauline ring about the searching and challenging statement made by Wesley on his return from Georgia: 'Are they plenteous in alms? Behold, I gave all my goods to feed the poor. Do they give their labour as well as their substance? I have laboured more abundantly than they all. Are they willing to suffer for their brethren? I have thrown up

---

[34] *Wesley's Works*, VIII.348. [35] *Journal*, I.94.

[36] *Letters*, I.166ff.; cf. *Journal*, II.159 and Tyerman, *Life and Times of John Wesley*, I.102ff.

[37] *Journal*, I.467.

[38] See Rattenbury, *Conversion of the Wesleys*, p. 43. While it would not be relevant here to consider whether Wesley's benevolence should have been directed more toward Epworth on the principle that 'charity begins at home', we may at least be permitted the passing thought.

my friends, reputation, ease, country; I have put my life in my hand, wandering into stange lands; I have given my body to be devoured by the deep, parched up with heat, consumed by toil and weariness, or whatsoever God should please to bring upon me.'[39]

And all this ante-dated 24th May 1738.

(4) *We would also rule out the suggestion that any intellectual change figured prominently in the Aldersgate experience.*[40] We might well hesitate to accept Dr Cannon's view that the Aldersgate experience is important because a new theology gained Wesley's allegiance on the date of that experience and made a mighty contribution to the development of his thought. 'Aldersgate stands at the crisis of Wesley's thought, as well as at the crisis of his religious experience and of his life.'[41]

That beliefs, to which Wesley had already given intellectual assent, were crystallized by the events of 24th May 1738 we have not the least doubt. Dr Cannon would appear, however, to telescope the stages of Wesley's intellectual and spiritual development, covering at least two months, and would seem to crowd them into one day. Wesley himself stated that as early as the 5th March, by the teaching of Peter Böhler,[42] he was 'clearly convinced of unbelief, of the want of that faith whereby alone we are saved.... Accordingly, Monday the 6th, I began preaching this new doctrine,[43] though my soul started back from the work.'[44]

Dr G. C. Cell gives us a more balanced interpretation of the facts here. 'The doctrine[45] found entrance into his preaching on 6th March 1738.... But it did not become the centre of gravity or gain complete ascendency and control over his teaching and preaching till 24th May 1738.'[46] Turning back to these events, in 1765, Wesley wrote: 'As soon as I saw the nature of saving faith clearly, namely, on Monday, 6th March 1738, I declared it without delay. And God began to work by my ministry as He never had done before.'[47]

Dr Cell emphatically points out that one of the most important of Wesley's concepts is his way of referring to, and reasoning

---

[39] *Journal*, I.423.   [40] cf. Winchester, *Life of John Wesley*, p. 54.
[41] Cannon: Theology of John Wesley, p. 68.   [42] See pp. 25ff., *infra*.
[43] For an examination of this 'New Doctrine', see Part II, ch. 1, pp. 53ff., *infra*.
[44] *Journal*, I.442.   [45] The Doctrine of Justification by Faith.
[46] *Rediscovery of John Wesley* (New York, 1935), p. 184.
[47] Wesley's *Short History of the People called Methodists* (1765).

about, what in his life went before and what came after 'I preached or knew salvation by faith'.[48] While Wesley's use of this clause, in writing to 'John Smith',[49] is taken to refer to 24th May 1738,[50] the statement can be applied to Aldersgate only if that event be viewed as the culmination of the intellectual and spiritual struggles which preceded it. And, as is revealed elsewhere in Wesley's writings, the intellectual content of his religious experience had been largely settled on 6th March and the days immediately following.

Dr Cell maintains that 'Wesley always read the objective significance of his conversion-experience in the spring of 1738 not primarily in terms of his personal feeling, but in terms of the religious principles involved.'[51] But, assuming this to be true, 'the religious principles involved' were those Wesley accepted in theory some two months before Aldersgate.

From a study of Wesley's conversations with Peter Böhler,[52] we learn that Wesley preached justification by faith as soon as he recognized its truth (i.e. on 6th March 1738), but that he did not *know the experience* till 24th May. After further contacts with Böhler, Wesley says, under the date 23rd April: 'Here ended my disputing. I could now only cry out, "Lord, help Thou my unbelief!" '[53]

There are comparatively few entries in Wesley's *Journal* between 7th March and 24th May 1738, but an examination of these supports the view that the period from 5th to 7th March is almost as important as 24th May. They are the days of his *intellectual* conversion.[54] It is clear that the distinctive feature of Aldersgate did not consist in any revolution in Wesley's *thinking*.

In the light of this examination of Wesley's pre-Aldersgate religious experience, it is easy to appreciate the refusal of some scholars to apply the word 'conversion' to 24th May 1738. Wesley himself hesitated to use the word by reason of its infrequent appearance in the New Testament. His religious life before Aldersgate has revealed little trace of those elements which are usually understood to constitute the pre-conversion state. This is borne out by the corrective notes which Wesley wrote in his later and maturer years, and with which he modified his earlier evaluation of his religious life before 24th

---

[48] Cell, op. cit., p. 184. [49] Archbishop Secker? *Letters*, II.65.
[50] Cell, op. cit., p. 184. [51] ibid. [52] *Journal*, I.442. See pp. 25ff.
[53] ibid., p. 455. [54] Rattenbury, *Conversion of the Wesleys*, p. 70.

May 1738.⁵⁵ If 'conversion' be used for Aldersgate, then another term would seem to be needed to refer to that religious revolution in which a life of blatant sin gives way to the new life 'in Christ'.

So far we have said much that is negative or destructive. This has been clearly necessary in order to prepare the ground for a constructive answer to the question: 'What is the distinctive feature of Wesley's Aldersgate experience?'

Our view is that 24th May 1738 was the first occasion on which John Wesley gained an assurance of personal salvation centred in a crucified Christ.⁵⁶ His Aldersgate Street experience was the foundation on which Wesley's doctrine of Assurance, or the Witness of the Spirit, was based.⁵⁷ 'The Witness of the Spirit is for Wesley really a theological name for "the heart strangely warmed".'⁵⁸

Wesley's religious transformation at Aldersgate was a Pentecostal experience.⁵⁹ The Methodist doctrine of the Spirit's witness was traced by Wesley to its source at Aldersgate when he wrote in 1767: 'It is confirmed in your experience and mine. The Spirit Himself bore witness to my spirit that I was a child of God, gave me an evidence thereof: and I immediately cried, "Abba, Father".'⁶⁰

Though Wesley later modified the harsh judgement he pronounced on his religious life before 24th May 1738 we cannot trace in his writings any serious reassessment of the nature and value of the Aldersgate experience. Even if afterwards he momentarily lost the sense of certainty first gained on 24th May, it does not follow that he did not really enjoy the distinctive experience on that memorable evening.

The interpretation here is supported by Wesley's own account of what happened at the meeting in Aldersgate Street. 'I felt my heart strangely warmed. I felt I did trust in Christ, Christ alone for salvation; and *an assurance was given me*, that he had taken away *my* sins, even *mine*, and saved *me* from the law of sin and death.'⁶¹

---

⁵⁵ *Journal*, I.422f. But cf. Dr G. C. Cell, *Rediscovery of John Wesley*, pp. 181f.
⁵⁶ For the full significance of this statement, see Part II, ch. 1, pp. 25ff., *infra*.
⁵⁷ For an examination of the doctrine, see Part II, *infra*.
⁵⁸ Lawson, *Notes on Wesley's Forty-Four Sermons*, p. 91.
⁵⁹ Note the comparison drawn between 'Pentecost' and the Aldersgate experience in Part III, ch. 6, pp. 142f., *infra*.
⁶⁰ *Sermons*, II.350. See Dr H. Watkin-Jones, *The Holy Spirit from Arminius to Wesley* (1929), p. 316.
⁶¹ *Journal*, I.475f. (first italics mine).

CHAPTER TWO

24TH MAY 1738—AN END AND A BEGINNING

IN THE earlier writings of Wesley there are references which imply that an inner sense of assurance increasingly became Wesley's chief quest—especially under the influence of the Moravians.[1]

The first instance dates back to his Oxford days. It appears in a letter written to his mother on 18th June 1725—a letter in which he criticizes a passage in Jeremy Taylor's *Holy Living and Holy Dying*.[2] Wesley quotes Taylor's words: 'Whether God has forgiven us or no we know not, therefore still be sorrowful for ever having sinned.'[3] Wesley comments as follows: 'I take the more notice of this last sentence, because it seems to contradict his own words in the next section, where he says that by the Lord's Supper all the members are united to one another and to Christ the head: the Holy Ghost confers on us the graces we pray for, and our souls receive into them the seeds of an immortal nature. Now, surely these graces are not of so little force, as that we cannot perceive whether we have them or no; and if we dwell in Christ, and Christ in us, which he will not do till we are regenerate, certainly we must be sensible of it. If his opinion be true, I must own I have always been in great error; for I imagined that when I communicated worthily, i.e. with faith, humility, and thankfulness, my preceding sins were *ipso facto* forgiven me. . . . But if we can never have any certainty of our being in a state of salvation, good reason it is that every moment should be spent not in joy but fear and trembling; and then undoubtedly we are of all men most miserable!'[4]

In a further letter to his mother, dated 29th July 1725, written also from Oxford, Wesley says: 'That we can never be so certain of the pardon of our sins as to be assured they will never rise up against us, I firmly believe. We know that they will infallibly do so if ever we apostatize, and I am not satisfied

---
[1] For the influence of Moravianism on Wesley, see pp. 20ff., 31ff., 53ff., *infra*.
[2] *Letters*, I.17ff.; cf. Bett, *Spirit of Methodism*, p. 111.
[3] *Holy Living and Holy Dying*, Ch. 4, § 7.
[4] *Letters*, I.19f.; Cell, *Rediscovery of John Wesley*, pp. 166f.

24TH MAY 1738—AN END AND A BEGINNING

what evidence there can be of final perseverance till we have finished our course. But I am persuaded we may know if we are *now* in a state of salvation, since that is expressly promised in the Holy Scriptures to our sincere endeavours, and we are surely able to judge of our own sincerity.'[5]

In Sermon 138, written in 1733, we find a remarkable anticipation of his later experience and doctrine of the 'Witness of the Spirit'. 'The Holy Spirit', writes Wesley, 'within us is the security of our salvation; he is likewise an earnest of it, and assures our spirits that we have a title to eternal happiness. "The Spirit of God beareth witness with our spirits that we are the children of God."[6] And in order that this testimony may be lively and permanent, it is absolutely necessary to attend carefully to the secret operation of the Holy Spirit within us. . . . In this sense, God is said . . . to have "sealed us, and to have given the earnest of his Spirit in our hearts".'[7]

Another early allusion to the necessity of the Spirit's witness appears in the Sermon on the 'Circumcision of the Heart', written also in 1733. Wesley holds that those who are born of God have 'the testimony of their own spirit with the Spirit which witnesses in their hearts that they are the children of God. Indeed it is the same Spirit who works in them that clear and cheerful confidence that their heart is upright toward God; that good assurance . . . that they are now in the path which leadeth to life.'[8] Later, in the same sermon, Wesley teaches that 'none is truly "led by the Spirit" unless that "Spirit bear witness with his spirit, that he is a child of God".'[9]

Dr George Eayrs believes that Wesley's 'quest for the assurance of divine pardon . . . drove him for long years over land and sea'.[10] Is this the purpose and the meaning which we should attach to a statement in a letter addressed to Dr Burton on 10th October 1735? Wesley writes: 'My chief motive . . . is the hope of saving my own soul. I hope to learn the true sense of the Gospel of Christ by preaching it to the heathen.' This interpretation is accepted by the Rev. Frank Baker: 'The Wesley brothers' mission to Georgia . . . was for both John and

---

[5] *Letters*, I.22.

[6] Romans 8:16. For an examination of the biblical basis of Wesley's doctrine, see Part III, pp. 103ff., *infra*.

[7] *Works*, VII.492; Lee, *John Wesley and Modern Religions*, p. 155.

[8] *Sermons*, I.271.   [9] ibid., p. 276.

[10] *John Wesley, Christian Philosopher and Church Founder*, p. 157.

Charles as much an attempt to find spiritual certainty for themselves as to proclaim the Gospel to the Red Indians.'[11]

On his return from Georgia, Wesley says: 'I want that faith which none can have without knowing that he hath it . . . for whosoever hath it . . . is freed from doubt, "having the love of God shed abroad in his heart, through the Holy Ghost which is given unto him"; which "Spirit itself beareth witness with his spirit, that he is a child of God".'[12]

After outlining his strivings after holiness, Wesley writes: 'I could not find that this gave me any comfort or any assurance of acceptance with God.'[13] 'Outwardly calm as he was before 1738', says T. E. Brigden, 'his journals reveal the distressing restlessness of soul until he realized the mystic peace by the witnessing Spirit of God.'[14]

In the summary of his spiritual pilgrimage with which he prefaces his account of 24th May 1738, Wesley says: 'Neither had I the witness of the Spirit with my spirit, and indeed could not; for I sought it not by faith, but as it were by "the works of the law". . . . I well saw that no one could, in the nature of things, have a sense of forgiveness and not *feel* it. But I felt it not.'[15]

'I continued thus to seek it', says Wesley, 'until Wednesday, 24th May.'[16] On that day his search for certainty ended.

Dr Cannon, in the earlier part of his book on *The Theology of John Wesley*, criticizes the view that assurance alone was the quest of Wesley's life. He argues that this is to mistake the by-product of a phenomenon for the phenomenon itself. 'True, assurance did come; but it came along with, and as an aspect of, something else.'[17] But can this argument be seriously regarded as a refutation of the view we have advanced? Dr Cannon is surely saying the obvious. In what other way did he suppose anyone could expect assurance to come? He is merely saying that assurance was not an entity in itself but was assurance of some *thing*—that the inner sense of certainty had an objective reference. And this is the very point he makes later in the same book. 'The witness of the Spirit assumes a role of cardinal significance in Wesley's theology, for it is the means whereby a man's justification is made manifest, the internal sign that the power of God has touched his life, that his sins

---

[11] *Charles Wesley as Revealed by His Letters* (1948), p. 20.   [12] *Journal*, I.424.
[13] ibid., p. 468.   [14] *New History of Methodism*, I.207.   [15] *Journal*, I.471.
[16] ibid., p. 472.   [17] op. cit., p. 68.

24TH MAY 1738—AN END AND A BEGINNING

have been forgiven, and that he has been set on the road to holiness and final salvation.'[18]

We saw in the previous chapter that certain writers have minimized the value of the Aldersgate experience on the ground that it lacked permanence in Wesley's later experience and thought. With reference to Wesley's religious experience on 24th May 1738, Dr Piette says that 'whether it be considered in its preparation, or be studied in itself and its results, it would seem to have been merely a quite ordinary experience whose effects time was quick to dull. Had it not been entered in the first extract of the *Journal*, it is quite possible that Wesley would have entirely forgotten all about it. In any case, subsequent appraisals, made after the lapse of many years, reduce to pitiable proportions the songs of praise and victory which first accompanied it.'[19]

In support of this depreciation of Wesley's Aldersgate experience, Dr Lee draws attention to the corrections made later by Wesley in his original estimate of his pre-Aldersgate religious life.

In his penetrating survey of his varied experiences in Georgia, Wesley wrote: 'I, who went to America to convert others, was never myself converted to God.'[20] Years after, Wesley added this modifying comment: 'I am not sure of this.'[21] Another statement which his maturer mind modified was: 'I am a child of wrath.' He tones this down by adding: 'I believe not.'[22]

It is not our intention to argue away these corrections. They are part of the evidence which could be adduced to show that Wesley undoubtedly revised some of his earlier judgements.[23] Dr Lee seems to imply, however, that these corrective notes seriously detract from Wesley's earlier evaluation of his Aldersgate experience. Acceptance of the evidence, we believe, does not necessarily commit us to this conclusion. Our view is that these corrections, assuming them to be authentic, only serve to show that Wesley came to realize that he had painted his pre-Aldersgate days in too dark a hue.

But Dr Lee has further evidence to present in support of his

---

[18] *Journal*, p. 215.   [19] *John Wesley in the Evolution of Protestantism*, p. 306.
[20] *Journal*, I.421.

[21] The authenticity of this note is emphatically denied by Dr G. C. Cell, *Rediscovery of John Wesley*, pp. 181f. These corrections first appear in Thomas Jackson's edition of the *Journal*. See Jackson's *Autobiography*, p. 234, and Curnock's remarks in his edition of Wesley's *Journal*, I.422.

[22] *Journal*, I.423.   [23] See Part II, ch. 2, pp. 61ff., *infra*.

depreciation of Aldersgate. This includes two entries in Wesley's *Journal* and a letter written to his brother Charles:

(1) The first entry is dated 14th October 1738—only five months after Aldersgate. 'I cannot find in myself the love of God, or of Christ . . . I have not that joy in the Holy Ghost;[24] no settled, lasting joy. Nor have I such a peace as excludes the possibility either of fear or doubt. When holy men have told me I had no faith, I have often doubted whether I had or no. . . . Although I have not yet that joy in the Holy Ghost, nor the full assurance of faith[25] . . . I nevertheless trust that I have a measure of faith, and am "accepted in the Beloved".'[26]

(2) The second entry in the *Journal*, dated 4th January 1739, is even more bewildering. 'My friends affirm I am mad, because I said I was not a Christian a year ago. I affirm I am not a Christian now. Indeed, what I might have been I know not, had I been faithful to the grace then given, when, expecting nothing less, I received such a sense of the forgiveness of my sins as till then I never knew. But that I am not a Christian at this day, I as assuredly know as that Jesus is the Christ. For a Christian is one who has the fruits of the Spirit of Christ, which . . . are love, peace, joy. But these I have not.'[27]

(3) The relevant part of John's letter to Charles, written on 27th June 1766, is as follows: 'I do not love God. I never did. Therefore I never believed in the Christian sense of the word. Therefore I am only an honest heathen, a proselyte of the Temple, one of the φοβούμενοι τὸν Θεόν.[28] . . . If I ever have had that faith, it would not be so strange. But I never had any other ἔλεγχος[29] of the eternal or invisible world than I have now; and that is none at all, unless such as fairly shines from reason's glimmering ray. I have no direct witness, I do not say that I am a child of God, but of anything invisible or eternal.'[30]

Other evidence might be quoted in support of Dr Lee's point of view:

(1) On 30th October 1738 Wesley wrote to his brother:

---

[24] References to the absence of joy are frequent in the *Journal* for the months immediately subsequent to 24th May 1738.

[25] πληροφορία πίστεως, Hebrews 10²². See Part III, ch. 4, pp. 128ff., *infra*.

[26] *Journal*, II.91; cf. Wesley's subsequent 'observations' on 16th December 1738—ibid., pp. 115f.

[27] ibid., p. 125.   [28] 'Those who fear God.'

[29] 'A proof, test', Hebrews 11¹.   [30] *Letters*, V.16.

'The πληροφορία πίστεως—the seal of the Spirit, the love of God shed abroad in my heart, and producing joy in the Holy Ghost—this witness of the Spirit I have not; but I patiently wait for it. . . . And, having seen and spoken to a cloud of witnesses abroad[31] as well as in my own country, I cannot but see that believers who wait and pray for it will find these Scriptures fulfilled in themselves. My hope is that they may be fulfilled in me. . . . Those who have not yet received joy in the Holy Ghost, the love of God, and the plerophory of faith (any or all of which I take to be the witness of the Spirit with our spirit that we are the sons of God), I believe to be Christians in that imperfect sense wherein I may call myself such.'[32]

(2) Looking back over the years, in 1772, to his 'Holy Club' days, Wesley writes in a nostalgic strain: 'Let me be again an Oxford Methodist! I am often in doubt whether it would not be best for me to resume all my Oxford rules, great and small. I did then walk closely with God and redeem the time. But what have I been doing these thirty years?'[33]

It is idle to pretend that these extracts from Wesley's post-Aldersgate writings present no difficulty. How the man who had written such glowing accounts as the entry in the *Journal* for 24th May 1738 could later express himself in these terms seems, at first thought, inconceivable. And yet are such fluctuations of spiritual experience peculiar to Wesley? Is not this the way of most, if not all, of the saints? The illumination of the mountain top is often dimmed by the shades of the valley.

It is significant that only two of these disconcerting passages from Wesley's pen are dated later that the beginning of 1739. It was in the early part of this year that Wesley began field-preaching and set in motion the mighty spiritual movement of the Methodist Revival. His pre-occupation with his inner religious consciousness gave way to an outward ministry in which could be seen the incontrovertible evidence of the workings of God's Spirit in the lives of men and women. 'Grace is never apparent and sensible to the soul', says Richard Baxter, 'but while it is in action; and therefore want of action must cause want of assurance.'[34]

We cannot deny, however, that there is some truth in Dr

[31] Moravian Settlements at Marienborn and Herrnhut. See pp. 31ff., *infra*.
[32] *Letters*, I.264. [33] ibid., VI.6.
[34] *The Saints' Everlasting Rest* (Reunion Edn., The Old Royalty Publishing Co.), p. 101.

Piette's contention that Wesley wrote little for over fifty years (1738–91) about the personal aspects of his Aldersgate experience. But an argument from silence is notoriously precarious. Were this the criterion by which the significance and influence of a spiritual experience were determined, then we must revise our estimate of the Baptism of Jesus and of Paul's illumination on the Damascus Road. Neither Jesus nor Paul made frequent reference to these pre-eminently important events—events which set the seal to lives of service that have made the world for ever different. In the case of Wesley, the silence can best be accounted for on the assumption that he never let the warm heart become a memory but tended the fires of Christian experience so well that it remained a present reality.[35]

Moreover, the permanent value of the Aldersgate experience —with assurance as its distinctive feature—is reflected in a number of references in Wesley's later writings:

(1) We have already noted the double system of chronology traceable in Wesley's voluminous works. 'In addition to the common way of timing events *anno domini* . . . there are scattered throughout the twenty-five volumes of his writings, references, not a few cases, but numbered by the score, to his conversion-experience, *anno meae conversionis*.'[36]

It would appear, however, that *some* of these references are to the early months of 1738, rather than to 24th May. Such phrases as 'thirty years ago' may sometimes point back to 6th March 1738, when Wesley gave intellectual assent to the doctrine of salvation by faith alone, rather than to 24th May, when the belief was translated into experimental knowledge.[37]

(2) There would appear to be an allusion to Aldersgate in Wesley's letter of 14th May 1765 addressed to the Rev. John Newton: 'I think on justification just as I have done any time these seven and twenty years.'[38]

(3) Another instance is found in a letter addressed to Dr Thomas Rutherforth, written by Wesley on 28th March 1768: 'You charge me . . . with maintaining contradictions. I answer: If all my sentiments were compared together, from the year 1725 to 1768, there would be truth in the charge; for during the latter part of this period I have relinquished several of my former sentiments. During these last thirty years I may have varied in some of my sentiments without observing it. . . . I

---

[35] Cell, op. cit., p. 27.   [36] ibid., p. 185.
[37] Rattenbury, *Conversion of the Wesleys*, pp. 22f.   [38] *Letters*, IV.298.

24TH MAY 1738—AN END AND A BEGINNING

believe there will be found few, if any, real contradictions in what I have published for near thirty years.'[39]

It is significant that Wesley does not deny contradictions and that he regards 1738 as the year when most of the changes in his sentiments were effected, after which, he maintains, there was a large measure of consistency. Wesley is doubtless referring to the revolutionary influence of Aldersgate.

Happily, however, there are other statements from Wesley's pen which testify more explicitly to the focal importance and the permanent value of the experience of 24th May 1738:

(1) An early and direct reference to the abiding influence of Aldersgate appears in a letter to his brother, Samuel, dated 30th October 1738: 'By a Christian I mean one who so believes in Christ as that sin hath no more dominion over him; and in this obvious sense of the word I was not a Christian till May the 24th last past.'[40]

(2) In estimating the place of the Aldersgate experience in Wesley's later life and thought, Dr Lee seems to have overlooked, or ignored, Wesley's correspondence with 'John Smith'. On 30th December 1745 Wesley writes: 'From 24th May 1738, "wherever I was desired to preach, salvation by faith was my only theme—that is, such a love of God and man as produces all inward and outward holiness, and springs from a conviction, wrought in us by the Holy Ghost, of the pardoning love of God." . . . And it is usually true that "it was for preaching the love of God and man that several of the clergy forbade me their pulpits" before that time, before 24th May, before I either preached or knew salvation by faith.'[41]

Further evidence could be quoted from Wesley's writings; but we believe that sufficient data have been adduced to establish the conclusion, not only that Aldersgate was the fulfilment of his quest for an inner sense of assurance, but that this distinctive feature of the Aldersgate experience on 24th May 1738 wielded a permanent influence over Wesley's subsequent life and thought.

[39] *Letters*, V.357f. [40] ibid., I.262f. [41] ibid., II.65.

CHAPTER THREE

THE EARLY INFLUENCE OF THE MORAVIANS

SCHOLARS have differed in assessing the value of the interaction of Methodism and Moravianism. 'In my judgement', says Dr H. B. Workman, 'the contact of Moravianism and Methodism is surface contact, which may easily be exaggerated.'[1] The opposite view, however, is taken by Dr Henry Bett: 'Methodism owes more . . . to Moravianism than to any other religious movement.'[2] As to which of these views more closely approximates to the true position, it is the purpose of this chapter to determine.

John Wesley's first meeting with the Moravians is in October 1735 on board the *Simmonds*, outward bound for Georgia. Wesley writes in his *Journal*: 'I began to learn German, in order to converse with the Moravians,[3] six and twenty of whom we have on board, men who have left all for their Master, and who have indeed learned of Him, being meek and lowly, dead to the world, full of faith and of the Holy Ghost.'[4]

In the survey of his religious pilgrimage with which he prefaced his entry in the *Journal* for 24th May 1738, Wesley writes as follows: 'In this refined way of trusting to my own works and my own righteousness . . . I dragged on heavily, finding no comfort or help therein till the time of my leaving England. On shipboard, however, I was again active in outward works; where it pleased God of His free mercy to give me twenty-six of the Moravian brethren for companions, who endeavoured to show me "a more excellent way". But I understood it not at first. I was too learned and too wise. So that it seemed foolishness unto me. And I continued preaching, and following after, and trusting in, that righteousness whereby no flesh may be justified.'[5]

Under the date, Sunday, 25th January 1736, Wesley writes: 'At seven I went to the Germans. I had long before observed the great seriousness of their behaviour. Of their humility they had given continual proof, by performing those servile offices

[1] *The Place of Methodism in the Catholic Church* (1921), p. 78.
[2] *The Spirit of Methodism* (1937), p. 50.
[3] In the later editions of the *Journal*, Wesley speaks of the Moravians as 'Germans'.
[4] *Journal*, I.110.   [5] ibid., pp. 469f.

for the other passengers which none of the English would undertake; for which they desired and would receive no pay, saying, "it was good for their proud hearts" and "their loving Saviour had done more for them". And every day had given them occasions of showing a meekness which no injury could move. If they were pushed, struck, or thrown down, they rose again and went away; for no complaint was found in their mouth. There was now an opportunity of trying whether they were delivered from the spirit of fear, as well as from that of pride, anger and revenge. In the midst of the psalm wherewith their service began . . . the sea broke over, split the mainsail in pieces, covered the ship, and poured in between the decks, as if the great deep had already swallowed us up. A terrible screaming began among the English. The Germans . . . calmly sang on. I asked one of them afterwards, "Was you not afraid?" He answered: "I thank God, no." I asked. "But were not your women and children afraid?" He replied mildly: "No; our women and children are not afraid to die." '[6]

A study of Wesley's Diaries and *Journal*, relating to the Georgian episode, reveals how frequently he was in contact with the Moravians. Wesley's association with the Moravians in the *Simmonds* had whetted his appetite for further information about the Moravian Church and their way of salvation with its dominant note of confidence and peace. Wesley, therefore, sought an early opportunity of conversing with August Gottlieb Spangenberg, whom he came to hold in very high esteem.

Spangenberg—the leader of the first contingent of Moravians to Georgia—had been a student at Jena and later became professor at the University of Halle. He was also the author of *Idea Fidei Fratrum*,[7] which purified the theology of the Moravian Church from some of the undesirable elements contributed by Count Zinzendorf. With reference to Spangenberg's book, Hagenbach writes: 'It is a devotional compendium so simply biblical and so far removed from all enthusiasm and everything objectionable, that, with few exceptions, every one must coincide with it who will grant that the Scriptures are the rule of our faith.'[8] It was Spangenberg's assurance of Christ's power to free from sin that relieved the anguish of Peter Böhler when the latter was studying at the University of Jena.[9]

[6] *Journal*, pp. 142f.   [7] Published in 1779. E. T. by Benjamin La Trobe.
[8] *Christian Church in Eighteenth and Nineteenth Centuries*, I.429f.
[9] *New History of Methodism*, I.196.

Wesley therefore, approached Spangenberg, shortly after his arrival, and sought his spiritual guidance. It proved to be a memorable interview for Wesley.

The entry in the *Journal* reads: 'I asked Mr Spangenberg's advice with regard to myself—to my own conduct. He told me he could say nothing till he had asked me two or three questions. "Do you know yourself? Have you the witness within yourself? Does the Spirit of God bear witness with your spirit that you are a child of God?" I was surprised and knew not what to answer. He observed it, and asked: "Do you know Jesus Christ?" I paused and said: "I know He is the Saviour of the world." "True," replied he, "but do you know He has saved you?" I answered: "I hope He has died to save me." He only added: "Do you know yourself?" I said: "I do." But I fear they were vain words. After my answering, he gave me several directions, which may the good God who sent him enable me to follow!'[10]

These words reveal, with unmistakable clearness, Wesley's need of a personal assurance of salvation. It is not improbable that the stress here laid by Spangenberg on the witness of the Spirit would remind Wesley of his father's dying words to him on this subject—'The inward witness, son, the inward witness, that is the proof, the strongest proof, of Christianity.'[11] It is significant that Wesley quoted his father's testimony in the first sermon he preached at Savannah.[12]

Looking back over the years, in 1771 Wesley said: 'Five and thirty years since,[13] hearing that wise man Mr Spangenberg describe the fruits of faith, I immediately cried out: "If this be so, I have no faith." He replied,[14] "*Habes fidem, sed exiguam*".'[15]

The growing admiration and sense of indebtedness which Wesley felt toward the Moravian community are reflected in a letter written by Wesley to Count Zinzendorf on 15th March 1736. 'I should not dare to interrupt your more weighty affairs with a letter of mine, did I not hold you to be a disciple of Him who would not have the smoking flax quenched nor the bruised reed broken. But since I am entirely convinced of this, I beg of you that in your prayers and the prayers of the Church that sojourns with you, I may be commended to God,

---

[10] op. cit., I.151.
[11] Dr George Eayrs, *Wesley, Christian Philosopher and Church Founder*, p. 149.
[12] *New History of Methodism*, I.192.   [13] i.e. 1736.
[14] 'You have faith, but it is weak.'   [15] *Letters*, V.281, VII.298.

THE EARLY INFLUENCE OF THE MORAVIANS 23

to be instructed in true poverty of spirit, in gentleness, in faith, and love of God and my neighbour.'[16] Wesley's deference is also seen in his readiness to accept the judgement of the Moravians on the question of his marrying Miss Sophia Hopkey.[17]

It must not be supposed, however, that Wesley accepted the Moravian teaching in Georgia uncritically. A significant entry appears in the *Journal* for 31st July 1737. 'Having been long in doubt concerning the principles of the Moravian Brethren . . . I proposed to them the following queries, to each of which is subjoined the substance of their answer.'[18] It is noteworthy that among the questions submitted by Wesley are the following: 'What do you mean by conversion?' 'What is Faith?' 'Is the Lord's Supper a means of grace?' It will be relevant to recall some of these questions in later chapters. With reference to Zinzendorf, Wesley went so far as to say on 1st August 1737: 'The Count's exposition of Scripture and method of public prayer fully convinced me that he likewise is but a man.'[19]

It is no part of our purpose here to trace Wesley's varying fortunes during his stay in Georgia. Suffice it to say that he considered his missionary labours a failure. 'All the time I was in Savannah', he wrote, 'I was thus beating the air.'[20] He appears, however, to have been unduly pessimistic, if we accept Whitefield's appreciation of Wesley's work in Georgia:[21] 'The good Mr Wesley has done in America is inexpressible. His name is very precious among the people; and he has laid a foundation that I hope neither men nor devils will ever be able to shake. Oh that I may follow him as he has followed Christ.'[22]

We need not pause to assess the relative accuracy of these judgements. Our interest lies in Wesley's state of mind and soul. At this juncture, he regarded his missionary enterprise as a failure. Whatever else Wesley might have achieved, he believed that he had failed in the fulfilment of his 'chief motive'.[23]

On 22nd December 1737 Wesley set sail for England on board the *Samuel*. He was a disillusioned man—much wiser and humbler than he was on the outward journey some two years

---

[16] *Letters*, I.195f.   [17] Moore, *Life of Wesley*, I.312.
[18] *Journal*, I.372.   [19] ibid., p. 375.   [20] ibid., p. 470.
[21] Whitefield arrived in Georgia on 7th May 1738.
[22] See Whitefield's *Journal*. Wesley himself gives a more optimistic account later. See *Journal*, I.435.
[23] *Letters*, I.188.

before. The return voyage was a time of heart-searching and self-examination. We find a revealing entry in the *Journal*, dated 8th January 1738:

'In the fullness of my heart, I wrote the following words: "By the most infallible of proofs, inward feeling, I am convinced,

'1. Of unbelief, having no such faith in Christ as will prevent my heart from being troubled; which it could not be, if I believed in God, and rightly believed also in Him.

'2. Of pride, throughout my life past; inasmuch as I thought I had what I find I have not.

'3. Of gross irrecollection; inasmuch as in the storm I cry to God every moment; in a calm, not.

'4. Of levity and luxuriancy of spirit, recurring whenever the pressure is taken off, and appearing by my speaking words not tending to edify; but most by my manner of speaking of my enemies.

'Lord, save, or I perish! Save me,

'1. By such a faith as implies peace in life and in death.

'2. By such humility as may fill my heart from this hour for ever, with a piercing uninterrupted sense, *Nihil est quod hactenus feci*;[24] having evidently built without a foundation.

'3. By such a recollection as may cry to Thee every moment especially when all is calm: Give me faith, or I die; give me a lowly spirit; otherwise, *mihi non sit suave vivere*.[25]

'4. By steadiness, seriousness, σεμνότης,[26] sobriety of spirit; avoiding as fire every word that tendeth not to edifying; and never speaking of any who oppose me, or sin against God, without all my own sins set out in array before my face.'[27]

Looking back, after his arrival in England, upon his missionary work in Georgia, Wesley wrote in the *Journal* under 3rd February 1738: 'Many reasons I have to bless God, though the design I went upon did not take effect, for my having been carried into that strange land, contrary to all my preceding resolutions. Hereby I trust He hath in some measure "humbled me and proved me and shown me what is in my heart". . . . Hereby God has given me to know many of His servants; particularly those of the Church of Herrnhut.'[28]

[24] 'That which hitherto I have done is nothing.' See Thomas à Kempis, *Imitation of Christ*, I.19.i.
[25] 'To me let it be no pleassure to live.'   [26] 'Gravity'; cf. 1 Timothy 2^2, 3^4.
[27] *Journal*, I.415f.   [28] ibid., p. 435.

THE EARLY INFLUENCE OF THE MORAVIANS

At this stage of his religious development, Wesley reviewed his own spiritual state in the Moravian dialect.[29] The simplicity and reality of the Moravians' faith sent him in more ardent search of a like assurance. Thus was Wesley prepared in mind and heart for his meeting with Peter Böhler in London on 7th February 1738—a day Wesley considered much to be remembered.[30] In his *Short History of the People called Methodists*, Wesley says: 'In all our steps we were greatly assisted by the advice and exhortations of Peter Böhler, an excellent young man, belonging to the society commonly called Moravians.'[31]

Peter Böhler was born at Frankfort-on-the-Main in 1712; he was thus nine years younger than Wesley. Brought up a Lutheran, he entered Jena University in 1731; and it was while he was studying here that he met Count Zinzendorf, whose influence was responsible for his joining the Moravian Church. From Pietism, Böhler inherited his experimental religion and certain views on justification by faith, which later he urged the Methodists to accept.[32]

After finding Böhler lodgings in London, Wesley tells us that he did not willingly lose any opportunity of conversing with him.[33] Whenever possible, they journeyed together.[34] 'All this time', writes Wesley, 'I conversed much with Peter Böhler; but I understood him not, least of all when he said,[35] *Mi frater, mi frater, excoquenda est ista tua philosophia.*'[36]

One is impressed by the humble way in which Wesley listened to Böhler's testimony. It is the eager co-operation of a man who desperately desires what he believes the other can give. With reference to John Wesley, Böhler reported to Zinzendorf that he was 'of a good natured disposition, and fully conscious of not believing in the Saviour as he ought, and was very ready to receive instruction'.[37]

This 'philosophy' of Wesley, however, was not going to be purged away as easily as Böhler might have thought. Wesley had just been, with his Moravian friend, on a visit to his beloved Oxford. One wonders if the old associations

---

[29] Rattenbury, *Conversion of the Wesleys*, p. 67. [30] *Journal*, I.436.
[31] *Works*, XIII.307. [32] See *Encyclopaedia of Religion and Ethics*, VIII.838.
[33] *Journal*, I.437. [34] ibid., p. 439.

[35] 'My brother, my brother, that philosophy of yours must be purged away.' Wesley and Böhler conversed in Latin, since Böhler knew little English, and presumably Wesley did not feel he had a sufficient grasp of German for this purpose.

[36] *Journal*, I.440. [37] J. P. Lockwood, *Memorials of Peter Böhler* (1868), p. 69.

as Fellow of Lincoln College accounted to some extent for this 'philosophic' element in Wesley's conversation. But, in any case, Böhler was not to be intimidated by Oxford! As we shall see later, it was not a characteristic of the Moravians to lack confidence in their claim to a grasp of true religion.

Under the date 4th March 1738 Wesley writes: 'I found my brother at Oxford, recovering from pleurisy; and with him Peter Böhler, by whom (in the hand of the great God) I was, on Sunday the 5th, clearly convinced of unbelief, of the want of that faith whereby alone we are saved.'[38] The qualifying phrase, 'with the full Christian salvation', is added as a note to this entry in the Standard Edition of the *Journal*.[39] This statement gives rise to a number of vital questions. What did he mean by 'convinced of unbelief'? In what sense did he lack 'that faith whereby alone we are saved'?

Wesley continues under the above date: 'Immediately it struck into my mind, "Leave off preaching. How can you preach to others, who have not faith yourself?" I asked Peter Böhler whether I should leave it off or not. He answered: "By no means." I asked: "But what can I preach?" He said: "Preach faith *till* you have it; and then, *because* you have it, you will preach faith." '[40]

We might pause here briefly to consider what Böhler meant by: 'Preach faith till you have it.' The exhortation must not be taken to mean: 'Preach what you don't believe till you believe it.' The truer interpretation would seem to be: 'Preach this doctrine, the truth of which your mind accepts, until it becomes your own experience.'[41]

Wesley goes on to say: 'Accordingly, Monday the 6th, I began preaching this new doctrine, though my soul started back from the work. The first person to whom I offered salvation by faith alone was a prisoner under sentence of death.'[42] The *Journal* tells of Wesley's journeys to different parts of the country in the course of which he commends 'this new doctrine' to his fellow travellers.

---

[38] *Journal*, I.442.

[39] Curnock comments as follows: 'This note is not in the first edition, or in *Works* (1771–4), or in Benson's edition (1809). It is either Jackson's, or, more probably, Wesley's.

[40] *Journal*, I.442.   [41] See Rattenbury, *Conversion of the Wesleys*, p. 71.

[42] *Journal*, I.442.

On 23rd March Wesley writes: 'I met Peter Böhler again,[43] who now amazed me more and more by the account he gave of the fruits of a living faith—the holiness and happiness which he affirmed to attend it. The next morning I began the New Testament again, resolving to abide by "the law and the testimony"; and being confident that God would hereby show me whether this doctrine was of God.'[44]

One could wish that Wesley had recorded in his *Journal* the substance of more of his vital conversations with Peter Böhler. The movement toward the Aldersgate experience seems too rapid, owing to the omission of some of the intermediate stages by which that spiritual height was reached. The review of his religious development, however, with which Wesley prefaced his account of 24th May 1738 helps to make up the deficiency. But, unfortunately, this review, while it gives the main sequence of events, includes few dates.[45]

This review, however, adds some valuable details. 'When Peter Böhler, whom God prepared for me as soon as I came to London, affirmed of true faith in Christ (which is but one) that it had these two fruits inseparably attending it, "dominion over sin and constant peace from a sense of forgiveness", I was quite amazed and looked upon it as a new Gospel. If this was so, it was clear I had not faith. But I was not willing to be convinced of this. Therefore I disputed with all my might, and laboured to prove that faith might be where these were not. . . . Besides I well saw no one could, in the nature of things, have such a sense of forgiveness, and not *feel* it. But I felt it not. If then, there was no faith without this, all my pretensions of faith dropped at once.'[46]

Wesley, therefore, insisted that Böhler's claim should be tested at the bar of Scripture and experience. Turning to the Scriptures, Wesley found that 'they all made against me, and I was forced to retreat to my last hold, "that experience would never agree with the *literal interpretation* of those Scriptures".' Böhler, however, soon supplied the experimental proof in the form of three 'living witnesses', who testified 'that a true living faith in Christ is inseparable from a sense of pardon for all past

---

[43] In Böhler's account of this interview both John and Charles are present. Lockwood, *Life of Peter Böhler*, p. 74.
[44] *Journal*, I.447.
[45] See Böhler's account in his letters of his contacts with the Wesleys. *World Parish*, Vol. II, No. 1 (New York, November 1949).
[46] *Journal*, I.471.

and freedom from all present sins'. Wesley writes: 'I was now thoroughly convinced.'[47]

Another interview takes place on 22nd April, which Böhler describes as 'a right searching conversation with the two Wesleys'.[48] Wesley's account is as follows: 'I met Peter Böhler again. I had now no objection to what he said of the nature of faith, namely, that it is (to use the words of our Church),[49] "a sure trust and confidence which a man hath in God, that through the merits of Christ his sins are forgiven and he reconciled to the favour of God".[50] Neither could I deny the happiness and holiness which he described as fruits of this living faith. "The Spirit itself beareth witness with our spirit that we are the children of God"[51] and "He that believeth hath the witness in himself"[52] fully convinced me of the former; as "Whatsoever is born of God doth not commit sin"[53] and "Whosoever believeth is born of God"[54] did of the latter.'[55]

By 'happiness' in this connexion, Wesley plainly means assurance of salvation or the witness of the Spirit. This interpretation is clear, not only from its association in the above passage with Romans 8^{16} and 1 John 5^{10}, but also from a study of at least two other quotations in the *Journal*.[56]

Wesley is baffled, however, by Böhler's claim that this experience is gained instantaneously. 'I could not comprehend', writes Wesley, 'what he spoke of an instantaneous work. I could not understand how this faith should be given in a moment: how a man could *at once* be turned from darkness to light, from sin and misery to righteousness and joy in the Holy Ghost. I searched the Scriptures again touching this very thing, particularly the Acts of the Apostles: but, to my utter astonishment, found scarce any instances there of other than *instantaneous* conversions; scarce any so slow as that of St Paul, who was three days in the pangs of the new birth. I had but one retreat left, namely, "Thus, I grant, God wrought in the *first* ages of Christianity; but the times are changed. What

---

[47] *Journal*, p. 472.   [48] *Moravian Messenger* (1875), p. 144.

[49] On Wesley's relationship with the Anglican Church on the question of Assurance, see Part V, pp. 179ff., *infra*.

[50] From the Homily 'Of Salvation'. See *London Quarterly Review* (January 1902), pp. 141f.

[51] Romans 8^{16}.   [52] 1 John 5^{10}.   [53] 1 John 5^{18}.

[54] 1 John 5^{1}. For an examination of the biblical basis of assurance, see Part III, pp. 103ff., *infra*.

[55] *Journal*, I.454.   [56] ibid., I.447, 471.

reason have I to believe that he works in the same manner now?"'[57]

Again the issue is decided on the ground of experience. 'On Sunday, the 23rd,' Wesley says, 'I was beat out of this retreat too, by the concurring evidence of several living witnesses, who testified God had thus wrought in themselves, giving them in a moment such a faith in the blood of His Son as translated them out of darkness into light, out of sin and fear into holiness and happiness. Here ended my disputing. I could now only cry out: "Lord, help Thou my unbelief!"'[58]

It is enlightening to study Böhler's account of what was doubtless the same incident. 'I took four of my English brethren', writes the Moravian, 'to John Wesley. They told, one after another, what had been wrought in them. Wesley and those that were with him were as if thunderstruck at these narratives. I asked John Wesley what he then believed. He said four examples were not enough. I replied I would bring eight more here in London. After a short time he stood up and said: "We will sing that hymn: *Hier legt mein Sinn sich vor Dir nieder.*"[59] During the singing of the Moravian version he often wiped his eyes.'[60]

This last sentence of Böhler's is very revealing; for it indicates, not only how closely the Moravian watched Wesley's spiritual evolution, but also the fact that the founder of Methodism was capable of deep religious feeling, as well as penetrating intellectual insight. The Moravian hymn here chosen by Wesley emanated from a Pietistic sphere influenced by 'the wise and good Professor Francke'.[61] It is one of many German hymns with which Wesley became familiar and which expressed an intensely Evangelical spirit. These hymns played no small part in the mental and spiritual preparation of Wesley's religious illumination at Aldersgate, on 24th May 1738.[62]

Wesley was again troubled by another twinge of conscience at the thought of commending to others an experience which as yet he did not share. 'I asked Peter Böhler again whether

[57] *Journal*, p. 454.   [58] ibid., p. 455.

[59] 'My soul before Thee prostrate lies', by C. F. Richter, from the Freylinghausen *Gesangbuch*, translated by Wesley for his *Psalms and Hymns*, 56 (Charlestown, 1737); *Lutheran Hymnal*, 355. The usual tune appears in Wesley's first *Tune-Book* (1742). Bett, *Hymns of Methodism*, pp. 16, 33.

[60] See Richard Green, *John Wesley, Evangelist*, p. 185.

[61] *Wesley's Letters*, VI.44.

[62] We shall examine the theological significance of Wesley's translations from German hymns in Part II, Chapter 4, pp. 82ff., *infra*.

I ought not to refrain from teaching others. He said, "No; do not hide in the earth the talent God has given you".'[63]

It was a sad day for Wesley when Böhler left England. His departure antedated Wesley's Aldersgate experience by twenty days. Writing in the *Journal* on 4th May 1738 Wesley says: 'Peter Böhler left London in order to embark for Carolina.'[64] Then follows a tribute which expresses how deeply Wesley felt himself indebted to his Moravian friend and spiritual guide. 'Oh, what hath God begun, since his coming to England! Such an one as shall never come to an end till heaven and earth pass away.'[65]

Wesley was 'a little refreshed' by a letter written by Böhler from Southampton before he set sail for the New World. He expresses his affectionate concern that Wesley 'may taste, and then see, how exceedingly the Son of God has loved you, . . . and that you may continually trust in Him, and feel His life in yourself. Beware of the sin of unbelief; . . . see that you conquer it this very day, through the blood of Jesus Christ. . . . So put Him in mind of His promises to poor sinners that He may not be able to refrain from doing for you what He hath done for so many others. . . .'[66]

Although Böhler had embarked for Carolina before Wesley's transforming experience at Aldersgate, it is plain that this young Moravian's zeal for, and experience of, a 'true, living faith' with its 'sense of forgiveness'[67] went a long way in the intellectual and spiritual preparation of Wesley for 24th May. It was this faith, as interpreted by Böhler, to which Wesley refers when he writes in the *Journal*: 'I continued thus to seek it . . . till Wednesday, 24th May.'[68]

[63] *Journal*, I.455.   [64] ibid., p. 457.
[65] ibid., p. 460. Curnock holds that this tribute was added at a much later date, as the content of the statement seems to imply.
[66] The letter was written in Latin. *Journal*, I.461.
[67] *Journal*, I.471.   [68] ibid., p. 472.

CHAPTER FOUR

A VISIT TO GERMANY

THERE were few people in England to nurture and guide Wesley after he had gained religious illumination and power at Aldersgate. Like Paul, after his encounter with Christ on the Damascus Road, Wesley felt the need of a retreat. For Wesley, however, it was not Arabia, but Marienborn and Herrnhut, Moravian settlements in Germany.[1]

The entry in the *Journal* for 7th June 1738 reads: 'I determined . . . to retire for a short time to Germany. . . . And I hoped the conversing with these holy men who were themselves living witnesses of the full power of faith, and yet able to bear with those that are weak, would be the means, under God, of so establishing my soul, that I might go on from faith to faith and "from strength to strength"!'[2]

Some three weeks after his Aldersgate experience Wesley set out accompanied by Benjamin Ingham and John Toltschig.[3] On 4th June they reached Marienborn. 'The family at Marienborn', Wesley says, 'consists of about ninety persons, gathered out of many nations. They live for the present in a large house hired by the Count. . . . 'Oh how pleasant a thing it is for brethren to dwell together in unity." '[4]

Wesley writes an enthusiastic letter to his mother, dated 6th July 1738, regarding his visit to Marienborn and his reception by Count Zinzendorf. 'The Count received us in a manner I was quite unacquainted with, and therefore know not how to express. I believe his behaviour was not unlike that of his Master . . . when He took the little children in His arms and blessed them. We should have been much amazed at him, but that we saw ourselves encompassed with a cloud of those who were all followers of him, as he is of Christ.'[5]

Benham says that Ingham was admitted to partake of the

---

[1] On the historical development, constitution, and doctrine of Moravianism, see *E.R.E.*, VIII.837ff.; Bett, *Spirit of Methodism*, pp. 55ff.; Harrison, *The Evangelical Revival and Christian Reunion*, pp. 32ff.
[2] *Journal*, I.482f.
[3] Toltschig had been driven to Herrnhut for refuge by the fierce persecution in Moravia in 1724. See *Charles Wesley's Journal*, I.106.
[4] *Journal*, II.10f.   [5] *Letters*, I.250; cf. I.251.

Holy Communion. 'But when the congregation saw Wesley to be *homo perturbatus*, and that his head had gained an ascendancy over his heart, and being desirous not to interfere with his plan of affecting good as a clergyman of the English Church[6] ... they deemed it not prudent to admit him to that sacred service.'[7]

This account lacks authenticity, and it must be borne in mind that Benham's book was not published till over a century after the alleged event.[8] Moreover, we can trace no reference to it either in Wesley's *Letters* or *Journal*. The incident, however, is not altogether improbable. The Holy Communion in the Moravian Community was rigidly fenced against all those who lacked full assurance. And, even after 24th May 1738 Wesley for a time was not without fluctuations of religious feeling and seasons of comparative uncertainty. It was, indeed, partly with a view to resolving these doubts and gaining a more continuous sense of assurance that he had travelled to Germany.

An entry in the *Journal* gives further expression to the purpose of Wesley's visit: 'I continually met with what I sought for, viz. living proofs of the power of faith; persons saved ... from all doubt and fear by the abiding witness of "the Holy Ghost given unto them".'[9]

On 12th July Wesley records Zinzendorf's answer to the question: 'Can a man be justified and not know it?'

'1. Justification is the forgiveness of sins.
'2. The moment a man flies to Christ he is justified.
'3. And has peace with God; but not always joy.
'4. Nor perhaps may he know he is justified till long after.
'5. For the assurance of it is distinct from justification itself.
'6. But others may know he is justified by his power over sin, by his seriousness, his love of the brethren, and his "hunger and thirst after righteousness" which alone prove the spiritual life to be begun.'[10]

On hearing the Count speak thus, Wesley says that he recalled what Peter Böhler had often said upon this head, which was to this effect:

'1. When a man has living faith in Christ, then he is justified.

[6] 'Peculiar Reasons', says Tyerman, *Life and Times of John Wesley*, I.198.
[7] Benham, *Memoirs of James Hutton*, p. 40.
[8] Simon, *John Wesley and the Religious Societies*, p. 205.
[9] *Journal*, II.13.   [10] ibid., II.13.

'2. This is always given in a moment.
'3. And in that moment he has peace with God.
'4. Which he cannot have without knowledge that he has it.
'5. And being born of God, he sinneth not.
'6. Which deliverance from sin he cannot have without knowing that he has it.'[11]

A comparative study of these two replies brings out very important differences regarding assurance. Böhler had maintained that a man cannot be justified without having peace with God and a knowledge that he has it. Zinzendorf, however, agrees that justification involves peace with God, but holds that he may not know he is justified, till long after.

Wesley must also have listened with great interest when Zinzendorf said that 'not always joy' accompanied the experience of justification; since, in the pages of the *Journal* immediately following 24th May, frequent references are found to the lack of joy in Wesley's religious life—a deficiency which then greatly troubled him.[12]

On 1st August 1738 Wesley reached Herrnhut, where he spent some hours in conversation with Christian David, who ranked as one of the best exponents of Moravian doctrine.[13] After recounting an unusual and hazardous religious development, the Moravian says that, under the influence of Pastor Schwedler, he first experienced the power of the gospel of Christ. 'Here I found the peace I had long sought in vain, for I was assured *my* sins were forgiven. Not indeed all at once, but by degrees; not in one moment, nor in one hour. For I could not immediately believe that I *was* forgiven, because of the mistake I was then in concerning forgiveness. I saw not then that the first promise to the children of God is, "Sin shall no more reign over you"; but thought I was to feel it in me no more from the time I was forgiven.'[14]

Christian David goes on to say: 'Neither saw I then that the being justified is widely different from the having the full assurance of faith. I remembered not that our Lord told His disciples before His death, "Ye are clean"; whereas it was not till many days after it that they were fully assured, by the Holy Ghost then received, of their reconciliation to God through His

---

[11] *Journal*, pp. 13f. [12] ibid., I.476ff.
[13] A middle-aged carpenter. Born at Senftleben on 31st December 1690.
[14] *Journal*, II.30.

blood.[15] The difference between these fruits of the Spirit was as yet hid from me; so that I was hardly and slowly convinced I had the one, because I had not the other.'[16]

Here Wesley gleaned further evidence that assurance is not an inseparable accompaniment of justification—that the latter may be received by the believer without the former. In the light of this, Wesley must have seen the need of re-assessing the meagre value he had attached to his pre-Aldersgate religious experience.

Christian David told Wesley that before the Moravian Church would judge a man to have true faith, or to be fit to receive the Lord's Supper, he must give satisfactory answers to certain questions, amongst which were the following:

(1) Are you fully assured, beyond all doubt or fear, that you are a child of God?
(2) In what manner, and at what moment, did you receive that full assurance?[17]

Another statement by Christian David is recorded in the *Journal*: 'I now clearly saw we ought not to insist on anything we *feel* any more than anything we *do*, as if it were necessary previous to justification or the remission of sins. I saw that least of all ought we so to insist on the full assurance of faith . . . as to exclude those who had not attained this from the Lord's Table, or to deny that they had any faith at all.[18] I plainly perceived that this full assurance was a distinct gift from justifying faith, and often not given till long after it.'[19]

Continuing the account of his religious experience, Christian David says: 'And now first it was that I had that full assurance of my own reconciliation to God through Christ. For many years I had had the forgiveness of my sins and a measure of the peace of God; but I had not till now that witness of His Spirit which shuts out all doubt and fear . . . I saw that what I had hitherto so constantly insisted on—the *doing* so much and *feeling* so much—were by no means essential to justification.'[20]

With these points in mind, we turn to the testimony of Michael Linner, the Eldest of the Church. He refers to the

[15] See 'The Apostolic Church', Part III, ch. 6, pp. 139ff., *infra*.
[16] *Journal*, II.30.   [17] ibid., II.35.
[18] Molther was among those who taught this (Part V, pp. 198ff., *infra*). It was probably on this ground that Wesley was excluded from the Holy Communion at Marienborn.
[19] *Journal*, II.35.   [20] ibid., p. 36.

great influence on his life of John 3¹⁶. 'I thought, "all"? Then I am one. Then He is given for *me*. But I am a sinner and He came to save sinners. Immediately my burden dropped off, and my heart was at rest.' The use of the personal pronoun here is reminiscent of Böhler's stress on the personal nature of salvation by faith, on which ground alone assurance could be gained. Michael Linner goes on to say that 'the full assurance of faith I had not yet; nor for the two years I continued in Moravia'. After some time, however, he is given that full sense of acceptance in Him which excludes all doubt and fear.

Michael Linner adds that the leading of the Spirit is different in different souls. His more usual method is to give, in one and the same moment, the forgiveness of sins and a full assurance of that forgiveness. 'Yet in many He works as He did in me—giving first the remission of sins, and after some weeks, or months or years, the full assurance of it.'[21] The Moravian's reference here to the varied operations of the Holy Spirit in different individuals is re-echoed, as we shall see, in Wesley's later writings.[22]

Wesley says that this great truth was further confirmed the next day by a conversation with David Nitschmann, one of the teachers and pastors in the Church.[23] Nitschmann testifies: 'In walking home I thought of an expression of Pastor Rothe's: "Only *suppose* these things are so; *suppose* there be a God." I said to myself: "Well, I will, I *do* suppose it." Immediately, I felt a strange sweetness in my soul, which increased every moment till the next morning. . . . This first sweetness lasted for six weeks, without any intermission.'[24]

The similarity of this description to Wesley's account of his Aldersgate experience is striking.[25] Both statements include the significant words 'felt' and 'strange'. The principal difference lies in the fact that, in the case of Nitschmann, the 'strange sweetness' lasted for six weeks, without the fluctuations of religious feeling which harassed Wesley in the months subsequent to 24th May 1738.

Nitschmann admits, however, that there was a weakness in his faith. 'I believed in God, but not in Christ. . . . For above four years I found no rest by reason of this unbelief; till one

---

[21] *Journal*, II.37.

[22] *Letters*, V.175, VII.298, VIII.110; cf. Simon, *John Wesley and the Religious Societies*, p. 207.

[23] *Journal*, II.37.   [24] ibid., p. 38.   [25] ibid., I.475f.

day ... those words shot into me: "God was in Christ reconciling the world to Himself." I thought: "Then God and Christ are one." Immediately my heart was filled with joy.'[26]

In recording Nitschmann's testimony, Wesley would be sure to recall his own misdirected faith prior to Aldersgate: 'I fixed not this faith on its right object; I meant only faith in God, not faith in or through Christ.'[27]

We now turn to the religious experience of Albinus Theodorus Feder, a student at Herrnhut. Despairing, like Wesley, of gaining salvation by his own strenuous efforts, he finally threw himself in faith on the mercy and power of Christ. 'In that moment', he explains, 'I found my heart at rest, in good hope that my sins were forgiven; of which I had a stronger assurance six weeks after, when I received the Lord's Supper here.'[28]

Two important features emerge from Feder's testimony. One is that there are degrees of assurance; the other that the Holy Communion can be a means, as in the case of Susanna Wesley, of leading believers into a deeper sense of Christian certainty.

Augustin Neisser tells Wesley that he received the witness of the Spirit gradually, but that, once he had gained assurance, he never lost it. 'In Him I found true rest to my soul, being fully assured that all my sins were forgiven. Yet I cannot tell the hour or the day when I first received that full assurance. For it was not given me at first, neither at once; but grew up in me by degrees. But from the time it was confirmed in me, I never lost it; having never since doubted, no, not for a moment.'[29]

David Schneider says: 'Before the time of my coming out of Moravia, I knew that my sins were forgiven. Yet I cannot fix on any particular time when I knew this first. For I did not clearly know it at once, God having always done everything in my soul by degrees.'[30] Schneider, however, suffered a spiritual relapse; but after the brethren at Herrnhut had cast lots,[31] they admitted him to the Lord's Table. 'And from that hour', says Schneider, 'my soul received comfort, and I was more and more assured that I had an advocate with the Father, and that I was fully reconciled to God by His blood.'[32]

---

[26] *Journal*, II.39.   [27] ibid., I.471.   [28] ibid., II.40.
[29] ibid., II.41.   [30] ibid., II.44.
[31] Wesley sometimes used this means for reaching a decision. *Works*, VIII.449.
[32] *Journal*, II.46.

Further evidence of the doctrine comes from Christopher Demuth, who begins his account by saying that his father, a little before he died, having been all his life-time under the law, received at once remission of sins and the full witness of the Spirit.[33] After some years of ardent seeking for God and of Jesuit persecution, Christopher is able to say: 'God gave me the full assurance that my sins were forgiven . . . and ever since it has been confirmed more and more by my receiving from Him every day fresh supplies of strength and comfort.'[34]

Wesley's visit to Herrnhut lasted nearly a fortnight. 'I would gladly', he wrote, 'have spent my life here. Oh when shall this Christianity cover the earth, as the waters cover the sea?'[35] On 12th August Wesley bade farewell to Herrnhut and on 16th September arrived back in London.[36]

How are we to assess this visit to the Moravian settlements of Marienborn and Herrnhut? We have observed how eagerly the founder of Methodism listened to these accounts of religious experience. It may be that Wesley's high regard for the Moravians made him somewhat credulous in accepting certain of their claims. While he heard much teaching in Germany that was scriptural, there were elements of doctrine not so securely based.[37] It would also appear that Moravian theology was not so clear cut as Böhler gave Wesley to understand, more particularly in regard to justification and assurance.[38]

We have already noted that, whereas Spangenberg in Georgia and Böhler in England had treated the witness of the Spirit as an inseparable accompaniment of salvation by faith, the Moravians at Herrnhut often spoke of assurance as *following* the forgiveness of sins. This offers an explanation of Wesley's statements about his not being a Christian in the months subsequent to 24th May 1738. By this, we do not mean that Wesley did not gain an assurance of salvation at Aldersgate Street after all; but that the fluctuations of feeling in Wesley's religious experience after 24th May are not necessarily a cause for despair. The testimonies of these representative Moravians show that seasons of uncertainty do not in themselves discount the believer's claim that he is a true child of God. There were few lapses, however, in Wesley's experience of assurance

[33] cf. the testimony to the Spirit's witness by Wesley's father on his death bed. *New History of Methodism*, I.168.
[34] *Journal*, II.47.   [35] Tyerman, *Life and Times of Wesley*, I.203.
[36] *Journal*, II.56, 63.   [37] Tyerman, op. cit., I.194.
[38] Piette, *John Wesley in the Evolution of Protestantism*, p. 312.

once he had thrown himself unreservedly, in the spring of 1739, into the all-absorbing task of the Methodist Revival.

We have already seen that there were certain elements in Moravianism of which Wesley and some of the leading Moravians disapproved. In addition to the murmurs of disapproval already quoted, there is a letter written at Marienborn by Wesley to Zinzendorf, in which, after speaking in high praise of his Moravian hosts, he goes on to say: 'I hope to see them at least once more, were it only to speak freely on a few things which I did not approve, perhaps because I did not understand them.'[39]

A similar note of disapproval is struck in a letter written by Wesley soon after his return to England. It is addressed to the Moravians at Marienborn and Herrnhut and dated September 1738. 'But', says Wesley, 'being fearful of trusting my own judgement, I determined to wait yet a little longer, and so laid it by unfinished.'

We quote those passages in the letter in line with this inquiry: 'Of some other things', writes Wesley, 'I stand in doubt, which I will mention in love and meekness. . . . Is not the Count all in all? . . . Are you in general serious enough? . . . Do you not fall into trifling conversation? Do you not magnify your own Church too much? . . . Do you love your enemies and wicked men as yourselves? Do you not mix human wisdom with divine, joining worldly prudence to heavenly? Do you not use cunning, guile, or dissimulation in many cases? Are you not of a close, dark, reserved temper and behaviour? . . . Have you that childlike openness, frankness, and plainness of speech so manifest to all in the Apostles and first Christians?'[40]

[39] *Wesley's Works*, XII.50.
[40] *Letters*, I.257f. See Part V, ch. 4, pp. 198ff., *infra*.

CHAPTER FIVE

THE TESTIMONY OF THE EARLY METHODISTS

WRITING to 'John Smith' on 28th September 1745 Wesley says: 'I am acquainted with more than twelve or thirteen hundred persons, whom I believe to be truly pious, and not on slight grounds, and who have severally testified to me with their own mouths that they do know the day when the love of God was first shed abroad in their hearts and when His Spirit first witnessed with their spirits that they were the children of God. Now, if you are determined to think all these liars or fools, this is no evidence to you; but to me it is strong evidence, who have for some years known the men and their communication.'[1]

Dr Henry Bett has shown how ill-founded is the belief that the majority of Wesley's helpers were ignorant.[2] Dr. T. B. Shepherd writes: 'An examination of two hundred who may claim to be the early preachers shows that, with the exception of half a dozen, they sprang from the lower middle class and classes above this; they were tradesmen, farmers, clerks, schoolmasters, or held better positions. Some of them were sprung from families of considerable wealth. . . . About one-fifth of them afterwards entered the Church of England or Dissenting Churches as clergymen or ministers.'[3]

We consider, first, the religious experiences of two men who gained a personal assurance of salvation before John Wesley himself—namely George Whitefield and Charles Wesley.

George Whitefield, born in 1714, was at the age of twenty-six 'the most brilliant and popular preacher the modern world has ever known'.[4] In 1732, he entered Pembroke College, Oxford, as a servitor. He became a member of the Holy Club to which John and Charles Wesley also belonged. His striving for a deeper spiritual experience was quickened by reading Henry Scougal's *The Life of God in the Soul of Man*. A fuller enlightenment came to him just seven weeks after Easter 1735 —three years before Wesley went to Aldersgate Street.

[1] *Letters*, II.47 (cf. p. 60); Simon, *John Wesley and The Methodist Societies*, p. 278; *Sermons*, II.350.
[2] *The Early Methodist Preachers* (1935), pp. 33–46.
[3] *Methodism and the Literature of the Eighteenth Century*, p. 144.
[4] *New History of Methodism*, I.257; cf. Shepherd, op. cit., pp. 169ff.

Whitefield writes: 'I was delivered from the burden that had so heavily oppressed me. The spirit of mourning was taken from me, and I knew what it was truly to rejoice in God my Saviour, and for some time could not avoid singing psalms wherever I was; but my joy gradually became more settled, and blessed be God, has abode and increased in my soul saving a few casual intermissions, ever since.'[5]

It is noticeable that the terms 'assurance' or 'witness of the Spirit' do not appear in Whitefield's account. This may be explained by the fact that such terminology was not widely current in the eighteenth century till it was introduced by the Moravians.[6] While the phraseology was absent, the experience of assurance was obviously present, including the spiritual fluctuations which Wesley also shared. For Wesley the place of illumination was Aldersgate, London; for Whitefield it was Oxford: 'I know the place; it may perhaps be superstitious, but whenever I go to Oxford, I cannot help running to the spot where Jesus Christ first revealed Himself to me, and gave me new birth.'[7]

Close attention should be given to the spiritual enlightenment of Charles Wesley—for two reasons. One is that it illustrates further the great influence wielded by the Moravians over the early Methodists. The other reason is that an examination of Charles Wesley's experience of assurance is essential in view of the theological significance of Methodist hymnology.[8]

After attending Westminster School, Charles gained a scholarship to Christ Church, Oxford. His brother, John, was then Fellow of Lincoln College, and a Greek Lecturer. John Wesley felt it incumbent upon him to advise Charles to take religion more seriously. Charles replied: 'What, would you have me to be a saint all at once?'[9] Later, however, he became more earnest in his search for reality in religion; and, during John's curacy at Wroote, he founded the Holy Club. In 1735, Charles was ordained deacon, then priest, in the Anglican Church. In October of the same year, he sailed for Georgia as secretary to General Oglethorpe, in company with his brother John, Benjamin Ingham, Charles Delamotte, and twenty-six Moravians under the leadership of Bishop David Nitschmann. On 5th February 1736 they landed at Savannah and a

[5] *New History of Methodism*, I.260. [6] See Part II, ch. 1, pp. 53ff., *infra*.
[7] *New History of Methodism*, I.260. [8] Part II, chs. 4 and 5, pp. 82ff., *infra*.
[9] Dr F. L. Wiseman, *Charles Wesley*, p. 26.

THE TESTIMONY OF THE EARLY METHODISTS 41

month later Charles took up his secretarial duties at Frederica. But he enjoyed no greater success in Georgia than did his brother; and was finally driven by ill health to return home. He landed in England on 3rd December 1736.[10]

On his return, Charles was received with honour by several high officials in the Church, the State, and the University.[11] An eminent career in the Church or the University seemed assured. 'But the hindrance was in himself. His mind was full of unrest and uncertainty.'[12]

About a fortnight after John Wesley, back in England, met Peter Böhler—7th February 1738—Charles began to teach Böhler English.[13] Charles Wesley records a bedside conversation on 24th February with Böhler. 'He asked me: "Do you hope to be saved?" "Yes." "For what reason do you hope it?" "Because I have used my best endeavours to serve God." He shook his head and said no more.'[14]

In the *Journal* for 28th April we read: 'Dr Cockburn came to see me; and a better physician, Peter Böhler, whom God had detained in England for my good. . . . He prayed over me, that now at least I might see the divine intention in this and my late illness. I immediately thought it might be that I should again consider Böhler's doctrine of faith; examine myself whether I was in the faith; and if I was not, never cease seeking and longing after it till I attained it.'[15]

Under 1st May, Charles Wesley writes: 'After receiving the sacrament, I felt a small anticipation of peace, and said, 'Now I have demonstration against the Moravian doctrine that a man cannot have peace without assurance of his pardon'.[16] I now have peace, yet cannot say of a surety that my sins are forgiven.'[17]

During his attack of pleurisy, Charles goes to live with Mr Bray, 'a poor ignorant mechanic, who knows nothing but Christ; yet by knowing Him, knows and discerns all things. Some time ago I had taken leave of Peter Böhler,[18] confessed my unbelief and want of forgiveness. . . . Mr Bray is now to supply Böhler's place.'[19]

Part of the entry in the *Journal* for 13th May reads: 'I joined

[10] *Journal of the Rev. Charles Wesley*, ed. by Thomas Jackson, I.1–55.
[11] ibid., pp. 73f.   [12] D. M. Jones, *Charles Wesley—A Study*, p. 64.
[13] *Journal of Charles Wesley*, I.82.   [14] ibid.   [15] ibid., p. 85.
[16] cf. *Letters of John Wesley*, II.109.   [17] *Journal of Charles Wesley*, I.85.
[18] The Moravian had left for missionary work.
[19] *Journal of Charles Wesley*, I.86.

with Mr Bray in prayer and Scripture and was so greatly affected, that I almost thought Christ was coming that moment.'[20] The next day Charles writes: 'At night my brother came, exceedingly heavy. I forced him (as he had often forced me) to sing an hymn to Christ, and almost thought He would come while we were singing.'[21]

Under the date, Wednesday, 17th May, Charles writes: 'Today I first saw Luther on the Galatians ... and found him nobly full of faith.... I laboured, waited, and prayed to feel "who loved *me*, and gave Himself for *me*".'[22]

This brief survey of Charles Wesley's spiritual development has already included references to two people who enjoyed an experience of assurance—namely, Böhler and Bray. Mention is now made of a third. Under 19th May, Charles writes: 'At seven Mrs Turner came and told me I should not rise from that bed till I believed. I believed her saying and asked, "Has God then bestowed faith upon you?" "Yes, He has." "Why, have you peace with God?" "Yes, perfect peace. ... I know all my sins are blotted out." '[23]

In the *Journal*, the entry for 21st May, Whit Sunday, is headed 'The Day of Pentecost'. Charles tells us that his brother and some friends called at 9 a.m. and that they sang a hymn to the Holy Spirit. Later he says that, as he was settling down to sleep, he heard a woman's voice: 'In the name of Jesus of Nazareth, arise, and believe, and thou shalt be healed of all thy infirmities.' 'The words struck me to the heart', says Wesley. 'I sighed, and said within myself, "Oh that Christ would but speak thus to me!" I lay musing and trembling: then thought, "But what if it should be Him?" ... I said, yet feared to say, "I believe, I believe!" '[24] Mrs Turner, Bray's sister, tells Wesley: 'It was I, a weak, sinful creature, spoke; but the words were Christ's: He commanded me to say them, and so constrained me that I could not forbear.'[25] She explained that, after a dream in which she saw Jesus Christ coming in white, she was 'commanded to go and assure me from Christ of my recovery, soul and body'.

Charles then writes: 'I rose and looked into the Scriptures. ... "And now, Lord, what is my hope? Truly my hope is even in Thee." ... "He has put a new song in my mouth." ... "Comfort ye, comfort ye, my people, saith your God, speak

---

[20] *Journal of Charles Wesley*, p. 87. [21] ibid. [22] ibid., p. 88.
[23] ibid., p. 89. [24] ibid., p. 90. [25] ibid., p. 91.

THE TESTIMONY OF THE EARLY METHODISTS 43

ye comfortably to Jerusalem . . . that her iniquity is pardoned. . . ."' 'In that hour', says Dr Wiseman, 'with Bray and Mrs Turner as his Aquila and Priscilla, the Methodist Apollos found peace with God and "rejoiced in hope of loving Christ".'[26] With reference to the same Sunday morning (21st May) John Wesley writes: 'I received the surprising news that my brother had found rest to his soul. His bodily strength returned also from that hour.'[27]

We have dealt at some length with the stages by which Charles Wesley reached the goal of Christian certainty, because it is to 21st May or 24th May (or both) that many of the early Methodists owe their assurance of sins forgiven. Our interest lies only in those elements in the lives of Wesley's followers which either confirm or correct Wesley's doctrine of assurance.

In the case of some of the early Methodists the direct influence of the Wesleys is very apparent. 'In the summer of that year [1760]', writes Jasper Robinson, 'I heard Mr Wesley preach, under one of whose sermons I was enabled to believe that my sins were forgiven.'[28] The doubts which assailed Wesley in the months succeeding Aldersgate are reflected in the experience of many of his followers.[29] William Black can testify: 'My burden dropped off; my guilt was removed; condemnation gave place to mercy, and a sweet peace and gladness was diffused throughout my soul.' But very soon uncertainty takes hold of him: 'I did not feel so clear an evidence as before, and began to question whether I had indeed found the Lord; whether the peace and comfort I had felt might not be from the devil.'[30] But assurance is recovered: 'I still held fast the beginning of my confidence, and felt the Spirit of the Lord bearing witness with my spirit that I was a child of God.'[31]

One of the most remarkable of Wesley's helpers was John Nelson, about whom Wesley writes in his *Journal* as follows: 'His relations and acquaintances soon began to inquire what he thought of the new faith; and whether he believed there was any such thing as a man's knowing that his sins were forgiven. John told them point-blank that this new faith, as they called

---

[26] *Journal of Charles Wesley*, p. 92; F. L. Wiseman, *Charles Wesley*, p. 49.

[27] *Journal of John Wesley*, I.464.

[28] *Lives of the Early Methodist Preachers*, VI.183; cf. V.296f. (Throughout the rest of this chapter we shall use only the title *Lives*.)

[29] cf. the case of Jonathan Reeves, who had peace, without fear or doubt, before he had 'that sense of pardon', *Journal*, II.109.

[30] *Lives*, V.250.   [31] ibid., p. 255.

it, was the old faith of the Gospel; and that he himself was as sure his sins were forgiven as he could be of the shining of the sun.'[32]

In his own biography, Nelson testifies to his relations that he has gained an experience of assurance. 'But', he says, 'they begged I would not tell any one that my sins were forgiven; for no one would believe me; and they would be ashamed to show their faces in the street.'[33]

Thomas Payne claims that God 'gave me the Spirit of adoption, crying "Abba, Father"; which Spirit witnessed with my spirit that I was a child of God'. But he goes on to explain that he 'imbibed that miserable notion' from Calvinism that every 'believer should come down from the mount. Hence I was persuaded that . . . I must doubt of my justification, which these wretched casuists lay down as one great mark of sincerity. For want of knowing better I listened to these till I lost the witness of the Spirit.'[34]

Alexander Mather recalls the day—14th April 1754—when, as he listened to Wesley preaching, 'God set my heart at liberty, removing my sins from me . . . which the very change of my countenance testified'. But in a matter of days his certainty is shaken: 'I began to think, "You fancy your sins are forgiven, but you are deceived." ' It was his wife who helped him recapture his assurance: 'I soon recovered my peace, which, by the mercy of God, I have not lost since.'[35]

An illustration of the degrees in which assurance was experienced appears in the autobiography of John Murlin. He speaks of a great deliverance on 1st April 1749, under the preaching of John Downes. 'I had now a calm serenity in my soul, and often much peace and joy; but I wanted a clearer manifestation of the pardoning love of God. And this He was pleased to give me soon after.'[36]

A psychological explanation of this fluctuating experience of assurance is given by Dr Caldecott. 'In two-thirds of the cases a series of vicissitudes after the first victory is recorded before a final harmony is won. Old emotions resume their force, in detachment or in opposition: . . . there are returns to love of amusement, to contentment with moral satisfactions, less

---

[32] *Journal*, III.12.

[33] *Lives*, I.37. For the unpopularity of the doctrine, see Part V, chs. 1-3, pp. 179ff., *infra*.

[34] *Lives*, II.282f.   [35] ibid., II.167f.   [36] *Lives*, III.294f.

frequently lapses into the coarser habits of the past, and sometimes the central emotion itself is reduced even to temporary disappearance: satisfaction fails, and only desire remains; in a few cases even that fades away and periods of emptiness have to be lived through.'[37]

To many of the early Methodists the doctrine of a personal assurance came, as it did to the Wesleys, as a new doctrine.[38] After listening to Charles Wesley preach, Thomas Mitchell records part of the incident as follows: "But when he told us we might know our sins forgiven in this life, yea, this very moment, it seemed to me a new doctrine, and I could not believe it at all. But I continued in prayer; and in a few days I was convinced of it, to my great joy. The love of Christ broke into my soul, and drove away all guilt and fear; and at the same time He filled my heart with love both to God and man."[39]

In a later chapter, we shall see how prominently the Bible figured in the life and thought of the Wesleys. It is not surprising, therefore, to find the Scriptures occupying a conspicuous place in the religious experience of their followers. Many references to assurance, therefore, are couched in the language of the New Testament, and often quote Romans $8^{15, 16}$, Galatians 2^{20}, and 4^6.[40]

On 3rd September 1758, Richard Whatcoat, being overwhelmed with guilt and fear, turned over the pages of Scripture in search of certainty. 'When I came to those words "the Spirit itself beareth witness with our spirit, that we are the children of God"; as I fixed my eyes upon them, in a moment my darkness was removed, and the Spirit did bear witness with my spirit that I was a child of God.'[41]

Dr Leslie F. Church points out that the basis of this assurance was always in the love of God and never in the work of man.[42] Confirmation of this is found in the testimony of George Shadford: 'I cried out . . . "God be merciful to me a sinner!" No sooner had I expressed these words than by the eye of faith . . . I saw Christ, my Advocate, at the right hand of God, making intercession for me. I believed He loved me, and gave Himself for me. In an instant the Lord filled my soul with Divine Love . . . when I read my Bible, it seemed an entirely new book.'[43]

---

[37] Caldecott, *The Religious Sentiment*, pp. 20f.
[38] See Part II, ch. 1, pp. 53ff., *infra*.   [39] *Lives*, I.242.
[40] See Part III, chs. 1 and 2, pp. 105ff., *infra*.   [41] *Lives*, V.314.
[42] Dr L F. Church, *The Early Methodist People*, p. 100.   [43] *Lives*, VI.150.

This leads to another factor in the early Methodists' experience of assurance—namely, that it was centred in Christ. John Gaulter said that under Wesley's discourses Joseph Cownley was fully enlightened. He then saw the impotence of his fastings and the insufficiency of his morality to purchase the favour of Heaven and that there was salvation only in Christ. He could find no rest until the Lord absolved him from his guilt, and gave him the witness and seal of pardon.[44] It was said of Jonathan Maskew that 'in a moment the burden of his sin was removed. . . . Thus the gloomy and poignant distress of his soul ended in the knowledge of the Divine favour, and the clear discovery and experience that true believers "have redemption through the blood of Christ, the forgiveness of sins".'[45]

Moreover, it is as a crucified Lord that Christ often appears to the consciousness of Wesley's helpers. 'By the eye of faith', says James Rogers, 'I had as real a view of His agony on Calvary as ever I had of any object by the eye of sense . . . such an inexpressible degree of approbation was communicated to my soul thereby, as I shall never forget. . . . In that moment my burden was gone; my heart was brought out of bondage into glorious liberty; and the love which I felt for God and all mankind was inexpressibly great.'[46]

In 1768, Wesley received a welcome letter giving news of the Methodist colonists in America. The writer of the letter was a layman, Thomas Taylor. In it, reference is made to Captain Webb and the stress he laid on assurance in his preaching. His doctrines were quite new to the hearers, for he told them that all their knowledge and profession of religion was not worth anything, unless their sins were forgiven and they had the witness of God's Spirit with theirs that they were the children of God.[47]

Many of the early Methodists shared the persecution which the Wesleys suffered, partly on account of their teaching concerning assurance. Wesley refers to the case of Edward Greenfield, who had been put in prison. 'I asked a little gentleman at St Just what objection there was to Edward Greenfield. He said, "Why, the man is well enough in other things; but his impudence the gentlemen cannot bear. Why, sir, he says he knows his sins are forgiven!"' Wesley adds the comment:

[44] *Lives*, II.4.   [45] ibid., IV.203.   [46] ibid., p. 286.
[47] Simon, *John Wesley, the Master Builder*, IV.228f.

'And for this cause he is adjudged to banishment or death!'[48]

Certainty of their place in the family of God explains, not only the sufferings the early Methodists endured, but also their courageous service. Such service represents that fruit of the Spirit without which no one can long lay claim to the Spirit's witness. The life of Francis Asbury is a glorious example of this fact—a devoted servant of God whose sacrificial labours vie even with those of John Wesley.[49] He became the pioneer bishop of the Methodist Episcopal Church of America which today numbers its members in millions. He sacrificed those things that many people count most dear; and found the sacrifice a joy. In 1771 he set sail for the New World—never to return. On the voyage he writes in his journal on 12th September 1771: 'Whither am I going? To the New World. What to do? To gain honour? No, if I know my own heart. To get money? No, I am going to live for God, and to bring others so to do.'[50]

The secret of this sacrificial service is in his certainty of God and in that assurance of salvation gained in his early life. 'On a certain time, when we were praying in my father's barn, I believe the Lord pardoned my sins and justified my soul. . . . I had obtained a clear witness of my acceptance with God.'[51]

These religious experiences reveal many features reminiscent of the Wesleys' spiritual pilgrimage. But, as Dr Leslie F. Church observes, 'There is so wide a range of personalities involved, even in the first generation of Methodists, that any kind of uniformity or approximation to the Wesley pattern can neither be expected nor desired'.[52] For the remainder of this chapter, therefore, consideration will be given to those experiences of assurance which do not easily, if at all, fall into the Wesley mould.

Any claim to inner certainty is liable to lead to statements of an extravagant nature.[53] The subjective aspect of religious experience may become so predominant that contact with the objective and historical side is dangerously weakened. Is such a tendency traceable in the lives of the early Methodists?

It must be admitted that reference is sometimes made to the seeing of visions and the hearing of voices.[54] Such phenomena,

---

[48] *Journal*, III.185.
[49] Eayrs, *Wesley, Christian Philosopher and Church Founder*, pp. 107ff.
[50] James Lewis, *Frances Asbury*, p. 22.   [51] ibid., p. 16.
[52] Church, *The Early Methodist People*, p. 103.   [53] See Part V, pp. 179ff., *infra*.
[54] See Theophilus Evans, *The History of Modern Enthusiasm from the Reformation to the Present Times* (London, 1756), pp. 115ff.

however, as Professor William. James has shown, are not to be summarily dismissed, but are to be treated as data for psychological examination.[55]

There is an incident in the life of Sampson Staniforth. It happened between 12 and 2 a.m., while he was on sentinel duty with the British Army at Ghent. 'As soon as I was alone, I kneeled down, and determined not to rise, but to continue crying and wrestling with God, till He had mercy on me. How long I was in that agony I cannot tell; but as I looked up to heaven, I saw the clouds open exceeding bright, and I saw Jesus hanging on the cross. At the same moment, these words were applied to my heart: "Thy sins are forgiven thee."[56] My chains fell off; my heart was free.[57] All guilt was gone, and my soul was filled with unutterable peace.'

Staniforth's experience is coupled by Matthew Arnold with that of Paul: 'Paul's conversion is for science an event of precisely the same nature as the conversions of which the history of Methodism relates so many. . . . The conversion of Paul is in itself an incident of precisely the same order as the conversion of Sampson Staniforth, a Methodist soldier in the campaign of Fontenoy. . . . Not the narrative, in the Acts, of Paul's journey to Damascus, could more convince us of its own honesty.'[58]

The midnight hour itself is enough to detract from the objective reality of this vision, and Staniforth himself gives it a subjective explanation: 'I then closed my eyes; but the impression was still the same. And for about ten weeks, while I was awake, let me be where I would, the same appearance was still before my eyes, and the same impression upon my heart, "Thy sins are forgiven thee".'[59]

The next instance comes from the life of Silas Told.[60] It occurred while he was listening to John Wesley preaching on the forgiveness of sins (John 12^{13}): 'I saw I could never be saved without knowing my sins were forgiven; and the Spirit of God sealed every word upon my heart. At the close of the

[55] See James, *Varieties of Religious Experience.*

[56] Mark 2^5; Luke 5^{20}; Matthew 9^2; Luke 7^{48}.

[57] *M.H.B.*, 371, verse 4; note here the influence of Scripture and Methodist hymnology.

[58] Matthew Arnold, *St. Paul and Protestantism* (1870), pp. 114f. Quoted by Shepherd, op. cit., p. 155.

[59] *Lives*, IV.122f.

[60] Wesley's *Journal*, VI.221; Eayrs, *Wesley, Christian Philosopher and Church Founder*, pp. 111f.; Shepherd, op. cit., pp. 156ff.; *New History of Methodism*, I.312.

discourse, however strange it may appear, a still small voice[61] entered my heart with these words, "This is the truth!" and instantly I felt it in my soul.'[62]

Another example is John Kirby's account of how he gained an assurance of salvation: 'I looked up, and it appeared to me as if the roof of my house was taken away, so that I saw the firmament. While I was wondering at this, a dark cloud arose, which I thought was a thunder-cloud. The cloud was drawn aside, and left in view Jesus Christ, all besmeared with blood. He looked upon me and said, "I have loved thee, and given myself for thee".[63] I felt the word in my heart, and all guilt, and fear and sorrow fled away. Now I know that I "have an Advocate with the Father, Jesus Christ the righteous, who is the propitiation for my sins".'[64]

What are we to make of these visions and voices? Do they invalidate their testimony to an experience of assurance? 'Criticism has sometimes been passed on these private journals', writes Dr Leslie F. Church, 'on the ground that they reveal their writers as self-centred and morbidly introspective. There is little justification for this, as a rule, so long as the whole record be taken into account.'[65]

As Dr Caldecott says, 'Though these young men describe unusually intense emotionality, they were not of ill-balanced nervous systems: they all lived vigorously, and most of them continued laborious pursuits until advanced old age; they were not fretting under disappointments, or depressed with the ennui of prematurely worn-out single emotions, the "sorrows of youth".'[66]

Moreover, in the wider fellowship of the class meetings, any individual excesses were checked and corrected. These accounts also came under the scrutiny of Wesley's penetrating insight and corrective judgement.[67]

The Holy Communion was a means of conveying a sense of forgiveness to some of the early Methodists. John Nelson writes: 'I went to the table with trembling limbs and heavy heart; but no sooner had I received, than I found power to

---

[61] 1 Kings 19^{12}.
[62] *The Life of Silas Told, written by himself* (City Road, London, 1789), p. 22. Quoted by Dr Church, *The Early Methodist People*, pp. 111f.
[63] cf. Galatians 2^{20}. [64] *Lives*, V.117.
[65] Church, op. cit., p. 113; cf. pp. 122f.
[66] Caldecott, *The Religious Sentiment*, pp. 7f.
[67] Flew, *The Idea of Perfection*, pp. 315f.

believe that Jesus Christ had shed His blood for me, and that God, for His sake, had forgiven my offences.'[68]

It was also at the Lord's Table where Susanna Wesley gained a sense of God's forgiveness. She tells John Wesley: 'Two or three weeks ago, while my son Hall was pronouncing those words, in delivering me the cup, "The blood of our Lord Jesus Christ, which was given for thee", the words struck through my heart, and I knew God for Christ's sake had forgiven *me* all *my* sins.'[69]

And there we must leave our examination of the religious experiences of the early Methodists. This experimental evidence is one of the two main criteria by which Wesley held that any claim to an inner certainty of salvation should be tested.[70] The other criterion is the Scriptural warrant, which we shall consider in Part III of this book.

[68] *Lives*, I.17.   [69] *Journal*, II.267; cf. pp. 36off.   [70] ibid., I.471.

Part Two
Assurance in its Theological Setting

CHAPTER ONE

'A NEW GOSPEL'?

IN Part I of this book, we have been concerned with the religious experiences in the eighteenth century upon which, in the main, Wesley based his doctrine of assurance. In Part II, we consider the theological implications of this experimental religion. It will not be possible, of course, to keep rigidly separate the experience and the theory of the doctrine.

What was it in Peter Böhler's teaching that appeared to Wesley as 'a new gospel' or a 'new doctrine'?[1]

Dr Piette maintains that the part which we must recognize Böhler's appearance to have played is not that of having initiated John Wesley into the Lutheran doctrine of faith without works. Böhler made him see the overwhelmingly important place which the love of God ought to occupy in the life of every truly Christian soul. In support of this interpretation, Piette quotes from the letter sent by Böhler to Wesley on 4th May 1738, where, argues Piette, 'Böhler refers to the intense practice of the love of God, in which, he says, Wesley does not believe'.[2]

We can only say that we have found little evidence to support this interpretation. To hold such a theory would call for the explaining away of too many passages in Wesley's voluminous writings where an interpretation in terms of the love of God could only be forced. One wonders, for example, how Piette would fit his interpretation to the following citation: 'They added . . . that this faith was . . . the free gift of God. . . . I resolved to seek it . . . by adding . . . continual prayer *for this very thing, justifying, saving faith*, a full reliance on the blood of Christ shed for me; a trust in Him, as my Christ, as my sole justification, sanctification, and redemption.'[3]

Wesley's comment on his fruitless excursion into, and hatred of, mysticism would also seem to refute Piette's theory. 'I had a plenary dispensation', writes Wesley, 'from all the commands of God: the form ran thus, "*Love is all*; all the commands beside

---

[1] *Journal*, I.442, 471.
[2] Piette, *John Wesley in the Evolution of Protestantism*, p. 307.
[3] *Journal*, I.472 (italics mine).

are only means of love: you must choose those which you feel are means to you, and use them as long as they are so".'[4]

Dr Lee maintains that it is impossible to claim that Wesley was taught the *doctrine* of justification by faith in 1738, *after* he returned to England.[5] This statement brings us to the heart of our inquiry in this chapter; and leads to a clearing of the ground for determining Böhler's distinctive contribution to Wesley's theological thought.

We must retrace our steps here in order to gain an insight into Wesley's thought on the nature of faith prior to his meeting with Peter Böhler. Despite Wesley's claim to be *homo unius libri*,[6] other books played a vital part in his spiritual development. Some of the religious books he had read before, and during, his visit to Georgia, as well as on the return voyage, must have wielded a considerable influence over him. In addition to Thomas à Kempis's *Imitation of Christ*[7] and the *Apostolic Constitutions*,[8] he was consulting, to quote his own words, 'small remains of Clemens Romanus, Polycarp and Ignatius'.[9]

Wesley held that Haliburton's *Life* was the best description of the Christian's inner spiritual experience.[10] The Scot, with whose conversion the book deals, says that there is forgiveness of sins through the redemption which is in Jesus, so that by this means God may be just in justifying even the ungodly that believe in him.[11]

Under the date, 24th January 1738, Wesley writes: 'My mind was now full of thought, part of which I write down as follows' —we quote only the relevant passages—'For many years I have been tossed by various winds of doctrine. . . . I was early warned about laying, as the Papists do, too much stress on outward works, or on faith without works.' He goes on to say that he had from the very beginning valued faith, the means of grace, and good works, since he believed that God would by them bring him in due time to the mind which was in Christ.[12]

[4] *Journal*, I.420 (italics mine). See Part V, chs. 4 and 5, pp. 198ff., *infra*.
[5] Lee, *John Wesley and Modern Religion*, p. 81.
[6] 'A man of one book', *Sermons*, I.32.   [7] Called by Wesley *Christian Pattern*.
[8] Of later date than Wesley at one time thought.
[9] *Works*, XIV.212. See Part IV, pp. 149ff., *infra*.
[10] Wesley's Preface to *Life of Haliburton* (1739), *Works*, XIV.212.
[11] *Works*, X.295f., *Life of Haliburton*.   [12] *Journal*, I.418f.

Wesley then makes some very significant observations. 'I fell among some Lutheran and Calvinist authors, whose confused and indigested accounts magnified faith to such an amazing size that it quite hid all the rest of the commandments ... being so terrified with the cry of merit or good works that they plunged at once into the other extreme.' Wesley adds that such English writers as Beveridge, Taylor and Nelson 'a little relieved me from these well-meaning, wrong-headed Germans'.[13]

Reviewing the fruitless effects of all his past strenuous endeavours, Wesley maintains that he had given at least intellectual assent to all the main theological aspects of the Christian faith. In the course of this penetrating examination, he says: 'Are they versed in the science of divinity? I too have studied it for many years. Can they talk fluently upon spiritual things? The very same could I do.' Later on, in this survey, Wesley claims 'a rational conviction of all the truths of Christianity'.[14]

In the light of this evidence, it seems difficult to deny that Wesley was at least intellectually acquainted with the *doctrine* of justification by faith before he met Peter Böhler. But there is other evidence, which demands that we define this situation more precisely. To the Wesleys and to their contemporaries the idea of *preaching* and *experiencing* justification by faith appeared to be an innovation. A denial of this would make nonsense of several statements on this subject in Wesley's writings.

One such statement is in a letter to Charles, dated 31st July 1747. John says: 'Some years ago we heard nothing about either justifying faith or a sense of pardon; so that, when we did hear them, the theme was quite new to us.'[15]

Another statement is dated 6th March 1738: 'I began preaching this new doctrine of salvation by faith alone, though my soul started back from the work.'[16] We recall also John's reference to the intellectual enlightenment which Charles gained in conversation with Böhler: 'It now pleased God to open his eyes; so that he also saw clearly the nature of that one true living faith, whereby alone, "through grace, we are saved".'[17]

The entry in Charles Wesley's *Journal* reads: 'Today I first

[13] *Journal*, p. 419. [14] ibid., I.422f. [15] *Letters*, II.108.
[16] ibid., p. 442f.; cf. Conference (1746), *Works*, VIII.290.
[17] Ephesians 2⁸. *Journal*, I.459.

saw Luther on the Galatians, which Mr Holland[18] had accidentally lit upon. We began and found him nobly full of faith. . . . I marvelled that we were so soon and so entirely removed from him that called us into the grace of Christ, unto another Gospel. Who could believe that our Church had been founded on this important article of justification by faith alone? I am astonished I should ever think this a new doctrine.'[19]

Does this quotation confirm, or conflict with, our conclusion that John Wesley was already conversant with the doctrine of justification by faith before he met Peter Böhler? It is a nice point; and it does not lend itself to any precise or emphatic statement.

One could argue, of course, that Charles might not have been acquainted with the doctrine of justification, even though his brother was. Or, one could hold that this passage refers only to the experiential aspect, and not to the verbal statement, of the doctrine of justification.

It seems impossible to determine the question merely on these grounds. Viewing the matter in the light of Charles Wesley's theological training, we believe that Charles *must* have been theoretically conversant with the doctrine before he fell under the spell of Böhler's teaching. Be this as it may, it does not necessarily affect our conclusion in the case of John Wesley.

The whole question, however, can be viewed from a different angle. The emphasis perhaps ought to be placed, not so much on 'justification by faith', as on 'justification by faith *alone*'. Dr W. R. Cannon appears to have this interpretation in mind when he says that it is at the point of faith, its nature and its function, that the radical change took place in Wesley's thought concerning justification. The Moravians taught that man is saved by faith alone.[20]

Whatever the extent of their acquaintance with the doctrine of justification prior to their contact with Böhler, the Wesleys had certainly attached great importance to good works. The measure of their earnestness and sacrifice in Christian service has already been considered in an earlier chapter. This is brought out by Wesley in the review of his religious life prefixed to 24th May 1738. In this review, Wesley says that prior to his Aldersgate experience he had many sensible comforts

---

[18] Probably the reader of Luther's *Preface to the Romans* on 24th May 1738; *Journal*, I.475.

[19] *Charles Wesley's Journal*, I.88.   [20] Cannon, *Theology of John Wesley*, p. 74.

which were short anticipations of the life of faith. Yet he had not 'the witness of the Spirit with my spirit, and indeed could not; for I sought it not by faith, but as it were by the works of the law'.[21]

It would appear that the very simplicity which characterized salvation by faith, as presented by the Moravians, was new to the Wesleys. It is significant that Böhler considered the simplicity of the doctrine as a reason for the Wesleys' hesitation in accepting it. In a letter to Zinzendorf, Böhler wrote: 'Our mode of believing in the Saviour is so easy to Englishmen, that they cannot reconcile themselves to it; if it were a little more artful, they would much sooner find their way into it.'[22]

Another aspect of Böhler's teaching—new to Wesley—was that conversion was instantaneous. Only after the evidence both from Scripture and from the 'living witnesses' had been examined would Wesley give his assent to this doctrine.[23] It was chiefly the stress on instantaneous conversion which gave rise to such a heated controversy when Wesley 'spoke clearly and fully at Blendon to Mr Delamotte's family'.[24] This aspect of Böhler's theology, however, did not hold Wesley's assent for long. Later he modified this emphasis on conversion 'in a moment' in favour of the sounder view that 'there is an irreconcilable variability in the operations of the Holy Spirit in the souls of men'.[25]

But perhaps the most important and distinctive feature of Böhler's contribution to Wesley's religious thought was the emphasis laid on the need of a *personal* faith in *Christ*. In other words, one of Wesley's deficiencies in the matter of faith appears to have consisted in its being either a faith merely in God or a vague sort of trust in Christ.

This limitation in Wesley's theological outlook is traceable in certain references he makes to his past religious pilgrimage. He was convinced that the cause of his uneasiness was unbelief and 'that the gaining a true, living faith was the "one thing needful".' He goes on to explain, however, that 'he fixed not this faith on its right object: I meant only faith in God, not faith in and through Christ.'[26] One recalls the vagueness of his faith in Christ as revealed in his conversation with Spangenberg in Georgia.[27]

---

[21] *Journal*, I.470f.   [22] *Methodist Magazine* (1854), p. 687.   [23] *Journal*, I.454f.
[24] ibid., p. 456; cf. *Charles Wesley's Journal*, I.84f.
[25] *Letters*, V.175, VII.298, VIII.110.   [26] *Journal*, I.471.   [27] ibid., p. 151.

The emphasis on the centrality of Christ in Böhler's exposition of saving faith appears to have been new even to the London Moravians.[28] 'To their astonishment, they saw, for the first time, that he who believeth in Jesus hath everlasting life; and it was with indescribable joy that they embraced the doctrine of justification through faith in Christ, and of freedom by it from the dominion and guilt of sin.'[29]

Wesley's search for certainty based on a personal, saving faith in Christ is reflected in a moving passage from his pen. 'If it be said that I have faith. ... I answer, so have the devils— a sort of faith. ... The faith I want[30] is "a sure trust and confidence in God, that, through the merits of Christ, my sins are forgiven"....[31] I want that faith which St Paul commends to all the world ... that faith which enables every one that hath it to cry out, "I live not, but Christ liveth in me; and the life which I now live, I live by faith in the Son of God, who loved me, and gave Himself for me." '[32]

Supporting our interpretation here concerning the centrality of Christ is Dr Cell's statement that Peter Böhler's 'new gospel' was 'a God-given faith in Christ'.[33] And the personal aspect of this 'new doctrine' is emphasized by Dr W. R. Cannon.[34] 'Anglicanism', he says, 'taught that man is saved by the merits of Christ's death'. But the Moravians saw this in a more personal light. Christ, they said, died for the world as a whole,[35] but the important thing is that He died for you as a person.[36] The same point is stressed in Böhler's letter to Wesley on 8th May 1738, in which he pleads that Christ 'may be manifested to *your* soul . . . how exceedingly the Son of God has loved *you* . . . and so you may . . . feel His life *in yourself* . . . believe in *your* Jesus Christ'.[37] The personal aspect of salvation by faith is indicated by Charles Wesley: 'I laboured, waited and prayed to feel "who loved *me*, and gave Himself for *me*".'[38]

Further confirmation of this point of view is given by a recent Anglican writer. 'Then came his [Wesley's] contact with the Moravians, from whom he learned that forgiveness is

---

[28] Tyerman, *Life and Times of John Wesley*, I.181. [29] *Hutton's Memoirs*, p. 27.
[30] Wesley, at a later date, adds the note: 'the faith of a son'.
[31] From the Anglican Homily 'Of Salvation'. [32] Galatians 2²⁰.
[33] Cell, *Rediscovery of John Wesley*, p. 134.
[34] Cannon, *Theology of John Wesley*, p. 74.
[35] Spangenberg, *Exposition of Christian Doctrine*, p. 199. [36] ibid., p. 196.
[37] *Journal*, I.461. (Italics mine, except the last.)
[38] *Charles Wesley's Journal*, I.88.

not a future possibility but a present reality. The well-grounded Christian does not believe *that* Christ *is* the Saviour of *mankind*, he believes *in* Christ *as his own* Saviour; does not vaguely trust that finally the merits of Christ may avail for him personally, but knows that they do so now. This is called "having an interest in" Christ—an "interest" in the sense of a legal right or claim on which one can boldly take one's stand. Indeed, it brings with it a boldness or freedom in approaching the presence of God (the Johannine παρρησία),[39] together with a peace of mind and power over sin. And all this is wrought in the soul through "faith". It was evident that Wesley had not this "faith".'[40]

We have already quoted evidence, in an earlier chapter, to show that Wesley was in search of assurance before his meeting with Böhler. Reference has been made to his criticism, in a letter to his mother, regarding Jeremy Taylor's disparagement of assurance;[41] to his father's dying words concerning the inner witness;[42] and to that important conversation in which Spangenberg asked Wesley: 'Have you the witness within yourself?'[43] Assurance is also referred to in a sermon by Wesley on the 'circumcision of the heart', based on Romans 2^{29}, and preached at St Mary's, Oxford, before the University as early as 1st January 1733.[44]

In the light of these facts, it might be questioned whether Böhler contributed anything new in regard to the doctrine of assurance. From the experiential point of view, this question has already been answered in an earlier chapter, where we saw that Böhler was the chief human means of leading Wesley into the Aldersgate experience.

From the doctrinal point of view, we have already gone a long way, in this chapter, towards an answer to the question. This is realized when assurance is viewed in its proper theological setting. Assurance, as Wesley came to understand it, is an assurance of *salvation*; salvation based on justification by faith *alone*; faith, not of a vague, general kind, but a *personal* faith centred in *Christ*; a Christ who 'loved *me* and gave Himself for *me*'.[45]

---

[39] See pp. 141f., *infra*.
[40] H. A. Hodges, 'A Neglected Page in Anglican Theology', art. in *Theology*, Vol. xlviii, No. 299, May 1945 (S.P.C.K., London).
[41] *Letters*, I.19f.
[42] Eayrs, *Wesley, Christian Philosopher and Church Founder*, p. 149.
[43] *Journal*, I.151.   [44] *Sermons*, I.271.   [45] Galatians 2^{20}.

Our conclusion is that Peter Böhler played a leading part in bringing home to Wesley an understanding of 'that faith whereby alone we are saved'.[46] It was largely under his influence and teaching that Wesley perceived that saving faith was not 'the faith of a heathen' or 'of a devil' or 'that which the apostles themselves had while Christ was yet upon earth'.[47] It was not only an assent to the whole gospel of Christ, but also a full reliance on the blood of Christ; a trust in the merits of His life, death and resurrection; a recumbency upon Him as our atonement and our life, *as given for* us, and *living in us*.[48]

Even if it be allowed that Böhler did not introduce Wesley to the idea and terminology of assurance, he certainly indicated the *personal* nature of the doctrine and emphasized the fact that assurance involved, not merely a general faith in God, but an individual trust in the redemptive work of Christ.

All this is implied in what we consider to be the *locus classicus* for the doctrine of assurance—namely, Wesley's account in the *Journal* of his Aldersgate experience: 'While he was describing the change which God works in the heart through faith in Christ, I felt my heart strangely warmed. I felt I did trust in Christ, in Christ alone, for salvation; and an assurance was given me that He had taken away *my* sins, even *mine*, and saved *me* from the law of sin and death.'[49]

---

[46] *Journal*, I.442.   [47] See Part III, ch. 6, pp. 139ff., *infra*.
[48] *Sermons*, I.38ff.   [49] *Journal*, I.476.

CHAPTER TWO

HOW THE DOCTRINE GREW

REFERENCES to the doctrine are traceable in Wesley's early writings. On 11th June 1738,[1] Wesley preached before the University of Oxford on Ephesians 2⁸. In this sermon, assurance is set forth as one of the privileges of salvation by faith.[2]

A significant letter, dated 28th September 1738, is addressed to the Rev. Arthur Bedford.[3] Wesley endorses three propositions laid down by Bedford, viz.:

'(1) That assurance of salvation is not of the essence of faith.
'(2) That a true believer may wait long before he hath it.
'(3) That, after he hath it, it may be weakened and intermitted by many distempers, sins, temptations and desertions.'[4]

A divergence of view arises, however, in the meaning each attaches to the phrase, 'assurance of salvation'. For Bedford it signifies to *persevere* in a state of salvation; for Wesley the phrase means only that we are *now* in a state of salvation. Wesley regards most of Bedford's exposition of the doctrine as an *ignoratio elenchi*,[5] and holds that his interpretation is supported neither by the Methodists, the Moravians, the Anglican Catechism, nor the Bible.

Wesley goes on to deprecate the use of the phrase 'assurance of salvation' on the ground that it is not found in Scripture, and prefers 'the assurance of faith'.[6] 'And even this I believe is not of the essence of faith, but a distinct gift of the Holy Ghost, whereby God shines upon His own work and shows us that we are justified through faith in Christ.'

Samuel Wesley writes to his brother John on 5th November 1738 asking 'whether he will own or disown, in terms, the necessity of a sensible information of God's pardon'.[7] John's

---

[1] *Not* 18th June, as given in *Works*, 1771.   [2] *Sermons*, I.43.
[3] Chaplain to the Prince of Wales. See *Arminian Magazine*, 1782, pp. 425ff.
[4] *Letters*, I.254ff.   [5] i.e. 'Ignoring the point in question'.
[6] See pp. 133ff., *infra*.
[7] *Priestley's Letters*, p. 88; Tyerman, *Life and Times of John Wesley*, I.192.

reply is dated 30th November: 'I believe every Christian . . . should pray for the witness of God's spirit. . . . In being a child of God, the pardon of his sins is included; therefore I believe the Spirit of God will witness this also. . . . This witness I believe is necessary for my salvation. How far invincible ignorance may excuse others I know not.'[8]

In a letter of 13th December 1738, Samuel maintains that John misinterprets the witness of the Spirit, and quotes as his authority a sermon by Bishop Bull.[9] John replies that Bull's sermon is full of manifest contradictions, both to Scripture and experience. Wesley denies that assurance continues equally clear in all as long as they continue in a state of salvation. It is true that some 'have felt no agonies at all, no anxious fears, no sense of dereliction. Others have.'[10]

On 26th March 1739, Samuel writes again to his brother. He argues that the witness of the Spirit is not necessary to salvation; quoting, in proof, the case of baptized infants and people of a gloomy constitution.[11] Answering these points, Wesley writes on 4th April 1739 that:

'(1) No kind of assurance . . . is essential to their salvation who die infants.
'(2) I believe God is ready to give all true penitents . . . a fuller sense of pardon than they had before they fell. I know this to be true of several; whether there be exempt cases, I know not.
'(3) Persons that were of a . . . gloomy constitution . . . I have known in a moment (let it be called miracle, I quarrel not) brought into a state of firm, lasting peace and joy.'[12]

Wesley, though unwilling, as he says, to continue an unprofitable dispute, sends another letter on 10th May to his brother Samuel, in which he reiterates his argument that it is an assurance of present pardon only; therefore not necessarily perpetual, nor irreversible.[13]

An important entry, relevant to our purpose, appears in the *Journal* for 25th January 1740. Wesley writes: 'One came to me in the evening to know if a man could not be saved without the faith of assurance. I answered . . . I never yet knew one soul thus saved without what you call "the faith of assurance"';

---

[8] *Letters*, I.274f.   [9] Whitehead's *Life of Wesley*, II.108f.   [10] *Letters*, I.279.
[11] Tyerman, *Life and Times of John Wesley*, I.193.   [12] *Letters*, I.290.
[13] ibid., p. 308.

I mean a sure confidence that, by the merits of Christ, he was reconciled to the favour of God.'[14]

In a sermon, the probable date of which is 6th June 1742, John Wesley holds that 'true religion . . . implies happiness as well as holiness . . . and a peace that banishes all doubt, all painful uncertainty; the Spirit of God bearing witness with the spirit of a Christian, that he is "a child of God".'[15] Wesley carries this idea a stage farther in a later sermon on 'the marks of the new birth', where he maintains that to be a child of God is so to *hope* in God through the Son of His love, as to have not only the testimony of a good conscience, but also the Spirit of God 'bearing witness with your spirits, that ye are the children of God'; whence cannot but spring the rejoicing evermore in Him through whom ye 'have received the atonement'.[16]

In the *Minutes* of the first Methodist Conference (1744), the question is raised: 'Does anyone believe, who has not the witness in himself, or any longer than he sees, loves, obeys God?' The answer given is: 'We apprehend not.'[17] This Conference defined justifying faith as a supernatural inward sense, or sight, of God in Christ reconciling the world unto Himself. The effect of such a faith is described as follows: 'First, a sinner is convinced by the Holy Ghost "Christ loved me and gave Himself for me"; this is that faith by which he is justified, or pardoned, the moment he receives it. Immediately the same spirit bears witness "Thou art pardoned; thou hast redemption in His blood" and this is saving faith, whereby the love of God is shed abroad in his heart.'

Two other relevant questions are considered at this Conference: 'Have all true Christians this faith? May not a man be justified and not know it?' The answer is: 'That all true Christians have this faith, even such a faith as implies an assurance of God's love, appears from Romans 8^{15}; Ephesians 4^{32}; 2 Corinthians 13^{5}; Hebrews 8^{10}; 1 John 4^{10}; and last 1 John 5^{19}.[18] And that no man can be justified and not know it appears further from the very nature of things, for faith after repentance is ease after pain, rest after toil, light after darkness.'[19]

Wesley's reply led the Conference to raise another pertinent

[14] *Journal*, II.333f.   [15] *Sermons*, I.153.
[16] ibid., I.294. The probable date is January, 1743.
[17] Question 8, *Minutes*, 25th June 1744; *Works*, VIII.276.
[18] See Part III., pp. 103ff., *infra*.
[19] *Works*, VIII.276; cf. Beet, *A Manual of Theology*, p. 240.

question regarding the uninterrupted continuance of the assurance of God's love and of the peace and joy arising from it. The answer given is reminiscent of Wesley's religious experience in the months immediately following Aldersgate: 'It is certain, a believer need never again come into condemnation. It seems he need not come into a state of doubt or fear or darkness; and that, ordinarily at least, he will not, unless by ignorance or unfaithfulness. Yet it is true that the first joy does seldom last long; that it is commonly followed by doubts and fears; and that God frequently permits great heaviness before any large manifestation of Himself.'

In September 1745, Wesley writes the first of his six letters to 'John Smith', who maintains that when a man is pardoned, it is immediately notified by the Holy Ghost, not by His imperceptibly working a godly assurance, but by such attestation as is easily discernible from reason or fancy. In his reply, dated 28th September 1745, Wesley says: 'I do not deny that God imperceptibly works in some a gradually increasing assurance of His love; but I am equally certain He works in others a full assurance thereof in one moment. And, I suppose, it is easily discernible from bare reason and fancy.'[20]

Later in the same year, on 30th December, Wesley writes another letter to 'John Smith', denying that there is any sense in which the attestation of the Spirit is infallible. Wesley goes on to say that when Christians have an assurance of pardon, 'they cannot possibly doubt of their having it; although it is very possible, when they have it not, they may doubt whether they had it or no'.[21]

Some months later, Wesley is in correspondence with the Rev. Thomas Church,[22] whom he described as 'a gentleman, a scholar and a Christian; and as such he both spake and wrote'.[23] In answer to Church's criticism, Wesley distinguishes different degrees of assurance. 'The one is an assurance that my sins are forgiven, clear at first, but soon clouded with doubt or fear; the other is such a plerophory or full assurance that I am forgiven, and so clear a perception that Christ abideth in me, as utterly excludes all doubt or fear, and leaves them no place—no, not for an hour. So that the difference between

[20] *Letters*, II.46.   [21] ibid., p. 59.

[22] Vicar of Battersea and author of *Remarks on the Rev. Mr John Wesley's Last Journal* (published 1744).

[23] *Works*, X.450.

HOW THE DOCTRINE GREW

them is as great as the difference between the light of the morning and that of the midday sun.'[24]

At the Methodist Conference of 1745 a number of vital doctrinal points are considered.[25] Among the questions raised and answered are the following:

(1) 'Is a sense of God's pardoning love absolutely necessary to our being in His favour? Or may there be exempt cases?'
'We dare not say there are not.'
(2) 'Is it necessary to inward and outward holiness?'
'We incline to think it is.'
(3) 'Is it indispensably necessary to final salvation . . . or . . . among those who never heard it preached?'
'Love hopeth all things. We know not how far any of these may fall under the case of invincible ignorance.'
(4) 'Does a man believe any longer than he sees a reconciled God?'[26]
'We conceive not. But we allow there may be infinite degrees in seeing God.'[27]

Further significant questions are considered at the Conference of 1746:

(1) It is admitted that a real difficulty attaches to the judging of individual cases, since it is not always possible to appreciate all the circumstances.
(2) Wesley holds, however, that sincere seekers will ultimately gain an experience of assurance.
(3) 'Are not the assurance of faith, the inspiration of the Holy Ghost, and the revelation of Christ in us, terms nearly of the same import?'
'He that denies one of them must deny all; they are so closely connected together.'
(4) 'Are they ordinarily, where the pure Gospel is preached, essential to our acceptance?'
'Undoubtedly they are; and, as such, to be insisted on, in the strongest terms.'
(5) 'Wherein does our doctrine now differ from what we preached at Oxford?'
'Chiefly in these two points:

---

[24] *Letters*, II.192. See next chapter and Part III, ch. 4, pp. 128ff., *infra*.
[25] *Minutes*, 2nd August 1745.   [26] See *Sermons*, II.346; *Letters*, V.358.
[27] *Works*, VIII.282.

'(a) We then knew nothing of that righteousness of faith, in justification; nor
'(b) Of the nature of faith itself, as implying consciousness of pardon.'
(6) 'May not some degree of the love of God go before a distinct sense of justification?'
'We believe it may.'[28]

Another letter, written on 25th March 1747 to 'John Smith', calls for attention. His correspondent has accused Wesley of inconsistency in that, having claimed for the believer a clear attestation of acceptance by the witness of the Spirit, he goes on to admit that these same persons at other times doubt or deny that they ever had such attestation. In reply, Wesley sums up his teaching on this matter as follows:

(1) 'A man feels in himself the testimony of God's Spirit that he is a child of God; and he can then no more deny or doubt thereof than of the shining of the sun at noonday.
(2) 'After a time this testimony is withdrawn.
(3) 'He begins to reason within himself concerning it; next, to doubt whether that testimony was from God; and, perhaps, in the end to deny that it was. And yet he may be all this time in every other respect "of sound memory as well as understanding".'[29]

Wesley defends himself against 'John Smith's' charge of teaching 'a thing impossible'. 'What is impossible?' asks Wesley. 'That the Spirit of God should bear a clear, perceptible witness with our spirit that we are the children of God? Surely no! . . . Or that the Spirit of God should cease to bear such witness? Neither can the possibility of this be denied. The thing, then, which is supposed impossible is this—that a man who once had it should ever doubt that he had it or no. . . . I verily believe, as it was the God of heaven who once shone in his heart to give the light of the knowledge of the glory of God, so it is the god of this world who hath now blinded his heart so that the glorious light cannot shine upon it.'[30]

Wesley then takes up his correspondent on the point that, while he must allow there is a testimony of the Spirit with our spirit that we are the children of God, he denies that such a testimony is a perceptible one. Wesley examines the situation

[28] *Works*, VIII.290. [29] *Letters*, II.89. [30] ibid., p. 90.

HOW THE DOCTRINE GREW

as follows: 'It is allowed (1) the Spirit of God (2) bears witness to my spirit (3) that I am a child of God. But I am not to perceive it. Not to perceive what? The first, second, or third particular? Am I not to perceive what is testified—that I am a child of God? Then it is not testified at all. This is saying and unsaying in the same breath. Or, am I not to perceive that it is testified to my spirit? Yea, but I must perceive what passes in my own soul![31] Or, lastly, am I to perceive that I am a child of God, and that this is testified to my spirit, but not to perceive who it is that testifies? Not to know it is the Spirit of God?'[32]

We come now to the Methodist Conference of 1747.[33] Having established the Scriptural basis of assurance,[34] Wesley inquires whether experience also does not show that justifying faith necessarily implies assurance. It is admitted that there may be exempt cases; and that we do not always know enough to judge a man's spiritual state unerringly. Yet it is held that those who lack a conscious faith are not true Christians, although it is not to be assumed that they will die in such a condition.[35]

In answer to the question, 'Is justifying faith a divine assurance that Jesus Christ loved me, and gave Himself for me?' the reply given is: 'We believe it is.'[36]

Wesley soon seems to have realized, however, that this was unguarded language.[37] In the following month, he studied the matter more closely and wrote down the findings of this re-examination in a letter to his brother Charles on 31st July 1747:

'By justifying faith I mean that faith which whosoever hath not is under the wrath and curse of God. By a sense of pardon I mean a distinct, explicit assurance that my sins are forgiven.

'I allow:

'(1) That there is such an explicit assurance.

'(2) That it is the common privilege of *real* Christians.

'(3) That it is *the proper Christian faith*, which purifieth the heart and overcometh the world.

---

[31] Is the influence of Descartes' (1596–1650) *Cogito ergo sum* traceable here? See p. 213, *infra*.

[32] *Letters*, II.92.

[33] This Conference was in session from 15th–20th June 1747, and was the largest yet held.

[34] See Part III, pp. 103ff., *infra*.   [35] Question 10, *Works*, VIII.293.

[36] *Minutes* (edited, 1862), p. 15; *Works*, VIII.291.

[37] Tyerman, *Life and Times of John Wesley*, I.551f.

'But I cannot allow that justifying faith is such an assurance, or necessarily connected therewith.

'Because, if justifying faith *necessarily* implies such an explicit sense of pardon, then everyone who has it not, and everyone so long as he has it not, is under the wrath and under the curse of God. But this is a supposition contrary to Scripture and also to experience.'[38]

Wesley goes on to argue that the assertion that justifying faith is a sense of pardon is contrary to *reason*; it is flatly *absurd*. For how can *a sense of our having received pardon* be the *condition* of our receiving it?[39]

We must now retrace our steps a little. We passed from a consideration of the minutes of Conference for June 1747 to this letter to Charles, written at the end of July, in order not to break the continuity of thought in Wesley's teaching on assurance.

Earlier, on 10th July, Wesley wrote another letter to 'John Smith', in which he criticized his correspondent's statement that there was once an inward, perceptible testimony of the Spirit, but that it was peculiar to the early ages of the Church. Wesley quotes the three ways in which 'John Smith' holds that the Holy Spirit can bear witness to our divine sonship:

(1) 'By external, miraculous attestations;
(2) 'By internal, plainly perceptible whispers;
(3) 'By His standing testimony in the Holy Scriptures.'

'The apostles', continues John Smith, 'had all these three, Origen and Chrysostom probably the two latter. But if St Bernard, several hundred years after, pretended to any other than the third, his neighbours would naturally ask for proof, either that it should be so by Scripture or that it was so by facts.'[40]

By an imaginary conversation between Chrysostom and one of his neighbours, Wesley argues that a true interpretation of such passages as Romans 8[16] refers to an inward, perceptible testimony.[41] Wesley again admits that it is possible for a man to experience the Spirit's witness and later to lose it—even to deny that the testimony was of God—while remaining of 'sound memory as well as understanding'.[42]

In reply to his correspondent's demand for proof, Wesley

[38] *Letters*, II.108f. [39] *Works*, XII.113. [40] *Letters*, II.101.
[41] ibid., p. 102. [42] ibid. II.103.

asserts that by their fruits we can distinguish those who truly have the witness of God's love from an enthusiastic pretender to it.[43]

Richard Tompson writes to Wesley on 10th July 1755, saying that he differs from him concerning assurance being essential to saving faith. He cannot accept the view that no person is a *true believer in Christ* but he who either certainly *knows*, or has known by the *immediate revelation of the Holy Ghost*, that his sins are forgiven.[44]

In the letter of 25th July, Wesley says: 'That you may clearly see wherein we agree or wherein we differ, I have sent you the Minutes of some of our late Conferences. Several concessions are made therein, with regard to assurance . . . some difficulties cleared and a few arguments proposed . . . and if you can show me that any further concessions are needful, I shall make them with great pleasure.'[45]

Wesley goes on to say: 'I think a divine conviction of pardon is directly implied in the evidence or conviction of things unseen. But if not, it is no absurdity to suppose that, when God pardons a mourning, broken-hearted sinner, His mercy obliges Him to another act—to witness to his spirit that He has pardoned him.'[46]

Richard Tompson sends a reply to Wesley on 15th August, in which he criticizes Wesley's statement that 'His mercy obliges Him to another act'. In answer to this criticism, Wesley, in his letter of 5th February 1756, says: 'My meaning is, the same compassion which moves God to pardon a mourning, broken-hearted sinner moves Him to comfort that mourner by witnessing to his spirit that his sins are pardoned.'[47]

In a letter to Tompson dated 18th February 1756, Wesley writes: 'You ask,

'(1) "Can a man who has not a clear assurance that his sins are forgiven be in a state of justification?" I believe there are some instances of it.

'(2) "Can a person be in a state of justification who, being asked: Do you know your sins forgiven? answers: I am

---

[43] *Letters*, II.105.

[44] This correspondence, written in 1755-6, was published in 1760 in a pamphlet of fifty-two pages, headed: 'Original Letters between the Reverend Mr John Wesley and Mr Richard Tompson, respecting the Doctrine of Assurance as held by the former: wherein that tenet is fully examined; with some Strictures on Christian Perfection.'

[45] *Letters*, III.137.   [46] ibid. III.138.   [47] ibid., III.161.

not certainly sure; but I do not entertain the least doubt of it?" I believe he may.

'(3) "Can any one know that his sins are forgiven while he doubts thereof?"

'Not at that instant when he doubts of it. But he may generally know it, though he doubts at some particular time.'[48]

Writing again to Tompson on 16th March, Wesley says: 'My belief in general is this—that every Christian believer has a divine conviction of his reconciliation with God. The sum of those concessions is, "I am inclined to think there may be some exceptions".'[49]

Writing to Dr Rutherforth on 28th March 1768, Wesley says that he hardly ever uses the word 'assurance', though some are very fond of the expression. He then declares his 'present sentiments' with regard to the doctrine:

(1) 'I believe a few, but very few, Christians have an assurance from God of everlasting salvation; and that is the thing which the Apostle terms the plerophory or full assurance of hope.

(2) 'I believe more have such an assurance of being now in the favour of God as excludes all doubt and fear. And this, if I do not mistake, the Apostle means by the plerophory or full assurance of faith.

(3) 'I believe a consciousness of being in the favour of God (which I do not term plerophory, or full assurance, since it is frequently weakened, nay perhaps interrupted, by returns of doubt or fear) is the common privilege of Christians fearing God and working righteousness.'[50]

Wesley allows a very significant exception. It is an important modification in the somewhat dogmatic strain that characterized most of his earlier teaching on assurance.

'Yet I do not affirm', he writes, 'there are no exceptions to this general rule. Possibly some may be in the favour of God and yet go mourning all the day long. But I believe this is usually owing either to disorder of body or ignorance of the gospel promises. 'Therefore', he continues, 'I have not for many years thought a consciousness of acceptance to be essential to justifying faith.'[51]

[48] *Letters*, III.163f.   [49] ibid., III.174.   [50] ibid., V.358.
[51] ibid., V.359. See R. N. Young, *The Witness of the Spirit*, pp. 52f.

At the age of eighty-five, Wesley looks back with regret upon the narrowness of his earlier views. 'Nearly fifty years ago', writes Wesley, 'when Preachers, commonly called Methodists, began to preach that grand Scriptural doctrine, salvation by faith, they were not sufficiently apprized of the difference between a servant and a child of God. They did not clearly understand, that even one "who feareth God, and worketh righteousness, is accepted of Him". In consequence of this, they were apt to make sad the hearts of those whom God hath not made sad. For they frequently asked those who feared God, "Do you know that your sins are forgiven?" and upon their answering "No", immediately replied, "Then you are a child of the devil". No; that does not follow. It might have been said, (and it is all that can be said with propriety) "Hitherto you are only a *servant*, you are not a *child* of God. You have already great reason to praise God that He has called you to his honourable service".'[52]

[52] cf. Dr L. F. Church, *Early Methodist People*, p. 97; *Works*, VII.199.

CHAPTER THREE

THE MAIN FEATURES OF WESLEY'S TEACHING

THE previous chapter has revealed some measure of development in Wesley's teaching. In his early writings, Wesley regards an experience of assurance as essential to salvation.[1] With the passing of the years, however, Wesley's teaching on assurance is gradually modified in the light of experience. It is allowed that there be 'exempt cases', 'infinite degrees of seeing God'; and that justifying faith does not necessarily involve a sense of pardon.[2] In 1755, Wesley is able to send Richard Tompson Minutes of previous Methodist Conferences in which 'several concessions are made' regarding assurance.[3] In 1768, he goes so far as to say: 'I have not for many years thought a consciousness of acceptance to be essential to justifying faith.'[4] Assurance comes to be recognized as the spiritual sense of Christian certainty which distinguishes 'a son' from 'a servant' of God.[5]

It must not be concluded, by reason of these modifications, that Wesley virtually came to regard this distinctive Methodist doctrine as unimportant; and, therefore, that he ceased to emphasize it. On the contrary, looking back over fifty years of evangelical preaching, Wesley can insist: 'We preach assurance as we always did, as the common privilege of the children of God; but we do not enforce it, under the pain of damnation.'[6]

In the previous chapter, we omitted Wesley's sermons on the 'Witness of the Spirit', written probably in 1746 and 1767. We postponed dealing with this material till now, since the sermons summarize Wesley's numerous references to assurance and also bring out the main points of his doctrine.

In Sermon 10 (1746), based on Romans 8[16], Wesley begins by admitting that 'many have mistaken the voice of their own imagination for this witness of the Spirit of God'.[7] This being

[1] *Journal*, II.333f.; *Letters*, I.274f., II.59, 90; *Sermons*, I.81.
[2] *Works*, VIII.282; *Sermons*, II.346; *Letters*, II.108f., V.358.
[3] *Letters*, III.137.   [4] ibid., V.358; cf. ibid., VII.61.
[5] Sermon, 106; *Works*, VII.199; *Journal*, I.423 note.
[6] Southey, *Life of Wesley*, I.295.
[7] *Sermons*, I.203. 'This delusion' of 'enthusiasts' will be more fully considered in Part V, pp. 179ff., *infra*.

so, it is not surprising if many reasonable men should question whether this witness be the privilege of ordinary Christians; and regard it only as an extraordinary gift of the Apostolic age.

Reference is made to the witness or testimony of our spirit, the foundation of which consists in those numerous texts of Scripture which describe the marks of the children of God.[8] But how do we know that we have those marks? We are immediately conscious of it, as we are that we are alive. 'You cannot but perceive if you love, rejoice, and delight in God . . . you must be directly assured if you love your neighbour as yourself.'[9] 'This is the testimony of our own spirit; even the testimony of our own conscience . . . or consciousness that we are inwardly conformed, by the spirit of God, to the image of His Son.'[10]

Attention is directed in this sermon to a consideration of that testimony of God's Spirit, which is superadded to, and conjoined with our spirit. How does He bear witness with our spirit that we are the children of God? Wesley admits that it is hard to find words in the language of men to explain 'the deep things of God'.[11] It is the difficulty, as Dr W. T. Stace says, of 'trying to think non-sensuous objects in a sensuous way'; and our problem is intensified by our having to express spiritual ideas in a language which has been formed at a materialistic stage in the history of mankind.

Despite the difficulty, Wesley attempts a definition, though with caution.[13] 'Perhaps one might say (desiring any who are taught of God to correct, to soften or strengthen the expression), the testimony of the Spirit is an inward impression on the soul whereby the Spirit of God directly witnesses to my spirit, that I am a child of God; that Jesus Christ hath loved me, and given Himself for me; and that all my sins are blotted out, and I, even I, am reconciled to God.'[14]

In a letter of 21st May 1781 addressed to Joseph Benson, Wesley says: 'I do not insist on the term "impression". . . . I will thank any one who will find a better; be it "discovery", "manifestation", "deep sense" or whatever it may be.'[15]

[8] *Sermons*, I.205.   [9] ibid., I.207.
[10] See *Sermons*, I.219ff.; also Part III, 121ff., *infra*.
[11] cf. J. A. Beet, *Manual of Theology*, p. 241.
[12] Dr W. T. Stace, *Critical History of Greek Philosophy*, pp. 10ff.
[13] cf. definition given by Dr H. B. Workman, *New History of Methodism*, I.26.
[14] *Sermons*, I.208.   [15] *Letters*, VII.61.

Wesley goes on to show that this testimony of the Spirit of God must needs ... be antecedent to the testimony of our own spirit.[16] He argues that the witness of our own spirit consists in our being holy of heart, and that this spiritual state is subsequent to our first experience of divine acceptance and pardon. 'We cannot know His pardoning love to us, till His Spirit witnesses it to our spirit.'[17]

In answer to the question, 'How does the Spirit of God "bear witness with our spirit that we are the children of God", so as to exclude all doubt, and evince the reality of our sonship?' Wesley employs a favourite piece of syllogistic reasoning:

'He that now loves God, that delights and rejoices in Him with an humble joy, an holy delight, an obedient love, is a child of God;
But I thus love, delight and rejoice in God;
Therefore, I am a child of God.'[18]

As to the manner in which the divine testimony is manifested to the heart, Wesley will not take upon himself to explain.[19] But the *fact*, Wesley holds, is incontestible; namely, that the Spirit of God does give the believer such a testimony to his adoption, that while it is present to the soul, he can no more doubt the reality of his sonship, than he can doubt of the shining of the sun, while he stands in the full blaze of his beams.[20]

With reference to the question as to how this joint testimony of God's Spirit with our spirit may be clearly distinguished from presumption and delusion, Wesley teaches that the Holy Scriptures abound with marks by which we can discern the real from the counterfeit. The genuine experience of the Spirit's witness is recognizable by the following features:

(1) *It is preceded by repentance*.

In support of this, Wesley quotes as authorities the Bible and the Anglican Prayer Book.

(2) *It is preceded by 'the being born of God'*.

In the words of Scripture, assurance follows an experience of passing 'from darkness to light', 'from the power of Satan unto God' and 'from death unto life'.[21]

---

[16] cf. Lindström, *Wesley and Sanctification*, p. 115. [17] *Sermons*, I.208.
[18] ibid., I.210. [19] cf. Beet, op. cit., p. 243.
[20] *Sermons*, I.210. [21] ibid., I.213.

(3) *It is accompanied by*
  (a) 'an humble joy', to which the presumptuous man is a stranger; and by
  (b) the keeping of God's commandments.[22]

After showing that the real witness is known intuitively and does not admit of a more minute and philosophical account, Wesley concludes this sermon by asserting that the best confirmation of the witness of the Spirit is the presence of the fruit of the Spirit in the new life in Christ.[23]

Wesley's second sermon on the witness of the Spirit, also based on Romans 8^{16}, was written and published in 1767.[24] The chief aim of this sermon appears to have been:

(1) To show that Wesley's views on assurance had not fundamentally changed since he wrote Sermon 10 in 1746.[25] He says, 'After twenty years' further consideration I see no cause to retract any part of this.'[26]
(2) To emphasize the *truth* of the doctrine by quoting, as confirmatory evidence, the experience of many whose lives had been changed by the Methodist preaching.[27]
(3) To provide answers to some of the charges levelled against the doctrine of assurance.[28]

We turn now to a closer examination of those parts which are most in line with our purpose and which are not merely repetitions of the previous sermon. In attempting to show how the witness of the Spirit is mediated to the believer, Wesley stresses the following points:

(1) That the witness of God's Spirit is not testified by any outward voice.
(2) And not always by an inward voice.
(3) Nor is it necessarily applied to the heart by texts of Scripture.
(4) 'But He so works upon the soul by His immediate influence, and by a strong, though inexplicable operation, that the stormy wind and troubled seas subside, and there is

---

[22] *Sermons*, I.214.   [23] ibid., I.217.
[24] Sermon 45 in *Standard Sermons*, edited by Curnock (1921); Sermon 11 in *Works* (1771).
[25] *Sermons*, I.199ff.   [26] ibid., II.345.
[27] See an earlier chapter, in Part I, pp. 39ff., *supra*, on assurance in the lives of the Early Methodists.
[28] See Part V, pp. 179ff., *infra*, for Wesley's defence against the charge of enthusiasm and heresy.

a sweet calm; the heart resting as in the arms of Jesus, and the sinner being clearly satisfied that God is reconciled, that all his "iniquities are forgiven, and his sins covered".'[29]

Wesley holds that on the following points there is general agreement:
(1) That there *is* 'a witness or testimony of the Spirit'.
(2) That 'the Spirit does testify with our spirit that we are the children of God'.
(3) That 'there is an *indirect* witness, or testimony, that we are the children of God', i.e. 'the testimony of a good conscience towards God'.[30]
(4) That there can be no 'real testimony of the Spirit without the fruit of the Spirit'.

'But the point in question', continues Wesley, 'is whether there be any *direct* testimony of the Spirit at all; whether there be any other testimony of the Spirit than that which arises from a consciousness of the fruit.'[31] Wesley holds that there is a *direct* testimony, on the ground that this is the plain meaning of the text, Romans 8[16].[32] 'It is manifest', he says, that 'here are two witnesses mentioned, who together testify the same thing; the Spirit of God, and our own spirit.'

Wesley maintains that—

(1) the testimony of our own spirit involves an inward sense 'of our sincerity' and a 'consciousness of our own good works';
(2) the testimony of God's Spirit is '*immediate* and *direct*, not the result of reflection or argumentation'.[33]

The sermon concludes with two important inferences:

(1) 'Let none ever presume to rest in any supposed testimony of the Spirit, which is separate from the fruit of it.'
The 'immediate consequences' of the witness of God's Spirit 'will be the fruit of the Spirit'. Though 'this fruit may be clouded for a while ... yet the substantial part of it remains'.
(2) 'Let none rest in any supposed fruit of the Spirit without the witness.'
'This is the privilege', says Wesley, of all the children of

---

[29] *Sermons*, II.345. [30] See Sermon 11, ibid., I.219ff. [31] ibid., II.346.
[32] See Part III, pp. 111ff., *infra*. [33] *Sermons*, II.349.

THE MAIN FEATURES OF WESLEY'S TEACHING

God, and without this we can never be assured that we are His children. So there is no need that we should ever more be deprived of either the testimony of God's Spirit or the testimony of our own, the consciousness of our walking in all righteousness and true holiness.'[34]

Wesley's exposition in these sermons is not impregnable. In Sermon 10, part 2, sections 6–8, it is shown that the witness of the Spirit is certified by the *fruit* of the Spirit.[35] With this Professor William James would agree: 'The real witness of the Spirit to the second birth is to be found only in the disposition of the genuine child of God.'[36] But this ignores Wesley's teaching in the same sermon, where it is held that the witness is immediately and directly perceived, if our spiritual senses are rightly disposed.[37] Wesley gives yet another turn to the circular reasoning when, on a later page, he holds that we can know that our spiritual senses are rightly disposed only by the testimony of our own spirit.[38] This confusion of ideas is dispelled when it is remembered that there is a joint testimony witnessing to the new life in Christ.

In tracing the doctrine of assurance in the teaching of Wesley, we noted several references to the fact that one could experience assurance in varying degrees. One such reference appears in a letter dated December 1751, to Dr George Lavington, in which Wesley writes:

(1) 'Some Christians have only . . . faith . . . mixed with doubts and fears.'
(2) 'Some have also the full assurance of faith, a full conviction of present pardon.'
(3) Others claim 'a full assurance of hope . . . a full conviction of their future perseverance'.[39]

Wesley points out that the faith which we preach as necessary to all Christians is the first of these, and no other. He did not deny the possibility of the second; but he believed that very few people had an assurance of their future perseverance.[40]

The first degree of assurance is that of faith in general, carrying with it the possibility of intermittent shades of doubt or fear.[41] Such a spiritual condition is exemplified in Wesley's

---

[34] *Sermons*, II.358f. [35] ibid., I.214f.
[36] James, *Varieties of Religious Experience*, p. 238. [37] *Sermons*, I.216.
[38] ibid., p. 217. [39] *Letters*, III.305f.; cf. III.162. [40] ibid., V.358.
[41] ibid., V.358.

own life—until, in 1739, resisting his introspective tendencies, he turned his attention to the objective tasks of the Methodist Revival.[42]

Few men are happy in the realm of definition; and Wesley is no exception when he attempts to define these degrees of assurance. In a latter to the Editor of *Lloyd's Evening Post*, written on 1st December 1760, Wesley sees the need to distinguish between faith and assurance.

(1) 'Faith is an evidence or conviction of things not seen, of God, and of the things of God. This is faith in general.'
(2) 'More particularly it is a divine evidence or conviction that Christ loved me and gave Himself for me.'
(3) 'When this evidence is heightened to exclude all doubt, it is the plerophory or full assurance of faith.'[43]

As compared with the first classification, which we quoted, he here omits all reference to the full assurance of hope and breaks up the first division into two:

(1) Faith in general.
(2) Personal faith in Christ's atonement.

Wesley appears to use 'faith' in at least two senses without always making clear which connotation is to be understood. At one time, he means 'faith in general', as in Hebrews 11^1; at another time he seems to mean 'a saving faith in Christ's atonement', accompanied by only a low degree of assurance.[44]

In reply to Richard Tompson's assertion that assurance is quite a distinct thing from faith, Wesley writes: 'The assurance in question is no other than the full assurance of faith; therefore it cannot be a distinct thing from faith, but only so high a degree of faith as excludes all doubt and fear. This plerophory, or full assurance, is doubtless wrought in us by the Holy Ghost. But so is every degree of true faith; yet the mind of man is the subject of both. I believe feebly; I believe without all doubt.' In the same letter, Wesley holds that there may be faith without full assurance, since there are lower degrees of faith not impervious to doubts.[45]

Another salient feature of Wesley's doctrine of assurance is the claim that it is *the direct witness of the Spirit.*

There is a testimony of the Spirit other than that which

---

[42] *Works*, I.106. [43] *Letters*, IV.116; cf. ibid., II.192, IV.126.
[44] cf. ibid., I.256. [45] ibid., III.16. See Part V, ch. 4, pp. 198ff., *infra*.

arises from a consciousness of the fruit of the Spirit.[46] The need for this had been borne out by Wesley's own experience prior to Aldersgate.[47] As Harald Lindström says, 'to ground the assurance only on the fruit is to go back to justification by works'.[48] And this testimony is 'an inward impression on the souls of believers, whereby the Spirit of God directly testifies to their spirit that they are children of God'.[49] This witness is *immediate* and *direct*, not the result of reflexion or argumentation.[50]

While we must be actually holy in heart before we can be conscious that we are so, the direct witness furnishes us with a knowledge of what God has done for us in Christ.[51] This divine witness comes to us while we are imperfect believers, assures us of His pardoning grace, and claims us through the inspiration of His love.[52]

As we have seen, Wesley held that no one should rest in any supposed fruit of the Spirit without this *direct* witness.[53] A display of moral virtues is no adequate substitute for that inner divine voice which testifies to the believer that he is a child of God.[54] 'With Wesley', says Dr Cell, 'the first and last word about Christian experience is never the human receptivity, nor the historical mediation. It is always the divine gift, it is always the work and witness of the Holy Spirit.'[55]

Wesley believed, moreover, that when man consciously sins, he loses this witness of the Spirit, since faith itself must die before a man can commit an actual sin.[56] This testimony is inevitably destroyed, not only by the commission of any outward sin, or the omission of known duty, but by giving way to any inward sin; in a word, by whatever grieves the Holy Spirit of God.[57]

This 'direct witness' is confirmed by the *'indirect witness' of the Spirit*.

The indirect witness may be described as the testimony of conscience or the evidence of a genuine Christian life.[58] To the pragmatic test, 'By their fruits ye shall know them', Wesley

---

[46] *Works*, V.132.   [47] *Journal*, I.421–4.
[48] Lindstrom, *Wesley and Sanctification*, p. 115.   [49] *Sermons*, II.357.
[50] ibid., p. 349.   [51] ibid., p. 354.   [52] ibid., I.203f.
[53] See Daniel Walton, *Witness of the Spirit*, pp. 41, 43.   [54] *Sermons*, II.358.
[55] Cell, *Rediscovery of John Wesley*, p. 20.   [56] *Works*, VIII.283.
[57] *Sermons*, II.343ff.; Watkin-Jones, *Holy Spirit from Arminius to Wesley*, p. 320.
[58] For Wesley's definition of conscience, see Sermons 11 (1746) and 105 (1788); cf. Dr W. R. Cannon, *Theology of John Wesley*, pp. 217ff.

submitted his doctrine of assurance.[59] He would not have his followers imagine that they had the direct witness of God's Spirit while their lives displayed no evidence of the fruit of the Spirit.

Wesley's insistence on the necessity of this indirect witness is the inevitable outcome of the practical Christian training of his childhood in the Epworth Rectory, and of the warning presented by the antinomian tendencies of Moravian Quietism.[60] In 1767, Wesley wrote: 'Let none ever presume to rest in any supposed testimony of the Spirit, which is separate from the fruit of it. If the Spirit of God does really testify that we are the children of God, the immediate consequence will be the fruit of the Spirit, even love, joy, peace, long-suffering, gentleness, goodness, fidelity, meekness, temperance.'[61]

Expressed psychologically, in the words of William James, Wesley's teaching on this point might be interpreted as stating that 'religion includes ... a new zest which adds itself to life ... an assurance of safety and a temper of peace, and, in relation to others, a preponderance of loving affections'.[62]

This indirect witness, as we have seen, is also termed 'the witness of our own spirit', the title given by Wesley to his Sermon No. 11.[63] When he displays the fruit of the Spirit, the believer may know that he is a child of God.[64] For Wesley, this aspect of assurance is the result of reason, or reflexion on what we feel in our own souls. Strictly speaking, it is a conclusion drawn partly from the word of God and partly from our own experience.[65]

From the beginning of his post-Aldersgate ministry, Wesley laid emphasis on this aspect of his doctrine of assurance. Later in life, as our historical survey has revealed, he came to realize that there were Christians in whose lives could plainly be found the fruits of the Spirit, but to whom there had not been vouchsafed a *consciousness* of their acceptance with God.[66] In other words, while it was *not* possible for a Christian to enjoy the direct witness of the Spirit without producing 'the fruit', it *was* possible for a person to exhibit Christian graces and yet be denied an inner sense of spiritual certainty.[67]

[59] *E.R.E.*, VIII.329f.   [60] See Part V, ch. 4, pp. 198ff., *infra*.
[61] *Sermons*, II.358.   [62] James, *Varieties of Religious Experience* (1902), pp. 485f.
[63] *Sermons*, I.219f.
[64] ibid., p. 210; cf. Lindstrom, *Wesley and Sanctification*, p. 115.
[65] *Sermons*, I.221f.   [66] *Letters*, V.235, VI.272f.; *Works*, VII.199.
[67] cf. the difficult question of 'good works before justification': Simon, *John Wesley and the Methodist Societies*, p. 259; *Works*, VIII.283.

THE MAIN FEATURES OF WESLEY'S TEACHING

The witness of the Spirit—both Direct and Indirect—is '*the common privilege*' *of all believers.*

We have seen that Wesley, with the passing of the years, came to relax his early emphasis on assurance as essential to salvation.[68] But he never ceased to hold that it was an experience for which *all* Christians should strive.[69] 'I believe', he wrote in 1768, 'a consciousness of being in the favour of God . . . is the common privilege of Christians fearing God and working righteousness.'[70]

Since the witness of the Spirit is a common privilege open to every believer, it is plain, as Dr Workman points out, that Wesley's doctrine of assurance involved as a necessary corollary an Arminian theory of the Atonement.[71] Dr G. P. Fisher, in his sympathetic exposition of 'the evangelical Arminianism of Wesley', says that 'this faith in the living power of the Holy Spirit . . . was the secret of the emphasis which was laid on assurance as a privilege attainable by all Christians'.[72]

[68] *Works*, VII.199.   [69] *Letters*, V.235.   [70] ibid., p. 358.
[71] Workman, *New History of Methodism*, I.34.
[72] Fisher, *History of Christian Doctrine* (1896), p. 392.

CHAPTER FOUR

THE DOCTRINE EXPRESSED IN SONG

DR J. A. BEET has pointed out that, while John Wesley has rendered immense service to English theology by calling conspicuous attention to important elements, previously overlooked, in the Christian message, the real embodiment of Methodist theology is the *Methodist Hymn Book*, and especially Charles Wesley's hymns.[1] There is hardly a doctrine of evangelical theology, claimed Dr F. Luke Wiseman, 'that is not rendered intelligible, attractive and edifying by his ready pen'.[2]

Charles Wesley wrote some of his hymns in order to expound or to defend the distinctive doctrines of Methodism—not least the doctrine of assurance. John Wesley himself was well aware of the theological value and range of his brother's poetical compositions. With reference to the edition of 1780, of which 93 per cent. were hymns from his brother's pen, John expressed the view that 'the judicious and candid reader may find clear explications of every branch of speculative and practical divinity'.[3] In the Preface to this collection, Wesley summed up its contents as a little body of practical and experimental divinity, and claimed, though it included only 525 hymns, that it contained all the important truths of our holy religion.

It is clear, therefore, that no inquiry into Methodist theology can ignore the hymns of Methodism. Their doctrinal value is manifest.

In the sphere of hymnology, John Wesley's chief work was that of a translator and editor. John *could*, and *did*, compose hymns, as revealed in the Grace Murray affair and by his unfinished paraphrase of Psalm 104.[4] With reference to John Wesley's literary gifts, Dr J. H. Whiteley says: 'He was one of the ablest of his generation, as is evidenced by his masterly translations of poems from German, French and Spanish sources. In these versions, he reproduced the full flavour of the

[1] *London Quarterly Review*, January 1921.
[2] Wiseman, *Charles Wesley and His Hymns*, p. 15.
[3] See Preface to *Pocket Hymn-Book* of 1785.
[4] *Poetical Works of John and Charles Wesley*, edited by Dr Osborn (1872), VIII.191 (hereinafter referred to as *Poetical Works*).

originals; a task demanding the highest powers of scholarship, insight, skill and taste both in thought and expression.'[5]

While Charles Wesley's poetic inspiration sprang mainly from his own sense of certainty on 21st May 1738, John's activity as a translator began long before Aldersgate. It was during his missionary visit to Georgia that Wesley came under the spell of German hymns.

The influence of heart and mind which the Moravians wielded over the Wesleys has already been assessed in earlier chapters. One of the things about the Moravians which gripped John was their singing. His learning German enabled him, not only to converse with them, but to open up with his pen for English-speaking peoples the wealth of German hymnody.

We shall need to bear in mind throughout our examination of Methodist hymns that data for the doctrine of assurance are found in many verses where such terms as 'assurance' or 'the witness of Spirit' do not appear. Conversely, we can expect to trace in some hymns such words as 'assurance' and 'witness', but they are to be ignored, since, as their context reveals, they do not bear a connotation in line with this inquiry.

One of the first of the Moravian hymns to engage John Wesley's pen was '*Verborgne Gottesliebe*'—'Thou hidden love of God'.[6] According to his *Plain Account of Christian Perfection*, Wesley translated this hymn in Savannah in 1736. It was printed in his *Psalms and Hymns* in 1738.[7] The author of the hymn was Gerhard Tersteegen.[8] His leaning towards an inner sense of contact with God is revealed in his plea for an inward Divine voice to convey to his soul an assurance of belonging to a God of love:

> 'Speak to my inmost soul, and say,
>   I am thy Love, thy God, thy All!
> To feel Thy power, to hear Thy voice,
> To taste Thy love, be all my choice.'[9]

The next quotation comes from Paulus Gerhardt.[10] Christian certainty for Gerhardt is nothing less than Christ's taking

---

[5] Whiteley, *Wesley's England*, p. 20.   [6] From *Geistliches Blumengärtlein* (1729).
[7] *Poetical Works*, I.71.
[8] 1697–1769. A translator and expounder of the mystic writers.
[9] Wesley's *Psalms and Hymns* (1738); *Methodist Hymn-Book* (1933), 433, v. 6 (hereinafter referred to as *M.H.B.*).
[10] 1607–76. A gifted and popular hymn-writer; a Lutheran pastor.

possession of his whole life as a 'constant flame' and reigning 'without a rival there'.

> 'O may Thy love possess me whole,
> My joy, my treasure, and my crown:
> Strange flames far from my heart remove;
> My every act, word, thought, be love.'[11]

One of the greatest hymns to be considered here is by Johann Andreas Rothe.[12] It is *'Ich habe nun den Grund gefunden'*—'Now I have found the ground wherein'.[13] The entire hymn is a living monument to a deep personal conviction of religious certainty.[14] The author represents the assurance of salvation as having its source in the love and mercy of God:

> 'O Love, Thou bottomless abyss,
> My sins are swallowed up in Thee!
> Covered is my unrighteousness,
> Nor spot of guilt remains on me,
> While Jesu's blood through earth and skies
> Mercy, free, boundless mercy! cries.'

Such an experience of God's love and boundless mercy is appropriated to the individual believer through the exercise of faith:

> 'With faith I plunge me in this sea,
> Here is my hope, my joy, my rest;
> Hither, when hell assails, I flee,
> I look into my Saviour's breast:
> Away, sad doubt and anxious fear!
> Mercy is all that's written there.'[15]

We have already mentioned Wesley's indebtedness to Spangenberg in an earlier chapter. This Moravian bishop was the author of that fine hymn, 'What shall we offer our good Lord?'[16] Wesley's admirable translation was printed in 1742 in his *Hymns and Sacred Poems*.[17] Spangenberg is assured of the redeeming grace of God by the evidence of a new life:

[11] *M.H.B.*, 430.2.
[12] 1688–1750. Lutheran pastor and author of some forty hymns.
[13] In Zinzendorf's *Christ-Catholisches Singe- und Bet-Buchlein* (1727).
[14] *Poetical Works*, I.279. Wesley met Rothe at Berthelsdorf during his visit to Germany; *Journal*, II.21, note; Simon, *John Wesley and the Religious Societies*, p. 210.
[15] *M.H.B.*, 375.3, 4.
[16] It appeared in the *Herrnhut Hymn-Book* (1737) and in the *Brethren's Hymn-Book* in 1778.
[17] *Poetical Works*, II.64.

> 'We all, in perfect love renewed,
>   Shall *know* the greatness of Thy power,
>   Stand in the temple of our God
>   As pillars, and go out no more.'[18]

Wesley's genius as a translator was not limited to German verse. Among the hymns relevant to our purpose, one comes from a Spanish, the other from a French, source. He translates a choice Spanish hymn of unknown authorship, which is included in his *Psalms and Hymns* in 1738.[19] The hymn begins, 'O God, my God, my all Thou art'. The writer claims a certainty of continuous Divine help and protection:

> 'In all I do I feel Thine aid;
>   Therefore Thy greatness will I sing,
>   O God, Who bidd'st my heart be glad
>   Beneath the shadow of Thy wing.'[20]

The other hymn, from the French, is composed by Antoinette Bourignon.[21] Her dramatic renunciation of marriage is expressed in the hymn from which we quote. The first line is: 'Come, Saviour, Jesu, from above.' It was included in Wesley's *Hymns and Sacred Poems* of 1739.[22] Having emptied her 'heart of earthly love', her chief desire is that God will answer her prayer and for Himself 'prepare the place'. To have the inward certainty that this has been accomplished is her highest hope and aspiration.

> 'Thee I can love, and Thee alone,
>   With pure delight and inward bliss:
>   To *know* Thou tak'st me for Thine own
>   O what a happiness is this'![23]

These, then, are the main verses relating to assurance in John Wesley's translations. They are indeed sparse—especially in comparison with the spate of references traceable in his brother's verse. But they are important for two reasons. First, they illustrate further the indebtedness of Wesley to the Moravians. Secondly, they provide additional evidence in support of a point of view we have already stressed—namely, that John Wesley was acquainted with the idea of assurance

---

[18] *M.H.B.*, 784.6. (Italics mine.)   [19] *Poetical Works*, I.174.
[20] *M.H.B.*, 471.7.   [21] 1616–80. A religious mystic and voluminous writer.
[22] *Poetical Works*, I.110.   [23] *M.H.B.*, 546.5.

before it was translated into his own personal experience at Aldersgate on 24th May 1738.

The fact that many of Charles Wesley's hymns express his own spiritual experience stresses the importance of the consideration we have already given to his religious life. We have also seen that many authorities have testified to the value of these hymns as a medium of conveying theological truth. Does this mean, therefore, that their author was a theologian? Most scholars would answer that he was not a theologian in the *formal* sense—not an *abstract* theologian. It was intuition that often seemed to guide him to the heart of spiritual reality. For this reason, his hymns have been likened to Augustine's *Confessions* and Bunyan's *Grace Abounding*.

The edition of 1780 is Charles Wesley's chief monument as a poet and evangelist,[24] and is the basis of all later hymn-books. It owes much, however, to John Wesley's insight, poetic appreciation, and critical power. The quality of this hymnal and its relevance to our inquiry are clearly revealed in John's Preface: 'In what other publication of the kind have you so distinct and full an account of Scriptural Christianity? such a declaration of the heights and depths of religion, speculative and practical? so strong cautions against the most plausible errors; particularly those which are now so prevalent? and so clear directions for making your calling and election sure; for perfecting holiness in the fear of God?'[25]

For the remainder of this chapter, we shall examine those hymns from Charles Wesley's pen which are closely associated, in time or in thought, with the personal experience of assurance gained by the Wesleys in May 1738.

Foremost among these is the one called 'the Wesleys' Conversion Hymn'.[26] It was written on Tuesday, 23rd May 1738. Under this date in his *Journal*, Charles writes: 'At nine[27] I began an hymn upon my conversion, but was persuaded to break off,[28] for fear of pride. Mr Bray coming, encouraged me to proceed in spite of Satan. I prayed to Christ to stand by me, and finished the hymn.'[29]

The entry for the following day reads: 'Towards ten my

[24] D. M. Jones, *Charles Wesley—A Study*, p. 269.
[25] Preface to the 1780 *Hymn-Book*.
[26] *Poetical Works*, I.91. [27] i.e. nine in the *morning*.
[28] Presumably at the end of verse 2, judging by the wording of the following verse. Wiseman, *Charles Wesley and His Hymns*, pp. 8f.
[29] *Journal of Charles Wesley*, edited Jackson (1849), p. 94.

brother was brought in triumph by a troop of our friends, and declared, "I believe". We sang the hymn with great joy, and parted with prayer.' The hymn is almost certainly 'Where shall my wondering soul begin?' This is doubtless the first recorded expression of the Wesleys' inner sense of spiritual certainty.[30]

Charles takes us in this hymn to the very heart of their new found assurance:

> 'Oh, how shall I the goodness tell,
>   Father, which Thou to me hast show'd?
> That I, a child of wrath and hell,
>   I should be called a child of God!
> *Should know, should feel my sins forgiven,*
>   Blest with this antepast of heaven!'[31]

A few weeks later, Charles Wesley wrote the hymn, 'And can it be that I should gain?' which, though a greater poem, does not possess the same degree of freshness and vividness as the 'Conversion Hymn'. A verse, omitted from the new *Methodist Hymn-Book* of 1933, is very much in line with our purpose here:

> 'Still, the inward voice I hear
>   That whispers all my sins forgiven;
>
>   .   .   .   .   .
>
> 'I feel the life His wounds impart
>   I feel my Saviour in my heart.'[32]

A verse of this hymn gives poetic expression to the telling phrase, 'legal night', by which Charles summed up his religious life prior to 21st May 1738. Based on Peter's liberation from prison,[33] the hymn provides a graphic picture of the Wesleys' deliverance from the night of bondage and doubt into the new day of freedom and certainty:

> 'Long my imprisoned spirit lay
>   Fast bound in sin and nature's night;
> Thine eye diffused a quickening ray—
>   I woke, the dungeon flamed with light;
> My chains fell off, my heart was free,
> I rose, went forth, and followed Thee.'[34]

---

[30] John Wesley's account was obviously written later. See *Journal*, I.475f.
[31] *Hymns and Sacred Poems* (1739); *M.H.B.*, 361.2. (Italics mine.)
[32] *Poetical Works*, I.105.   [33] Acts xii.
[34] *Hymns and Sacred Poems* (1739); *M.H.B.*, 371.4.

This contrast between the 'legal night' and the 'new day' has many echoes in Charles Wesley's writings. A year after this illumination had come to him, he wrote a hymn 'for the Anniversary Day of One's Conversion'.[35] Two passages illustrate the point under discussion here:

> 'On this glad day the glorious Sun
>   Of righteousness arose;
> On my benighted soul He shone,
>   And fill'd it with repose.'[36]

The other passage is even more vivid:

> 'He breaks the power of cancelled sin,
> He sets the prisoner free.'[37]

The same idea is embodied in a line from another hymn to which we must give careful attention:

> 'The morning breaks, the shadows flee.'[38]

This quotation is from 'Wrestling Jacob', not only the greatest of the 'Conversion hymns', but perhaps Charles Wesley's finest literary production. Dr Watts regarded this one hymn as being worth all the verses he himself had written.[39] It tells the story of the Wesleys' spiritual conflict and victory under the figure of Jacob's struggle with the angel at Peniel.[40]

> 'Wrestling I will not let Thee go
> Till I Thy name, Thy nature, *know*.'

Then penitential despair proves to be the prelude to spiritual confidence and conquest:

> 'Yield to me now; for I am weak,
>   But confident in self despair;
> Speak to my heart, in blessings speak,
>   Be conquered by my instant prayer;
> Speak or Thou never hence shalt move,
> And tell me if Thy name is Love.
>
>   .   .   .   .   .
>
> 'Tis Love! 'Tis Love! Thou diedst for me!
> I hear Thy whisper in my heart.'

At last, his strenuous prayer gains for him the assurance of personal salvation:

---

[35] *Poetical Works*, I.299. [36] *Hymns and Sacred Poems* (1740). [37] *M.H.B.*, 1.5.
[38] *Poetical Works*, II.173. [39] *Works*, XIII.514. [40] Genesis 32[24-31].

> 'I know Thee, Saviour, who Thou art,
> Jesus, the feeble sinner's Friend.
>
> . . . . .
>
> 'Thy mercies never shall remove;
> Thy nature and Thy name is Love.'[41]

We saw, in an earlier chapter, that in the teaching of Spangenberg and Böhler the personal nature of assurance was emphasized. This is brought out by Charles in a hymn written shortly after he had entered into this new experience:

> 'Take me now, possess me whole,
> Who *for me, for me*, hast died.'[42]

The same note is struck in the anniversary hymn from which we have already quoted:

> 'Then with my heart I first believed,
> Believed with faith divine;
> Power with the Holy Ghost received
> To call the Saviour *mine*.
>
> 'I felt my Lord's atoning blood
> Close to *my* soul applied;
> *Me, me*, He loved—the Son of God—
> For me, for me, He died!
>
> . . . . .
>
> 'His blood can make the foulest clean,
> His blood avail'd *for me*.'[43]

While it is not possible to give a precise date for more than a few of the hymns, there is another that must be set in the early days of the Methodist Revival. It was originally entitled, 'Justified, but not Sanctified'. It contains the following significant lines:

> 'I feel my pardon seal'd in blood;
> Saviour, Thy love I wait to feel.
>
> . . . . .
>
> 'I *know* Thou wilt accept me now
> I *know* my sins are now forgiven!'[44]

[41] *Hymns and Sacred Poems*, 1742; M.H.B., 339.3, 4, 6, 7, 9.
[42] M.H.B., 97.1. See Dr Bett: *The Hymns of Methodism*, p. 94.
[43] *Poetical Works*, I.299.
[44] Rattenbury, *The Evangelical Doctrines of Charles Wesley's Hymns*, pp. 252f.

A reference to the spiritual illumination of 21st May is traceable in 'A Morning Hymn', which James Montgomery deemed among the finest Charles Wesley had written:[45]

> 'Joyless is the day's return
> Till Thy mercy's beams I see,
> Till Thou inward light impart,
> Glad my eyes, and warm my heart.
>
> 'Visit Then this soul of mine;
> Pierce the gloom of sin and grief;
> Fill me, Radiancy divine;
> Scatter all my unbelief;
> More and more Thyself display,
> Shining to the perfect day.'[46]

As we saw in our examination of assurance in the testimonies of the early Methodists, John Wesley encouraged his helpers to write an account of their religious experiences. The founder of Methodism, however, was reluctant to carry out his own instructions. When pressed to do so, Wesley is said to have replied by quoting the first two verses of his brother's hymn: 'O Thou who camest from above.' The theme is closely related to the account given by Wesley of his sense of certainty gained on 24th May 1738.[47] It must have been impossible for Wesley to repeat the following verse from his brother's pen without going back in thought to his own 'heart-warming' experience at Aldersgate:

> 'O Thou camest from above
> The pure celestial fire to impart,
> Kindle a flame of sacred love
> On the mean altar of my heart.'[48]

---

[45] *Hymns and Sacred Poems* (1740).
[46] *Poetical Works*, I.224; *M.H.B.*, 924.2, 3.   [47] *Journal*, I.475f.
[48] *Short Hymns on Select Passages of Scripture* (1772); *Poetical Works*, IX.58; *M.H.B.*, 386.1.

CHAPTER FIVE

THE SPIRIT'S WITNESS IN CHARLES WESLEY'S HYMNS

IN THIS chapter, we consider the remaining data for the doctrine of assurance in Charles Wesley's hymns. It would appear that this evidence can best be presented under various theological heads; for the doctrine of assurance has ramifications that go far and wide in the realm of theology. Indeed, every facet of theological truth is linked to many others and cannot be fully understood unless it is seen in relation thereto.

In tracing assurance in the teaching of Wesley, we saw that the One who bore witness with our spirits that we were the children of God was the Holy Spirit. It is not surprising, therefore, that in several of Charles Wesley's hymns the Spirit is related to the doctrine of assurance.

The theme of 'Wrestling Jacob' is reiterated in a later hymn, where the place of the angel, however, is taken by the Holy Spirit:

'The Spirit of interceding grace
  Give us in faith to claim;
To wrestle till we see Thy face,
  And know Thy hidden name.'[1]

To the penitent sinner the Holy Spirit gives assurance and a sense of acceptance:

'Come, holy celestial Dove,
  To visit a sorrowful breast,
My burden of guilt to remove,
  And bring me assurance and rest!
Thou only hast power to relieve
  A sinner o'erwhelmed with his load,
A sense of acceptance to give,
  And sprinkle his heart with the blood.'[2]

The hymn goes on to crave the inner certainty of having found Divine favour and the consciousness of pardon:

[1] *Poetical Works*, V.176; *Hymns and Sacred Poems* (1749); *M.H.B.*, 736.3.
[2] *Hymns of Petition and Thanksgiving for the promise of the Father* (1746); *Poetical Works*, IV.195.

> 'The sense of Thy favour inspire,
> And give me my pardon to feel.'[3]

It is the Spirit who conveys to the believer the assurance of regeneration through the merit of Christ's blood:

> 'His Spirit answers to the blood,
> And tells me I am born of God.'[4]

For the Wesleys, the source of that inner transformation by which their heart was 'strangely warmed' and their soul enlightened was the Spirit of God.

> 'Refining Fire, go through my heart,
> Illuminate my soul:
> Scatter Thy life through every part,
> And sanctify the whole.'[5]

Far from being an experience which the believer is to receive only at some future date, the inward witness is given *now* by the Holy Spirit:

> 'Holy Ghost, no more delay;
> Come, and in Thy temple stay;
> Now Thine inward witness bear,
> Strong, and permanent, and clear.'[6]

Charles Wesley's finest verses on the Spirit are those expressive of his own aspiration or experience. A clear and comprehensive statement on assurance is found in a hymn composed in 1740:

> 'Come, Holy Ghost, all-quickening fire,
> Come, and my hallow'd heart inspire,
>   Sprinkled with the atoning blood:
> Now to my soul Thyself reveal,
> Thy mighty working let me feel,
>   And know that I am born of God.'[7]

Then follows a reference to 'the joint witness' of the Spirit:

> 'Thy witness *with my spirit* bear,
> That God, my God, inhabits there.'[8]

---

[3] *M.H.B.*, 294.1, 3.
[4] *Poetical Works*, II.323; *Hymns and Sacred Poems* (1742), Part II; *M.H.B.*, 368.4.
[5] *Hymns and Sacred Poems* (1740); *Poetical Works*, I.328; *M.H.B.*, 387.6.
[6] *Poetical Works*, I.192; *Hymns and Sacred Poems* (1739); *M.H.B.*, 568.4.
[7] *Hymns and Sacred Poems* (1740); *M.H.B.*, 553.1.   [8] *Poetical Works*, I.240.

Our certainty of salvation is strengthened by the Spirit's unveiling of God, by His cultivating within us the divine nature, and by His setting upon our lives the seal of God's ownership:

> 'Send us the Spirit of Thy Son,
> To make the depths of Godhead known,
>   To make us share the life divine;
> Send Him the sprinkled blood to apply,
> Send Him our souls to sanctify,
>   And show and seal us ever Thine.'[9]

A verse which appeared in *Hymns on the Lord's Supper*, published in 1745, calls on the Holy Spirit as One who can effectively testify to the Passion of Christ and who will call to mind the Master's way of salvation for the individual soul:

> 'Come, Thou witness of His dying;
>   Come, Remembrancer divine,
> Let us feel Thy power, applying
>   Christ to every soul, and mine.'[10]

It is also the office of the Holy Spirit to bear witness to our regenerate life:

> 'Come, Holy Ghost, my heart inspire!
> Attest that I am born again.'[11]

The assurance granted to the believer by the Spirit is an assurance of *salvation*. In the hymns are instances where a link between an inner certainty and an experience of salvation is traceable:

> 'Thou waitest to be gracious still;
>   Thou dost with sinners bear,
> That, saved, we may Thy goodness feel,
>   And all Thy grace declare.'[12]

Salvation for Charles Wesley, however, is meaningless without the Cross of Christ. No inquiry into the theological significance of Methodist hymnology can proceed far without discovering that all roads lead to Calvary.[13] This partly explains the frequent repetition of the phrase:

---

[9] *Hymns for Whit-Sunday* (1746); *Poetical Works*, IV.165; *M.H.B.*, 730.2.
[10] *Ibid*, II.226; *M.H.B.*, 765.3.
[11] *Hymns and Sacred Poems* (1740); *Poetical Works*, I.307; *M.H.B.*, 280.4.
[12] *M.H.B.*, 49.2; *Poetical Works*, IX.55; *Short Hymns on Selected Passages of Scripture* (1762).
[13] Manning, *Hymns of Wesley and Watts*, p. 43.

"'Tis Thine the blood to apply.'[14]

How then do the hymns link the doctrine of assurance to the message of the Cross? It is not necessary to submit here all the illustrative passages that might be quoted. A few representative verses will serve our purpose.

There is a very graphic couplet in that well-known hymn, 'Let earth and heaven agree', in which the inner certainty of salvation is bound up with the historic death of Christ on 'the tree':

> 'See there my Lord upon the tree!
> I hear, I feel, He died for me.'[15]

In another hymn, Charles Wesley makes a touching plea that sinners might know the efficacy of Christ's death:

> 'Come, sinners, see your Maker die,
> And say, was ever grief like His?
> Come, *feel* with me His blood applied:
> My Lord, my Love is crucified.'[16]

There is a mystic tone about another hymn in which are enumerated some of the 'proffered benefits' sinners can 'embrace':

> 'A pardon written with His blood
> The tears that tell your sins forgiven.'[17]

One of Charles Wesley's many references to the blood of Christ is here associated with an inward sense of freedom from sin:

> 'O for a heart to praise my God,
> A heart from sin set free,
> A heart that always feels Thy blood
> So freely spilt for me.'[18]

This confidence in the atoning merit of Christ's redemptive work conveys to the believer an inner sense of security that no outer tempest can possibly overthrow:

---

[14] Rattenbury, *The Evangelical Doctrines of Charles Wesley's Hymns*, p. 176.
[15] *Hymns on God's Everlasting Love* (1741), No. XI, reprinted in *Arminian Magazine* (1778); M.H.B., 114.5; *Poetical Works*, III.71.
[16] M.H.B., 186.2; *Poetical Works*, II.74; *Hymns and Sacred Poems* (1742).
[17] *Hymns and Sacred Poems* (1749); M.H.B., 325.2, 3; *Poetical Works*, V.64.
[18] *Hymns and Sacred Poems* (1742); *Poetical Works*, II.77; M.H.B., 550.1.

> 'Who in the Lord confide,
> And feel His sprinkled blood,
> In storms and hurricanes abide,
> Firm as the mount of God.'[19]

The main text on which John Wesley based his teaching on the Witness of the Spirit was Romans 8[16]: 'The Spirit Himself beareth witness with our spirit that we are the children of God.'[20] It is not surprising, therefore, that Charles Wesley, in his hymns, presents an assurance, not only of sins forgiven, but of acceptance by God into His family. In other words, a positive aspect of the doctrine of assurance is adoption; and it is this high estate to which there is, as Romans 8 and Galatians 4 reveal, the witness of God's Spirit.

Wesley held that at Aldersgate Street he was raised from the status of 'a servant' of God to the rank of 'a son'.[21] This distinguishing feature of the true child of God is reflected in his brother's hymns, where it is adoption rather than justification that figures as the characteristic doctrine of salvation.[22]

In *Hymns and Sacred Poems*, 1740, there is a hymn headed 'Groaning for the Spirit of Adoption', the first verse of which begins:

> 'Father, if Thou my Father art,
> Send forth the Spirit of Thy Son.'[23]

The hymn goes on to reveal the quality of life enjoyed by those who are truly members of God's spiritual family:

> 'When shall I hear the inward voice
> Which only faithful souls can hear?
> Pardon, and peace, and heavenly joys
> Attend the promised Comforter.
>
> 'Come, Holy Ghost, my heart inspire!
> Attest that I am born of God;
> Come, and baptize me now with fire.'[24]

Few lines are more crammed with theology than those to which we now turn. They clearly reveal the important place

---

[19] *Poetical Works*, VIII.111; *M.H.B.*, 700.1; *Psalms and Hymns* (1743).

[20] See Part II, ch. 3, pp. 73ff., *supra*, and Part III, ch. 2, pp. 111ff., *infra*.

[21] *Journal*, I.423.

[22] Rattenbury, *Evangelical Doctrines of Charles Wesley's Hymns*, pp. 256f.; cf. Pope: *Compendium of Theology*, III.116; Stevens, *Theology of the New Testament*, p. 440.

[23] *Poetical Works*, I.307.   [24] *M.H.B.*, 280.2, 4.

which adoption holds in the Wesleys' doctrine of assurance. The hymn is addressed to the Holy Spirit:

> 'True witness of my sonship, now
>   Engraving pardon on my heart,
>   Seal of my sins in Christ forgiven.
>
> . . . . .
>
> 'Come then, my God, mark out Thine heir,
>   Of heaven a larger earnest give;
> With clearer light Thy witness bear,
>   More sensibly within me live;
> Let all my powers Thine entrance feel,
> And deeper stamp Thyself the seal.'[25]

An assurance of adoption implies a new relationship between God and the sinner—namely, one of reconciliation. Then can the believer know the wonder of pardon and share the fearlessness and confidence of the children of God:

> 'My God is reconciled,
>   His pardoning voice I hear;
> He owns me for His child,
>   I can no longer fear,
> With confidence I now draw near,
> And Father, Abba, Father! cry.'[26]

The same truth shines out in another hymn:

> 'If now the witness were in me,
> Would He not testify of Thee
>   In Jesus reconciled?
> And should I not with faith draw nigh,
> And boldly Abba, Father! cry,
>   And know myself Thy child?'[27]

The theme of God's love is echoed in many hymns where reference is also made to assurance. It is the attribute of love which is most conspicuous on the Godward side in the personal experience of divine pardon:

> 'Tell me now, in love divine,
> That Thou hast pardoned me.'[28]

---

[25] *Hymns and Sacred Poems* (1740); *Poetical Works*, I.164; *M.H.B.*, 299.3, 4.
[26] *Poetical Works*, II.323; *M.H.B.*, 368.5.; *Hymns and Sacred Poems* (1742).
[27] *Hymns for those that seek and those that have redemption in the blood of Christ* (1747); *Works*, IV.235; *M.H.B.*, 376.4.
[28] *Poetical Works*, VI.461; *Hymns for Children* (1763), No. 99; *M.H.B.*, 59.4.

In this matter, Charles Wesley is as sure and as dogmatic as the writer of the First Epistle of John.[29]

> 'God is love, I *know*, I *feel*;
> Jesus lives, and loves me still.'[30]

Wesley admits that godly fear has a part to play in the divine plan of redemption; but this is subordinated to the forgiving love of God:

> 'If I have only known Thy fear,
> And followed with a heart sincere
>   Thy drawings from above,
> Now, now the further grace bestow,
> And let my sprinkled conscience *know*
>   Thy sweet forgiving love.
>
> '*Short of Thy love* I would not stop,
> A stranger to the gospel hope,
>   *The sense of sin forgiven*;
> I would not, Lord, my soul deceive,
> Without the *inward witness* live,
>   That antepast of heaven.'[31]

John Wesley was much disturbed by the absence of joy in the religious experience which immediately followed Aldersgate.[32] Once the Revival was launched, however, and Wesley had lost himself in his endless labours, he gained that lasting happiness which is always a by-product for those whose chief end is to bring in God's Kingdom. Joy shone in the faces of those early Methodists into whose lives had come a sense of certainty—a joy so contagious that it led countless others into the same glad assurance.

All this is reflected in Charles Wesley's hymns. There is a definite lilt in the verse:

> 'My God I am Thine;
> What a comfort divine,
> What a blessing to know that my Jesus is mine!'[33]

---

[29] See Part III, ch. 3, pp. 123ff., *infra*.
[30] *Hymns and Sacred Poems* (1740); *Poetical Works*, I.271; M.H.B., 358.4.
[31] *Hymns for those that seek and those that have redemption in the blood of Jesus Christ* (1747); *Poetical Works*, IV.235; M.H.B., 376.2, 3.
[32] *Journal*, I.476ff.
[33] *Hymns and Sacred Poems* (1749); *Poetical Works*, V.24; M.H.B., 406.1.

The connexion between happiness and assurance is revealed very clearly in the words:

> 'How happy every child of grace
> Who knows his sins forgiven!'[34]

It is a 'quiet joy', for it has its setting in the serenity of those who have been initiated into God's spiritual family—a joy which defies definition and which is known only to those who have a knowledge of salvation:

> 'We all partake the joy of one,
> The common peace we feel,
> A peace to sensual minds unknown,
> A joy unspeakable.'[35]

It is at the table of the Lord that this supreme bliss can be effectively realized:

> 'Thy presence makes the feast;
> Now let our spirits feel
> The glory not to be expressed,
> The joy unspeakable.'[36]

In 1747, Charles Wesley wrote a hymn based on the Scriptural narrative of the Great Supper.[37] A verse which has since been omitted from the *Methodist Hymn-Book* links the knowledge of 'sins forgiven' with 'the joy of heaven':

> 'Excused from coming to the feast!
> Excused from being Jesu's guest!
> From knowing now your sins forgiven,
> From tasting here the joys of heaven.'[38]

In the verses already quoted from Charles Wesley's poetical works, we recall the frequent use of the word 'feel'. This might lead the casual observer to conclude that the Methodist poet based salvation on feeling. But this conclusion would be ill-founded, since it would ignore the counter-influence of Charles Wesley's hymns on the Lord's Supper, some of which were designed in part as an antidote to the individualistic extravagances of Moravian Quietism.

---

[34] *Poetical Works*, VI.216; *Funeral Hymns*, 2nd series (1759); *M.H.B.*, 627.1.
[35] *Hymns for those who seek and those who have redemption in the blood of Jesus Christ* (1747); *Poetical Works*, IV.252; *M.H.B.*, 745.5.
[36] *Poetical Works*, III.273; *Hymns for the Lord's Supper* (1745); *M.H.B.*, 761.3.
[37] Luke 14$^{16-24}$.   [38] *Poetical Works*, IV.274.

A subjective tendency is obviously linked to the doctrine of assurance, and we must consider some of the evidence:

> 'Loud and strong their voices be,
>   Small, and *still*, and *inward* Thine.'[39]

In a hymn where the influence of Milton seems traceable, Charles Wesley says:

> 'To attend the whispers of Thy grace
>   And hear Thee *inly* speak.'[40]

One wonders how John Wesley, with his detestation of mysticism, allowed the following lines to pass through his critical, editorial mesh:[41]

> 'Fill me with all the life of love;
>   In mystic union join . . .'[42]

While some of Charles Wesley's verses were designed to be an exposition of *true* 'stillness', there are lines which Molther and his followers could have quoted with great effect:

> 'For the small and inward voice
>   I wait with humble awe;
> Silent am I now and still,
>   Dare not in Thy presence move.'[43]

Charles Wesley, however, defended the doctrine of assurance in the teeth of bitter attacks—attacks launched on the ground that the doctrine savoured too much of 'enthusiasm'. One of his greatest hymns in support of assurance begins:

> 'How can a sinner know
>   His sins on earth forgiven?'[44]

The defence of the doctrine lies in the realm of personal experience, as the second verse shows:

> 'What we have felt and seen
>   With confidence we tell,
> And publish to the sons of men
>   The signs infallible.'[45]

---

[39] *Poetical Works*, I.97; *Hymns and Sacred Poems* (1739); *M.H.B.*, 97.5.
[40] *Poetical Works*, I.304; *M.H.B.*, 460.4; see *Paradise Lost*, IV.639.
[41] Rattenbury, op. cit., pp. 303f.
[42] *Hymns and Sacred Poems* (1740); *Poetical Works*, I.225; *M.H.B.*, 464.4.
[43] *M.H.B.*, 465.2; *Poetical Works*, II.263; see Part V, ch. 4, pp. 198ff., *infra*.
[44] *Hymns and Sacred Poems* (1749), see Part V, ch. 1, pp. 179ff., *infra*.
[45] *Poetical Works*, V.363.

But it is a distinctive experience. The confidence with which we 'publish to the sons of men' our certainty depends on the *quality* of that experience which 'we have felt and seen'.

This is revealed in a later verse, in which Charles expresses what has been called 'the indirect witness', or 'the witness of our own spirit':

> 'His Spirit to us He gave,
>   And dwells in us we know;
> · The witness in ourselves we have,
>   And *all its fruits we show*.'[46]

In other words, Charles Wesley teaches in his hymns what his brother stresses in his sermons—namely, that the witness of God's Spirit must be checked and certified by the fruit of the Spirit in our lives. The new life in Christ is the best answer to the charge of subjectivism.

We have so far quoted only the first section of this inspiring hymn. There are four other parts—none of which appears in modern Methodist hymn-books. The second section enlarges on the theme developed in the first—namely, that Christian conversion effects a complete change in the believer's life and is the best guarantee that our assurance is not a mere fanatical individualism:

> 'Redeem'd from all his woes,
>   Out of his dungeon freed,
> Ask, how the prisoner knows
>   That he is free indeed!'

There is a touch of impressive satire as the argument proceeds:

> 'The gasping patient lies!
>   In agony of pain
> But see him light arise
>   Restored to health again.
>
> 'And doth he *certainly* receive
>   The knowledge of his cure?
> And am I *conscious* that I live
>   And is my pardon sure?'

The third section argues that assurance can be appreciated only by those who possess spiritual discernment:

[46] *M.H.B.*, 377.7.

> 'Tell us no more, we cannot know
>   On earth the heavenly powers,
> Or taste the glorious bliss below,
>   Or feel that God is ours.
>
>   .   .   .   .   .
>
> 'For us who have received our sight
>   Ye fain would judges be
> And make *us* think there is no light
>   Because *ye* cannot see.'[47]

An assurance of forgiveness is the best incentive to seek a life bearing the pattern of Christ's; and this in turn will strengthen one's certainty of a place in God's family:

> 'My God! I know, I feel Thee mine,
>   And will not quit my claim,
> Till all I have is lost in Thine
>   And all renewed I am.'[48]

It would be difficult to find a clearer statement on 'the witness of our own spirit' than the one given in the following lines:

> 'Your faith by holy tempers prove,
>   By actions show your sins forgiven.'[49]

Or, in a verse reminiscent of the Epistle of James:

> 'Thus may I show the Spirit within,
>   Which purges me from every stain;
> Unspotted from the world and sin,
>   My faith's integrity maintain;
> The truth of my religion prove
> By perfect purity and love.'[50]

And there we must end our excursion into Methodist hymnology. The interpretation of the doctrine of assurance in the hymns is in line, generally speaking, with the teaching of John Wesley. There is, however, one marked difference which calls for comment. In Wesley's writings, we traced frequent reference to the varying degrees in which a believer may be

---

[47] D. M. Jones, *Charles Wesley*, pp. 273f.; *Hymns and Sacred Poems* (1749).
[48] *Poetical Works*, I.328; *Hymns and Sacred Poems* (1740); *M.H.B.*, 387.1.
[49] *Short Hymns on Selected Passages of Scripture* (1762); *M.H.B.*, 229.2; *Poetical Works*, XIII.86.
[50] James 1^{27}; *Poetical Works*, XIII.167; *M.H.B.*, 605.5.

assured of his salvation.[51] There is very little evidence of these degrees of assurance in the hymns. Not only would such an analysis of experience be somewhat cumbersome for versification; it would have proved a mode of thought and expression alien to Charles Wesley's temperament and poetic genius.

Our inquiry here does not claim to be exhaustive, but is an attempt, within the aim and scope of this book, to indicate the main aspects of assurance in the Wesleys' poetical works.

[51] *Letters*, III.305f.; see Part II, ch. 3, pp. 77f., *supra*, and Part III, ch. 4, pp. 128ff., *infra*.

Part Three
Assurance in the New Testament

CHAPTER ONE

THE BIBLE AND THE WESLEYS

'FROM a child', wrote John Wesley in 1789, 'I was taught to love and reverence the Scriptures, the oracles of God.'[1] He read the Bible regularly at home, at school and at the university.[2] It was mainly in the arena of Scripture where Wesley engaged Peter Böhler in intellectual combat.[3] It was with words from the Book of God upon his lips—Τὰ μέγιστα ἡμῖν καὶ τίμια ἐπαγγέλματα δεδώρηται ἵνα γένησθε θείας κοινωνοὶ Φύσεως[4]—that he went out in search of assurance on the memorable day which led him to Aldersgate Street.[5]

Writing to John Newton on 14th May 1765, Wesley wrote: 'In 1730 I began to be *homo unius libri*,[6] to study no book but the Bible.'[7] It is unfortunate that such a prolific writer as Wesley should give us such meagre information about the Holy Club at Oxford. But one thing is certain; the members not only read, but studied the Bible.[8] In his *Short History of Methodism*, Wesley says that in 1788 he and his helpers were resolved to be Bible Christians at all events; and, wherever they went, to preach with all their might plain, old Bible Christianity.[9]

The Bible was the supreme authority in all Wesley's theological teaching.[10] Many parts of his sermons are a catena of Scriptural texts.[11] In a letter to Richard Tompson, dated 5th February 1756, Wesley says that the united testimony of even such authorities as the ancient Fathers and the Reformers would not suffice to establish an unscriptural doctrine. 'Therefore', continues Wesley, 'we must be determined by higher evidence. And herein we are clearly agreed: we both appeal

---

[1] *Works*, XIII.272.

[2] i.e. at Epworth, at Charterhouse and at Oxford: *Journal*, I.465f.

[3] ibid., p. 471.

[4] 2 Peter 1⁴: 'There are given unto us exceeding great and precious promises, even that ye should be partakers of the divine nature.'

[5] *Journal*, I.472.   [6] 'A man of one book.'   [7] *Letters*, V.299.

[8] *Works*, VIII.348, XI.367; Piette, *John Wesley in the Evolution of Protestantism*, pp. 283ff.

[9] *Works*, VIII.349.   [10] See Tyerman, op. cit., I.532.

[11] e.g. Wesley's Sermon on 'Scriptural Christianity', *Sermons*, I.87ff.; *Letters*, IV.116.

"to the law and to the testimony".'[12] In his second sermon on the Witness of the Spirit, written on 4th April 1767, Wesley endorses the proposition that experience is not sufficient to prove a doctrine which is not founded on Scripture.[13]

In a letter to James Harvey, dated 20th March 1739, Wesley says: 'Permit me to speak plainly. If by Catholic principles you mean any other than scriptural, they weigh nothing with me. I follow no other rule, whether of faith or practice, than the Holy Scriptures.'[14]

Wesley was inclined to seek Divine guidance by a fortuitous opening of the Scriptures, taking the first passage he lit upon as the answer to his query.[15] The practice was fairly common in Wesley's time—and is found in some quarters even today.[16] Many instances appear in Wesley's *Journal* where the result is often unsatisfactory.

Wesley often quoted indiscriminately from the Old and New Testament. He could not be expected to have much appreciation of 'progressive revelation', though he did indicate that the Old Testament was not the standard of Christian experience.[17]

Wesley believed that all Scripture is infallibly true.[18] Soame Jenyns' tract, *The Internal Evidence of the Christian Religion*, is criticized by Wesley on the ground of its asserting that 'all Scripture is not given by inspiration of God, but the writers of it were sometimes left to themselves and consequently made some mistakes'. Wesley retorted: 'Nay, if there be any mistake in the Bible, there may as well be a thousand. If there be one falsehood in that book, it did not come from the God of truth.'[19]

It is revealing to observe what Wesley calls his 'short, clear, and strong argument to prove the divine inspiration of the holy Scriptures'. Wesley states: 'The Bible must be the invention either of good men or angels, bad men or devils, or of God.'

(1) 'It could not be the invention of good men or angels; for they neither would nor could make a book, and tell lies all

---

[12] *Letters*, III.159; see Hastings on the Bible as the ground of assurance, *The Christian Doctrine of Faith*, p. 312.
[13] *Sermons*, II.352; see Lindstrom, *Wesley and Sanctification*, p. 5; cf. Frost, *Die Autoritatslehre in den Werken John Wesleys*, pp. 88f.
[14] *Letters*, I.285; cf. *Works*, VII.423.
[15] See Simon, *John Wesley and the Religious Societies*, p. 263.
[16] Bibliomancy is traceable to the Early Church, which derived it from the Greek-Roman practice of divination by the casual opening of Homer and Virgil (see Sugden, *Sermons*, II.97); *Works*, VIII.449.
[17] *Letters*, IV.11.   [18] *Sermons*, I.249; see also I.205.   [19] *Journal*, VI.117.

the time they were writing it, saying, "Thus saith the Lord", when it was their own invention.
(2) 'It could not be the invention of bad men or devils; for they would not make a book which commands all duty, forbids all sin, and condemns their souls to hell to all eternity.
(3) 'Therefore, I draw this conclusion, that the Bible must be given by divine inspiration.'[20]

It is no part of our purpose here to offer any criticism of Wesley's clear, if unconvincing, argument.[21]

Wesley was not *homo unius libri*, however, in the sense that he consulted, or was influenced by, no other books. On the contrary, he had such an insatiable zest for reading that he held a unique position among the educated men of his century.[22] Indeed, a large part of this book is concerned with the influence which the writings of others wielded over Wesley. It is significant that the same letter, in which he spoke of himself as *homo unius libri*, expresses his indebtedness to three books: Jeremy Taylor's *Holy Living*, and William Law's *Serious Call* and *Christian Perfection*.[23]

Not only was Wesley's literary horizon wide; his critical power in Scriptural matters was far from inactive, particularly in regard to exposition and the correctness of the English translations. 'The Scriptures', he writes to Dr Conyers Middleton on 4th January 1749, 'are clear in all necessary points, and yet their clearness does not prove that they need not be explained.'[24] He points out, however, that even the children of God are not agreed as to the interpretation of many places in holy writ.[25] Wesley therefore gives a general rule for interpreting Scripture: 'The literal sense of every text is to be taken, if it is not contrary to some other texts; but in that case the obscure text is to be interpreted by those which speak more plainly.'[26] Wesley's method of interpretation is described more fully in the Preface to his *Sermons* (1746): 'In His presence, I open, I read His book. . . . Is there a doubt concerning the meaning of what I read? . . . I lift up my heart to the Father of Light: Lord, is it not Thy word, "If any man lack wisdom let him ask of God?" . . . Thou hast said, "If any man be willing to do Thy will, he shall know". I am willing to do, let me know,

[20] *Works*, XI.484. [21] See Cell, *Rediscovery of John Wesley*, p. 13.
[22] Simon, *John Wesley and the Religious Societies*, p. 58. [23] *Journal*, V.117.
[24] *Letters*, II.325. [25] *Sermons*, II.154. [26] *Letters*, III.129.

Thy will. I then search after and consider parallel passages of Scripture, "comparing spiritual things with spiritual." I meditate thereon with all the attention and earnestness of which my mind is capable. If any doubt remain, I consult those who are experienced in the things of God; and then the writings whereby, being dead, they yet speak. And what I thus learn, that I teach'.[27]

Wesley's criticism of the Authorized Version was not always well founded. On 14th September 1785, he wrote: 'I preached ... on Psalm 74[12]. In the old translation it runs, "The help that is done upon the earth, God doeth it Himself". A glorious and important truth. In the new, "Working salvation in the midst of the earth". What a wonderful emendation! Many such emendations there are in this translation; one would think King James had made them himself.'[28] Wesley was here in error and the Authorized Version correct, as he himself would have discovered if he had examined the Hebrew text:[29]

וֵאלֹהִים מַלְכִּי מִקֶּדֶם פֹּעֵל יְשׁוּעוֹת בְּקֶרֶב הָאָרֶץ

He was aware, however, that certain parts of the Old Testament were liable to mislead those who had not sufficiently grasped the high moral and spiritual character of the God whom Jesus revealed. It is significant that, in drawing up the Sunday services for American Methodism, Wesley omitted many psalms as being highly improper for the mouths of a Christian congregation.[30]

It is plain, however, that Wesley did not regard the Authorized Version of 1611, or, indeed, any other *translation*, as infallible—though, as we have seen, he did attach infallibility to the Bible as it was originally written. In the main, Wesley's many divergencies from the Authorized Version were notable improvements. This is clearly seen in his *Notes on the New Testament*, published in 1754. The notes are based on Wesley's own translation, which in numerous instances is a remarkable anticipation of the Revised Version of 1881.[31]

Moreover, Wesley had been Greek Lecturer at Lincoln College, Oxford, which meant that he brought an intimate

---

[27] *Sermons*, I.32.   [28] *Journal*, VII.114.
[29] Psalm 74[12]: 'Yet God is my King of old, working salvation in the midst of the earth.'
[30] *Works*, XIV.304.
[31] See Simon, *John Wesley and the Advance of Methodism*, pp. 263ff.

knowledge of the Greek language to his Biblical studies. His *Notes on the New Testament* were based on sound and wide scholarship—his own and that of others, among whom stands out pre-eminently 'that great light of the Christian world', Bengel.[32]

Such, then, is the place of the Bible in Wesley's life and thought. This is the framework in which we must set our examination of those texts of Scripture on which Wesley built his doctrine of Christian certainty. It is not our intention to quote *all* the Biblical passages or phrases incorporated by Wesley in his treatises on assurance, since this would be both tedious and fruitless. Wesley wove words of Scripture into many of his sentences. So much so that, were we to look up every Scriptural reference, we should repeatedly find ourselves introduced to a context alien to our immediate purpose here.

Before we examine the Biblical passages on which Wesley based his doctrine, we need some acquaintance with the main Greek terms which underlie the New Testament doctrine of assurance.

(1) Ἀσφάλεια. It is used in the Septuagint to translate בֶּטַח, which means 'confidence' or 'security'. ἀσφάλεια is used in this sense in Acts 5[23], and 1 Thessalonians 5[3]. In Luke 4, it signifies 'the certainty which results from learning that teaching accords with the fact'.[33]

(2) Πίστις, in Acts 17[31], has the meaning of 'pledge' or 'guarantee'; and the reference here is to the certainty of judgement, 'whereof He hath given assurance [πίστιν] unto all men, in that He hath raised Him from the dead' (R.V.).

(3) Συμμαρτυρέω (συν-μαρτυρέω) usually means 'to bear witness with', and appears in Romans 2[15], 8[16], and 9[1]. It signifies a joint witness, as indicated by the prepositional prefix συν. The simple verb μαρτυρέω is found much more frequently in the New Testament, and used also by some classical writers, in the sense of affording proof. Examples of this use are John 5[36], 10[25], and Acts 14[3, 17]. Strathman, however, takes συμμαρτυρεῖ (Romans 8[16]) to mean simply 'certifies'.[34]

(4) Πληροφορία. This is the most frequent term for assurance in the New Testament and in the Patristic writers. The passive form of the verb means 'to be fully persuaded, to be

---

[32] *Notes on the New Testament*, Preface, p. 6. Cell, *Rediscovery of John Wesley*, p. 13.
[33] *E.R.E.*, III.325.
[34] Kittel's *Theologisches Woerterbuch zum Neuen Testament*, IV.515f.

fixed and firm', and is found in Romans 4^{21}, 14^5 and Colossians 4^{12}. The noun signifies 'full assurance', 'confidence'.[35] It is used in conjunction with συνέσεως (Colossians 2^2, 'understanding') ἐλπίδος (Hebrews 6^{11}, 'hope'), and πίστεως (Hebrews 10^{22}, 'faith'). Πληροφορία is used absolutely in 1 Thessalonians 1^5 and the correct interpretation is 'full assurance'—the R.V. margin 'much fulness' being inadequate.

(5) Ὑπόστασις is translated 'assurance' in Hebrews 11^1.[36] It probably involves here the idea of 'steadiness', 'firmness', 'confidence', or a deed which gives reality or a guarantee.

[35] See also Grimm, *Greek-English Lexicon of the New Testament.*
[36] Hastings, *Dictionary of the Bible*, I.107.

CHAPTER TWO

THE DIRECT WITNESS

IN THIS chapter we consider the Scriptural warrant for Wesley's teaching on the direct witness of the Spirit. The *locus classicus* here is Romans 8¹⁶.[1] On this text Wesley based both his sermons on the 'Witness of the Spirit'.[2] He translates it thus: 'The Spirit itself beareth witness with our spirit, that we are the Children of God'. In Sermon 10, Wesley comments on the text as follows: 'The apostle has just said, in the preceeding verse, "Ye have received the Spirit of adoption, whereby we cry, Abba, Father"; and immediately subjoins, αὐτὸ τὸ Πνεῦμα (some copies read, τὸ αὐτὸ Πνεῦμα) συμμαρτυρεῖ τῷ πνεύματι ἡμῶν ὅτι ἐσμὲν τέκνα Θεοῦ; which may be translated, "*The same Spirit* beareth witness to our spirit, that we are the children of God".... But I contend not.'[3] This rendering is given also in his *Notes on the New Testament*.[4]

But Wesley is in error here, as Dr Sugden points out. There appears to be no trace of a reliable New Testament manuscript with the reading: τὸ αὐτὸ Πνεῦμα. Wesley does well to link the text with the preceding verse; but not on this Greek construction. Moreover, the translation 'The Spirit *itself*' is possible only because the pronoun αὐτὸ is neuter in order to agree with neuter noun πνεῦμα. In view of the doctrine of the personality of the Holy Spirit, however, the Revisers in 1881 rightly rendered the phrase: 'The Spirit *Himself*'.

Wesley is again on shaky ground when he says that the prefix συν (συν-μαρτυρεῖ) denotes only that the Spirit bears witness *at the same time* that He enables us to cry, 'Abba, Father'.[5] Paul's use of the compound verb to imply concurrent testimony is supported by other passages in the New Testament.

Dr Beet considers Wesley's first sermon (1746) on the witness of the Spirit unsatisfactory—one reason being that Wesley does not relate Romans 8¹⁶ *sufficiently* to the preceding verses.[6] But the second sermon, written some twenty years

---

[1] *Works*, VIII.83ff., 94ff., XII.94f.; cf. Hastings, *The Christian Doctrine of Faith*, p. 344.
[2] 1746 and 1767. *Standard Sermons*, I.199ff., II.341ff.   [3] *Sermons*, I.204.
[4] *Notes on the New Testament* (1754), p. 377.   [5] *Sermons*, I.204; see also pp. 134f.
[6] Beet, *London Quarterly Review*, January 1921.

later (1767), represents his more mature thought; and here Romans 8:16 is viewed in its larger context.[7] The previous two verses read: 'For as many as are led by the Spirit of God, these are the sons of God. For ye received not the spirit of bondage again unto fear; but ye received the spirit of adoption, whereby we cry, Abba, Father.'

In the sermon of 1767, Wesley raises the question as to the nature of the Spirit's witness in Romans 8:16. 'μαρτυρία', he says, 'may be rendered either (as it is in several places) "the witness" or less ambiguously "the testimony" or "the record".' 'The testimony now under consideration', continues Wesley, 'is given by the Spirit of God to and with our spirit: He is the Person testifying. What He testifies to us is "that we are the children of God".'[8]

On the 'spirit of bondage', Wesley gives us an interesting comment in his *Notes*. It refers, he says, to those operations of the Holy Spirit by which the soul, on its first conviction, feels itself in bondage to sin, to the world, to Satan, and to the wrath of God. This and 'the Spirit of adoption' are one and the same Spirit, manifesting itself in various operations, according to the circumstances of the persons.[9]

It cannot be said that Wesley's exegesis commands general approval. The Revised Version prints 'spirit' in both places with a small 's', and therefore neither commends nor condemns Wesley's exposition. Dr C. H. Dodd differs from both Wesley and the Revised Version. He paraphrases this passage as follows: 'You have received no slavish spirit. . . . No; you have received the Spirit of sonship.'[10] Dr A. E. Garvie plainly disagrees with Wesley. He holds that 'the spirit' is neither the human nor the divine Spirit, but 'a more general use of the term to express a mood, habit or state of feeling'. He interprets 'bondage' as 'a servile temper, a slavish disposition'; and 'adoption' he literally defines as 'placing as son'.[11]

In the words of Dr H. B. Swete: 'As the slave is marked by the slavish spirit, so the filial spirit is the sure sign of sonship. . . . It inspires the daily paternoster of the Church; . . . it is a joint-witness with their own consciousness that they

[7] *Sermons*, II.348.
[8] ibid., p. 344. For an able treatment of 'adoption', see Dr W. E. B. Ball, *St Paul and the Roman Law*.
[9] *Notes on the New Testament*, p. 377.
[10] Dodd, *Romans* in *Moffatt New Testament Commentary*, p. 128.
[11] Garvie, *Romans* in the *Century Bible*, p. 191.

possess the nature as well as the right of sons. There is no return in their case to the state of fear in which they lived under the Law, for they know God to be their Father, and themselves His accepted sons.'[12]

Closely linked with this passage in Romans is Galatians 4⁵⁻⁷: 'That He might redeem them which were under the law, that we might receive the adoption of sons. And because ye are sons, God sent forth the Spirit of His Son into our hearts, crying, Abba, Father. So that thou art no longer a bondservant, but a son; and if a son, then an heir through God.'

In his second sermon on 'the Witness of the Spirit', Wesley draws attention to this parallel passage, and adds this significant comment: 'Is not this something *immediate* and *direct*, not the result of reflection or argumentation? Does not this Spirit cry, "Abba, Father", in our hearts, the moment it is given, antecedently to any reflection upon our sincerity . . . ? All these texts then, in their most obvious meaning, describe a direct testimony of the Spirit.'[13] We are not concerned here with the soundness of Wesley's argument, but only with its Biblical basis.[14]

'We must love God', says Wesley, 'before we can be holy at all, this being the root of all holiness. Now, we cannot love God, till we know He loves us: "We love Him because He first loved us"!; and we cannot know His love to us, till His spirit witnesses it to our spirit.'[15]

Wesley's exposition on this Galatian passage recalls the distinction he drew between his pre-Aldersgate and his post-Aldersgate religious life.[16] Before 24th May 1738 he had the faith of 'a servant', but on that memorable day he gained a new spiritual experience which gave him an inward testimony that he was 'a son'.[17]

Dr J. A. Beet makes some illuminating comments on these two key passages—Romans 8¹⁶ and Galatians 4⁵, ⁶. In an attempt to answer the question, 'How do the Spirit of God and man's own spirit "bear witness that we are the children of God"?' he holds that the cry, 'Abba, Father' is both human ('*we cry*') and superhuman ('*in whom* we cry'). He argues that the words 'our spirit' refer to the nobler side of our nature. On the other hand, the Holy Spirit, by prompting the cry, affords

---

[12] Swete, *The Holy Spirit in the New Testament*, pp. 218f. [13] *Sermons*, II.349.
[14] See Part II, ch. 3, pp. 76ff., *supra*; Part III, ch. 5, pp. 134ff., *infra*.
[15] *Sermons*, II.349. [16] *Notes on the New Testament*, p. 470. [17] *Journal*, I.423.

proof of, or bears witness to, our sonship. Without this divine initiative, we should have no right to approach Him as 'Father'. The Holy Spirit is the source both of our filial confidence and of that divine power whereby we subdue those passions that vitiate our sonship and prolong our state of bondage. An assurance is gained that carries with it a sense of pardon and the confidence of being 'joint-heirs with Christ'.[18]

The importance of the assurance of adoption in Pauline theology is stressed by Dr G. B. Stevens: 'We reach the apostle's most characteristic thought in his doctrine of the Spirit's witness in the believer assuring him of his sonship to God.'[19] Dr Stevens believes that, in Paul's view, the Holy Spirit is the cause of the *assurance* of sonship rather than the cause of the *fact* of sonship. With this Dr Rattenbury agrees, and quotes Galatians 4[6] as evidence: ' "Because ye *are* sons, God sent forth the Spirit of His Son into your hearts, crying, Abba, Father"—not to make you sons, but "because ye are sons".'[20]

Dr H. B. Swete offers a similar interpretation: 'The Spirit ... is sent into the hearts of the adopted sons, because it is the very Spirit of sonship. It does not make them sons, for they are such by their union with the Incarnate Son, but it makes them conscious of their sonship.'[21]

A comparison of Galatians 4[6] and Romans 8[15] would suggest that in the former the Holy Spirit is mainly responsible for uttering the cry 'Abba, Father', whereas in the latter the human activity ('we cry') is clearly stated. Dr R. N. Young holds that these two Pauline passages are 'harmonized by the fact that it is not at His instance, or through Him, but in Him ... that the cry is uttered'. It involves the simplest, and, at the same time, the intensest expression of our religious life.[22] In the words of Dr Pope: 'Though it is our own spirit regenerate that as it were naturally says, "Abba, Father", it is the Holy Spirit in our spirit: the distinction between the regenerate spirit and the Holy Spirit is nearly lost in the New Testament.'[23] Dr Stevens would resolve the difficulty by observing that the

---

[18] Beet, *New Life in Christ*, pp. 74ff.
[19] Stevens, *Theology of the New Testament*, p. 440.
[20] Rattenbury, *Testament of Paul*, p. 175.
[21] Swete, *Holy Spirit in the New Testament*, pp. 204f.
[22] Young, *The Witness of the Spirit* (1882), p. 72.
[23] Pope, *Compendium of Christian Theology*, III.116.

Spirit inspires in the heart the conviction of sonship which is expressed in the cry, 'Abba, Father'.[24]

We may appear to have lingered somewhat long over these two passages from Romans 8 and Galatians 4. But this is the measure of their importance as basic texts for Wesley's teaching on the direct witness of the Spirit. Some texts appearing under this head in Wesley's writings receive such casual treatment at his hands that we should achieve little by pausing to consider them. Others, however, are more worthy of note; and to these we now turn.

The first is part of Galatians 2^{20}. In an attempt to define the testimony of God's Spirit, Wesley says that it is 'an inward impression on the soul, whereby the Spirit of God directly witnesses to my spirit, that I am a child of God; that *Jesus hath loved me, and given Himself for me*'.[25]

The text recalls the influence of the Moravians, and especially that of Peter Böhler.[26] We saw, in earlier chapters, that the faith Wesley lacked prior to Aldersgate Street was a personal trust in a crucified Christ.[27] It was this Scriptural truth which formed the basis of that new and powerful experience of the Spirit on 24th May 1738, issuing for Wesley in an assurance of salvation.[28]

The latter part of the text—paraphrased by Wesley in the Sermon quoted—also played a prominent part in Charles Wesley's spiritual transformation on 21st May 1738. 'Today I first saw Luther on the Galatians ... who was greatly blessed to me, especially his conclusion of the second chapter. I laboured, waited, and prayed to feel "who loved *me*, and gave Himself for *me*".'[29]

A reference to this Scripture appears in the *Minutes of Conference* for 1747. The question is asked: 'Is justifying faith a divine assurance that Christ loved me, and gave Himself for me?' The answer given is: 'We believe it is.'[30] Again, in a letter of 1st December 1760, addressed to the Editor of *Lloyd's Evening Post*, Wesley says that faith is a divine evidence or conviction that Christ 'loved me and gave Himself for me'.[31]

---

[24] Stevens, op. cit., p. 441.   [25] *Sermons*, I.208.
[26] See Part I, ch. 3, pp. 20ff., *supra*.
[27] *Journal*, I.461; see Part II, ch. 1, pp. 53ff., *supra*.   [28] ibid., pp. 442, 475f.
[29] *Journal of Charles Wesley*, edited Jackson, I.88.
[30] *Works*, VIII.291; cf. Tyerman, *Life and Times of Wesley*, I.551f.
[31] *Letters*, IV.116; cf. *Sermons*, II.450; *Letters*, III.222.

This text also gives a needful link between the inner or subjective aspect of assurance and its outward or historical aspect in the death of Christ.[32] It also serves to emphasize Wesley's argument that the direct witness of the Spirit has its source in the Love of God, which is antecedent to our love for Him and the witness of our own spirit.[33]

We come now to 1 Corinthians 2[12]. This text is linked to Romans 8[16] in the *Plain Account of Christian Perfection*, in which Wesley argues that the Spirit witnesses, not only to our being 'children of God in the lowest sense', but also to our being such in the higher sense of sanctification.[34] 1 Corinthians 2[12] in the Revised Version reads: 'But we received, not the spirit of the world, but the spirit which is of God; that we might know the things which are freely given to us by God'.[35] Commenting on this verse in his *Notes on the New Testament*, Wesley says that the spirit of the world is not properly received, for the men of the world always had it. But Christians receive the Spirit of God, which before they had not.[36]

The interjected negative clause οὐ τὸ πνεῦμα τοῦ κόσμου and the impersonal use of πνεῦμα form a parallel to the passage in Romans 8[15] (οὐ γὰρ ἐλάβετε πνεῦμα δουλείας πάλιν εἰς Φόβον). In his *Notes*, Wesley does not define 'the spirit of the world', but he would doubtless regard it, with Meyer, Evans, and Edwards, as a system of organized evil with its own principles and its own laws; though the interpretation of Heinrici and Lightfoot—'the Spirit of human wisdom, of the world as alienated from God'—is more in line with New Testament usage.[37]

This, then, is the 'spirit of the world' from which those who enjoy the witness of God's Spirit and an assurance of salvation are delivered. As in Romans 8[15], the Revisers print πνεῦμα in 1 Corinthians 2[12] with a small 's' in both places—'the spirit of the world . . . the spirit which is of God'—which presumably implies that in their view πνεῦμα is to be interpreted impersonally on each occasion. The latter instance is comparable, therefore, to 'the spirit of adoption' (πνεῦμα υἱοθεσίας) in Romans 8[15]; 'the only spirit', says Dr Massie, 'that can really

---

[32] See Pope, *Compendium of Christian Theology*, III.113ff.

[33] *Sermons*, I.208.   [34] *Works*, XI.421.   [35] Pope, op. cit., p. 128.

[36] Wesley, *Notes on the New Testament*, p. 404; cf. *Sermons*, I.228f.

[37] Robertson and Plummer, 1 Corinthians in *International Critical Commentary*, p. 45. See also Gifford's *Commentary on Romans*, 8[15].

come into contact with the "Spirit that is of God", and, in childlike temper, learn and receive of Him.'[38]

From the Greek structure of 1 Corinthians 2[12], it appears that we cannot confidently identify τὸ πνεῦμα τὸ ἐκ τοῦ θεοῦ with the Person of the Holy Spirit—a difficulty which Wesley does not seem to have appreciated and for which he offers no explanatory comment. He quotes the phrase, however, as though it referred to God's Spirit.[39] In this connexion, Dr Plummer points out that the distinction between the Personal Spirit of God (1 Corinthians 2[11]), dwelling in man (Romans 8[11]), and the spirit (in the sense of the higher element in man's nature), inhabited and quickened by the Holy Spirit, is subtle and difficult to fix with accuracy.[40]

Dr Plummer holds that πνεῦμα here refers to 'the *gift* rather than the Person of the Spirit'; though later he adds: 'The Person is in the gift, and the activity of the recipient is the work of the Divine Indweller'.[41] While 1 Corinthians 2[12] may not directly or explicitly refer to the Holy Spirit, it is plain from the larger context in which this verse is set that the Spirit of God is the source or agent of that spiritual discernment whereby we 'know the things which are freely given to us by God', things which 'the natural man receiveth not . . . because they are spiritually judged'.[42]

We turn now to the Conference of 1747, the *Minutes* of which record Wesley's answers to a number of objections raised against the witness of God's Spirit—objections couched in the language of Scripture—two of which call for brief notice here.

First, we take Question 7: 'But does not Paul say even of himself, "I know nothing by myself; yet am I not hereby justified"?'[43] We need do little more here than quote Wesley's reply: 'He does not say of himself here, that he was not justified or that he did not know it; but only, that though he had a conscience void of offence, yet this did not justify him before God'.[44] Wesley *might* have added that this was an instance where the testimony of one's own conscience or spirit needs the direct and certifying evidence of the Spirit of God.[45]

Next we consider Question 8 in the same *Minutes*. 'But does he [Paul] not disclaim any such assurance in those words,

[38] Massie, *Corinthians*, in *The Century Bible*, p. 150.   [39] *Works*, XI.421.
[40] Robertson and Plummer, op. cit., p. 46.   [41] ibid.
[42] 1 Corinthians 2[9-16].   [43] *Works*, VIII.292; 1 Corinthians 4[4].
[44] cf. G. G. Findlay, *Fellowship in the Life Eternal*, p. 303.
[45] See *Sermons*, II.358f.

"I was with you in weakness, and in fear, and in much trembling"?'[46] In answer, Wesley says: 'By no means. For these words do not imply any fear either of death or hell. They express only a deep sense of his own utter insufficiency for the great work wherein he was engaged.'

Later in this inquiry boldness (παρρησία) will present itself as a characteristic of those who enjoy the witness of the Spirit.[47] Does Paul's admission here that he experienced a degree of 'weakness' (ἀσθενεία), fear (Φόβος), and trembling (τρόμος) imply that the Apostle's sense of Christian certainty was deficient?

The explanation given by Wesley—as far as that goes—is generally approved by the commentators. Scholars have suggested several reasons for Paul's self-effacement.[48]

Dr Plummer says that it was not the Gospel which he had to preach that made him tremble: he was 'not ashamed' of that (Romans 1[16]). Nor was it fear of personal danger. It was rather 'a trembling anxiety to perform a duty'.[49] The combination of Φόβος and τρόμος appears only in Pauline writings,[50] and is taken by Dr Massie to signify a 'nervous anxiety for the proper performance of duty'.[51]

In the light of these critical comments, we accept the view that an experience of the direct witness of the Spirit, far from being ruled out by Paul's self-depreciatory language, is the kind of spiritual foundation we should expect as the source of such an expression of reliance on God and of 'a genuine humility in face of the importance and difficulty of the task'.[52]

Another question in these *Minutes* of Conference (1747) deals with a similar point: 'Does he [Paul] not exclude Christians in general from such an assurance, when he bids them "work out" their "salvation with fear and trembling"?'[53] Wesley answers as follows: 'No more than from love; which is always joined with filial fear and reverential trembling. And the same answer is applicable to all those texts which exhort a believer to fear.'[54]

---

[46] 1 Corinthians 2[3]; *Works*, VIII.292.
[47] See 'The Apostolic Church', Part III, ch. 6, pp. 141f., *infra*.
[48] *1 Corinthians* in *I.C.C.*, p. 31; *Cambridge Greek Testament*, p. 49; *Century Bible*, p. 145; *Expositor's Greek Testament*, p. 776.
[49] Robertson and Plummer, *1 Corinthians* in *I.C.C.*, pp. 31f.
[50] See 2 Corinthians 7[15]; Philippians 2[12]; Ephesians 6[5].
[51] Massie, *1 Corinthians* in *The Century Bible*, p. 145.
[52] Parry, *1 Corinthians*, Cambridge Greek Testament, p. 49.
[53] *Works*, VIII.202; Philippians 2[12].   [54] ibid.

A further explanation is found in a letter written by Wesley on 1st December 1760 to the Editor of *Lloyd's Evening Post*. Appropriately enough, the interpretation here offered links together a number of the texts which we have already been considering. Assurance is regarded as 'a divine evidence or conviction that Christ loved *me* and gave Himself for *me*. This directly leads us to *work out our salvation with fear and trembling*; not with slavish, painful fear, but with the utmost diligence, which is the proper import of that expression'.[55]

Wesley bases his doctrine of assurance mainly on passages from Paul and from the First Epistle of John—the *former* providing the chief Scriptural evidence for the *direct* witness of the Spirit, the *latter* for the *indirect* witness. With this broad division most scholars would agree; though there is much overlapping.

1 John 5^{10} is evidence for the *direct* witness and is quoted by Wesley in another letter to the Editor of the *Lloyd's Evening Post*:[56] 'He that believeth on the Son of God hath the witness in him....' Wesley himself adds little in the way of explanatory comment. In his *Notes*, he merely says: 'He that believeth on the Son of God hath the testimony, the clear evidence of this, in himself.'[57]

Dr G. G. Findlay sums up this verse as 'subjective confirmation' and comments as follows: ' "He who believes on the Son of God" . . . finds "within himself" the confirmation of the witness he received. His inner consciousness and the fruits of faith in his life[58] verify the witness of God about Christ which he has accepted.'[59]

The phrase 'The witness in himself' (τὴν μαρτυρίαν ἐν ἑαυτῷ) is interpreted by Dr W. H. Bennett to mean: 'The witness of the Holy Spirit to his spirit; and the testimony of the spiritual experiences that come through faith in Christ.'[60]

Dr David Smith sees in the text 'a subtle and profound analysis of the exercise of soul which issues in assured faith'. He indicates three stages:

(1) '*Believe God*' (πιστεύειν τῷ θεῷ). 'Accept . . . the historical manifestation of God in Christ.'

---

[55] *Letters*, IV.116.   [56] ibid., p. 126.   [57] *Notes on the New Testament*, p. 611.
[58] cf. 1 John 2^5, $3^{10, 19, 24}$, 4^{17}, $5^{2, 4, 18}$; John 7^{38}, 14^{12}.
[59] Findlay, *Fellowship in the Life Eternal*, p. 390.
[60] Bennett, *General Epistles* in *The Century Bible*, p. 317.

(2) *'Believe in the Son of God'* (πιστεύειν εἰς τὸν υἱὸν τοῦ θεοῦ). 'Make the believing self-surrender which is the reasonable and inevitable consequence of contemplating the Incarnation.'

(3) *'The Inward Testimony'* (τὴν μαρτυρίαν ἐν ἑαυτῷ). 'The testimony is no longer external in history but an inward experience and therefore indubitable.'[61]

And there we must leave our examination of the main Biblical passages on which Wesley based that aspect of his doctrine of assurance dealing with the *direct* witness of the Spirit.[62]

[61] David Smith, *1 John* in *Expositor's Greek Testament*, p. 196.

[62] Further criticism as to the adequacy of this Biblical basis is postponed until a later chapter, pp. 133ff., *infra*.

CHAPTER THREE

THE INDIRECT WITNESS

WE TURN in this chapter to the principal texts upon which Wesley based the *indirect* witness of the Spirit. This aspect of Wesley's doctrine of assurance is sometimes referred to as 'the witness of our own spirit', or 'the fruit of the Spirit'.

We consider first the text which Wesley chooses for his sermon on 'The Witness of Our Own Spirit'.[1] He translates it: 'This is our rejoicing, the testimony of our own conscience, that in simplicity and godly sincerity, not with fleshly wisdom, but by the grace of God, we have had our conversation in the world'[2]—a translation almost identical with the Authorized Version (1611) and with that in his *Notes on the New Testament*.[3]

His choice of text, however, is unfortunate. Uncertainty attaches to the reading of the Greek on which important parts of this sermon are built. The word ἁπλότητι (simplicity) should be replaced by the better attested reading ἁγιότητι (holiness).[4] This was observed by the Revisers (1881), who render the verse: 'For our glorying is this, the testimony of our conscience, that in holiness and sincerity of God, not in fleshly wisdom but in the grace of God, we behaved ourselves in the world.'

The emendation of the Greek, however, does not meet every deficiency. The subject matter of the context, in which this verse is set, is not in harmony with the main aims of the sermon. 'There is no reference', says Dr Sugden, 'to his consciousness of acceptance with God, or the witness of his conscience to that.'[5] Paul's primary purpose here is to vindicate himself against the charge of corruption brought against him by certain opponents at Corinth.[6]

We come now to 2 Corinthians 13⁵. This text was quoted by Wesley in a letter of 5th February 1756 to Richard Tompson, as a Scriptural warrant for the assertion that all Christians

---

[1] *Sermons*, I.221ff.   [2] 2 Corinthians 1¹².   [3] *Notes on the New Testament*, p. 440.

[4] ἁπλότητι in ℵ′, D E, G, L, the Latin and Syriac versions. ἁγιότητι in ℵˣ, A, B, C, K, M, P, 17, 37, 73. When written in 'uncial' letters, the two words are almost identical.

[5] Sugden, *Standard Sermons*, I.219.

[6] See Dr J. H. Bernard, *2 Corinthians* in *Expositor's Greek Testament*, p. 42.

have such a faith as implies a consciousness of God's love.[7] The Revised Version renders the verse: 'Try your own selves, whether ye be in the faith; prove your own selves. Or know ye not as to your own selves, that Jesus Christ is in you? unless indeed ye be reprobate.'

Wesley makes a significant comment in his *Notes*: ' "Know ye not yourselves, that Jesus Christ is in you?" All Christian believers know this, by the witness and fruit of His Spirit.'[8] Dr Bernard observes: 'Their own consciousness of the power of Christ's grace is the best proof that his preaching to them was Divinely authorized; he "begat them in Christ Jesus" ' (1 Corinthians 4[15]).[9]

With reference to the testimony of our own spirit, Wesley says that 'the foundation thereof is laid in those numerous texts of Scripture which describe the marks of the children of God; . . . as every man applying those Scriptural marks to himself may know whether he is a child of God. Thus, if he know, first, "as many as are led by the Spirit of God", into all holy tempers and actions, "they are the sons of God"; secondly, I am thus "led by the Spirit of God"; he will conclude, "Therefore I am a son of God".'[10]

The substance of this syllogistic argument—a type of reasoning to which Wesley was much attracted—is plainly irrefutable. It is the word of Christ in another form: 'By their fruits ye shall know them.'[11] In his second sermon on 'The Witness of the Spirit' (1767), Wesley says: 'If the spirit of God does really testify that we are the children of God, the immediate consequence will be the fruit of the Spirit, even "love, joy, peace, long-suffering, gentleness, goodness, fidelity, meekness, temperance".'[12]

Commenting on these words from Galatians 5[22], the Rev. Frederick Rendall says: 'Since the object of this verse is to exhibit the harmony between the fruit of the Spirit and the restraints of the law, those qualities only are specified which affect man's duty to his neighbour.'[13] πίστις in this passage is therefore correctly translated—as in the Revised Version—

---

[7] *Letters*, III.160.   [8] *Notes on the New Testament*, p. 461.
[9] Bernard, *2 Corinthians, Expositor's Greek Testament*, p. 116.
[10] Romans 8[14]; *Sermons*, I.205.
[11] Matthew 7[16, 20]; cf. Professor Wm. James, *Varieties of Religious Experience* (1902), pp. 485f.
[12] Galatians 5[22]; *Sermons*, II.358.
[13] Rendall, *Galatians, Expositor's Greek Testament*, p. 188.

'faithfulness' rather than 'faith'.[14] Dr W. F. Adeney makes the comment: 'The Spirit vitalizes, and therefore does not simply do works, but rather develops fruit. Here is the idea of Christian character growing and ripening.'[15]

From the first Epistle of John, Wesley gathers many texts in support of this aspect of his doctrine of assurance. In Sermon 10 (1746), after quoting evidence from Paul, Wesley writes: 'Agreeable to this are all those plain declarations of St John, in his First Epistle: "Hereby we know that we do know Him, if we keep His commandments" (2^3). "Whoso keepeth His word, in him verily is the love of God perfected: hereby know we that we are in Him"; that we are indeed the children of God (verse 5). "If ye know that He is righteous, ye know that every one that doeth righteousness is born of Him" (verse 29). "We know that we have passed from death unto life, because we love the brethren" (3^{14}). "Hereby we know that we are of the truth, and shall assure our hearts before Him" (verse 19); namely, because we "love one another, not in word, neither in tongue, but in deed and in truth". "Hereby know we that we dwell in Him, because He hath given us of His" loving "Spirit" (4^{13}). And "Hereby we know that He abideth in us, by the" obedient "Spirit which He hath given us" (3^{24}).'[16]

Before examining these texts, we observe Wesley's commendation of John and his brief analysis of the indirect witness. Wesley considers it improbable that anybody was farther advanced in the grace of God and the knowledge of our Lord Jesus Christ than the Apostle John and the fathers to whom he wrote. 'Notwithstanding which, it is evident, both the apostle himself, and all those pillars of God's temple, were very far from despising those marks of their being the children of God; and that they applied them to their own souls for the confirmation of their faith. Yet all this is no more than rational evidence, *the witness of our spirit*, our reason or understanding. It all resolves into this: Those who have these marks are children of God: but we have these marks: therefore we are children of God.'[17]

Dr G. G. Findlay points out that St John affirms the essential twofold fact of the Christian consciousness, that divine inner conviction of the child of God concerning his sonship, described by Paul in Romans 8^{16}; but 'St John puts the two testimonies

---

[14] The Greek word admits of both meanings.
[15] Adeney, *Galatians, Century Bible*, p. 328.   [16] *Sermons*, I.205f.   [17] ibid.

in the reverse order, proceeding from the outward to the inward, from the ethical to the spiritual, from effect to cause and from fruit to seed. . . . First, the practical and human evidence of loving deeds, next there is discovered, lying behind this activity, the mystical and divine evidence supplied by the indwelling of the Holy Spirit of Jesus Christ!'[18]

Wesley quotes three verses from the second chapter of John's First Epistle—namely, verses 3, 5 and 29. He adds little, however, in the way of comment on these passages. What there is appears mostly in his *Notes on the New Testament*,[19] and it is too meagre to warrant the inclusion here of any quotations. Yet Wesley is laying a sure Scriptural foundation in recognizing the evidential value of these texts.

In reference to these verses, Dr Findlay says, 'St John affirms . . . the disciplinary element in Christian experience; he never allows us, for many paragraphs, to get away from the plain ethical conditions of fellowship with God: "He *that keeps His commandments* (comp. 2[3-5], 7ff., 29f., 3[4ff.], 5[2f.], 18ff.) dwells in God and God in him." Union between God and the creature is possible only on terms of the latter's *obedience*; and the path of obedience is marked by the fence of "the commandments".'[20]

Dr C. H. Dodd sees in the reference here to a knowledge of God 'the central idea of . . . gnosticism'.[21] Some scholars would trace this knowledge back to Greek intellectualism. True knowledge for Plato consisted in the eternal and unchangeable essence of things as opposed to 'opinion' with its variable phenomena.[22] In the Hellenistic period, however, the Greek spirit lost its sense of certainty. Philosophers, therefore, turned to the religious 'mysteries' for a 'knowledge' of God which rational knowledge had failed to provide.

Moreover, the Old Testament also treated 'the knowledge of God' as a goal of human aspiration (Jeremiah 9[24], 31[34]). But for the Hebrew, 'to know God' consisted primarily in an understanding and fulfilling of His law, rather than in an exercise of the reason or in the sharing of a mystical experience.

A blending of these somewhat diverse principles—from Greek philosophy and Hebrew religion—is traceable in the New Testament, especially in the Johannine writings. In the

---

[18] Findlay, *Fellowship in the Life Eternal*, p. 290.
[19] *Notes on the New Testament*, pp. 603, 605f.   [20] Findlay, op. cit., p. 297.
[21] Dodd, *Johannine Epistles, Moffatt New Testament Commentary*, p. 29.
[22] See Stace, *Critical History of Greek Philosophy*, pp. 183ff.

Fourth Gospel, 'to know God' is to experience His love in Christ and to return that love in obedience.[23] In the First Epistle, John has to counter the views of those contemporaries, who, though claiming a superior knowledge of God, neglected the practical ethics that are integral to the true Christian faith.

For John, therefore, a personal assurance of salvation and a certainty of knowing God could not be divorced from the fulfilling of God's ethical commands. One wonders if John called to mind the words of the great Master: 'Why call ye me Lord, Lord, and do not the things that I say?'

The next verse from Wesley's list to be considered is 1 John 3^{14}: 'We know that we have passed out of death into life, because we love the brethren.'[24] In his *Notes*, Wesley comments thus: ' "We know"—as if he had said, We ourselves could not love our brethren unless we were "passed from" spiritual "death to life".'[25]

Once again the ethical test is prominent. As with Paul, 'The fruit of the Spirit is love . . .' (Galatians 5^{22}). Our possession of a genuine love for others is a mark whereby we can be assured that we share the spiritual life of the children of God. The exercise of this love is the fulfilling of 'a new commandment' (John 13^{34}), which transcends and includes all the rest. The first word in the original Greek of this text is ἡμεῖς. It is emphatic and can be understood to imply: 'Whatever the world may say, *we* know.'[26]

The Greek of 1 John 3^{19} presents a number of difficulties. The chief are:

(1) The interpretation of πείσομεν.
(2) The meaning of the repeated word καρδία.
(3) The repetition of ὅτι.
(4) The punctuation between verses 19 and 20.

The word πείσομεν in the Revised Version is translated 'shall assure' (future indicative of πείθω), with 'persuade' in the margin. This verb is usually followed by an objective clause announcing a fact or belief, but ' "that God is greater than our hearts" . . . is not a truth brought home to us by loving our brethren and relieving their wants (1 John 3^{16-18})'.[27]

---

[23] John 14^{15-24}, 17^3. [24] *Sermons*, I.205.
[25] *Notes on the New Testament*, p. 607.
[26] Smith, *1 John, Expositor's Greek Testament*, v. 186.
[27] Findlay, op. cit., pp. 294f.

It follows, therefore, that the second ὅτι of verse 20 is not 'that' of statement but 'because' of reason. Verse 20 does not state the *content* of assurance, but indicates the *ground* of assurance. Moreover, the Revisers regarded the first ὅτι, not as a conjunction, but as a relative pronoun ὅ τι. Scholars differ in the interpretation of μείζων ('greater than'). Some consider it to imply that God is 'greater than our heart' in the sense of 'greater in mercy' and therefore ready to grant an assurance of pardon. On the other hand, Wohlenberg and Findlay understand μείζων to mean 'greater in knowledge and consequently more severe in judgement'.[28]

In the light of these critical comments, we accept the translation: 'By this we shall know that we are of the truth, and shall assure our heart before Him, whereinsoever (ὅ τι ἐάν) our heart condemn us; because (ὅτι) God is greater (in mercy) than our heart, and knoweth all things.'

Though Wesley quotes only 1 John 3[19], our examination of the Greek text has revealed the necessity of taking verses 19 and 20 together, thus involving an alteration in the punctuation at the junction of the verses—ἡμῶν ὅ τι ἐάν.[29]

Ἐν τούτῳ at the beginning of verse 19 also presents a difficulty, in that it could be taken as referring either to what precedes, or what follows, this text. It could refer to the previous verse, in which it is said that love should express itself not merely 'in word, neither with the tongue, but in deed and in truth'. Or, it could relate to the succeeding verse: 'because God is greater than our heart, and knoweth all things'.[30]

Wesley accepts the former alternative—as do we—though it is contrary to the common usage of the writer. Commenting on the words: 'And hereby we know', Wesley says, 'We have additional proof by this operative love.'[31] The words 'that we are of the truth', Wesley takes to mean 'have true faith, and are the children of God'. He explains the phrase, 'And shall assure our hearts before Him', as signifying, 'shall enjoy the assurance of His favour'. 'The heart', he says, 'is the conscience'—conscience being a word not found in John's writings.[32]

Wesley's comments here would gain general acceptance. Of the two possible paraphrases given by Dr C. H. Dodd, we

---
[28] Wohlenberg, *Neue Kirkliche Zeitschrift* (1902), pp. 636ff.; Findlay, *Expositor*, November, 1905.
[29] See Dr R. N. Young, *Witness of the Spirit*, p. 42.
[30] cf. Brooke, *Johannine Epistles*, I.C.C., p. 100.
[31] See also *Sermons*, I.206.   [32] *Notes on the New Testament*, p. 607.

prefer the following—substantially that of Moffatt: 'By what I have said we may be sure that we belong to the truth, and reassure our heart in His presence, whenever our heart condemns us; because God is greater than our heart and knows all.'[33] We could wish for this verse fewer textual and exegetical difficulties. But, despite these, it may be safely included among those Scriptural passages on which can be based the doctrine of the indirect witness of the Spirit.

The remaining two verses from John's First Epistle, quoted by Wesley as 'marks of the children of God' or as illustrating 'the testimony of his own spirit', are 3^{24} and 4^{13}. Wesley quotes the whole of 4^{13}, but only the latter half of 3^{24}. It is doubtful, however, whether we can admit these texts as evidence for the *indirect* witness.[34]

It is the *direct* witness to which they would seem to bear testimony. Wesley would appear to recognize this; for, in adding them to his list of texts in support of 'the witness of our own spirit', he inserts a qualifying adjective before the word 'Spirit' in both verses—'*loving* Spirit' in 4^{13} and '*obedient* Spirit' in 3^{24}.[35] But the inclusion of these adjectives does not strengthen Wesley's claim that they are Biblical evidence for the *indirect* witness. Moreover, in his *Notes*, Wesley himself links the latter part of 3^{24} with the *direct* witness of God's Spirit, who 'witnesses with our spirit that we are His children'.[36]

[33] Dodd, *Johannine Epistles, Moffatt New Testament Commentary*, p. 92.
[34] cf. Pope, *Compendium of Christian Theology*, III.121.
[35] *Sermons*, I.206.   [36] *Notes on the New Testament*, p. 608.

CHAPTER FOUR

DEGREES OF ASSURANCE

BRIEF reference has already been made in earlier chapters to Wesley's views on the degrees of assurance.[1] There we noted inconsistencies in the presentation of this aspect of his doctrine. Here we must deal more fully with this feature of Wesley's teaching as we consider it in the light of its setting in the New Testament.

Wesley appears to have recognized four stages of faith showing an increasing sense of certainty:

(1) 'Faith in general.'
(2) 'More particularly . . . a divine . . . conviction that Christ loved me and gave Himself for me.'
(3) 'The plerophory or full assurance of faith.'[2]
(4) 'An assurance from God of everlasting salvation . . . the plerophory or full assurance of hope.'[3]

Wesley defined 'faith in general' as 'faith in an evidence or conviction of things not seen, of God, and of the things of God'. The definition given here is clearly based on Hebrews 11¹: 'Now faith is the assurance of things hoped for, the proving of things not seen' (R.V.).

The word translated 'assurance' in the Revised Version is the Greek term ὑπόστασις, and means, says Dr Marcus Dods, 'literally foundation, that which stands under; hence, the ground on which one builds a hope, naturally gliding into the meaning of "assurance", "confidence".'[4]

'Assurance' (ὑπόστασις) in this text, however, is *not* an 'assurance of personal salvation centred in a crucified Christ'.[5] If it were, this would deny the distinction which Wesley seeks to draw between 'faith' and 'assurance'.[6] Moreover, it is faith (πίστις), not ὑπόστασις, which is the subject of this verse. Faith is here represented as πραγμάτων ἔλεγχος οὐ βλεπομένων

[1] Part II, chs. 2 and 3, pp. 70; 77ff., *supra*.
[2] *Letters*, IV.116; cf. II.192, IV.126.   [3] ibid., V.358.
[4] Dods, *Hebrews, Expositor's Greek Testament*, p. 352; ὑπόστασις has also been translated 'title deeds'; see J. H. Moulton, *From Egyptian Rubbish Heaps*, p. 27.
[5] cf. Hebrews 3¹⁴; 2 Corinthians 9⁴, 11¹⁷; cf. Wesley, *Notes on the New Testament*, p. 564.
[6] In a letter to the Editor of *Lloyd's Evening Post* dated 1st December 1760.

—'an evidence', says Wesley, 'a divine evidence and conviction... of things not seen.... It implies both a supernatural evidence of God, and of the things of God.'[7] This was the kind of faith which Wesley knew prior to Aldersgate.[8]

We now examine in greater detail the important phrase, 'Full assurance of faith'. It appears in Hebrews 10[22], and is a translation of πληροφορία πίστεως. Wesley gives the Greek this rendering in his *Notes on the New Testament*, but he offers no interpretative comment.[9] In a number of instances where the phrase appears in Wesley's writings, the text from which it comes is not mentioned.[10]

In a letter to Dr Rutherforth dated 28th March 1768, Wesley refers to 'such an assurance of being now in the favour of God as excludes all doubt and fear' as interpreting what 'the Apostle means by the plerophory or full assurance of faith'.[11]

But not all the relevant data offer so clear an explanation as the statement just quoted. It is, for instance, confused with entire sanctification by Arvid Gradin, the Moravian. Gradin's account reads: 'Repose in the blood of Christ; a firm confidence in God, and persuasion of His favour; the highest tranquillity, serenity, and peace of mind, with a deliverance from every fleshly desire, and cessation of all, even inward sins.'[12]

But it is freedom from doubt and fear rather than from every fleshly desire that is essential to full assurance.

In a letter to Arthur Bedford, dated 28th September 1738, we find an even more confusing statement. Wesley writes: 'This πληροφορία πίστεως, however we translate it, I believe is neither more nor less than hope; or a conviction, wrought in us by the Holy Ghost, that we have a measure of the true faith in Christ, and that, as He is already made justification unto us, so *if* we continue to watch, strive, and pray, He will gradually become our sanctification here and our full redemption hereafter. This assurance I believe is given to some in a smaller, to others in a larger degree....'[13]

At least two statements here are at variance with other

[7] *Works*, VI.46; see Peake, *Hebrews, Century Bible*, p. 210.

[8] *Journal*, I.424; cf. Wesley's Letter to Wm. Law, 6th January 1756; *Works*, IX.496.

[9] *Notes on the New Testament*, p. 563.

[10] *Letters*, III.161, IV.116, VI.323, VII.57; *Works*, VIII.290.

[11] *Letters*, V.358. It is evident from this, and his *Notes*, that Wesley regarded Paul as the author of Hebrews. See *Notes on the New Testament*, p. 543; *Letters*, I.255, III.305.

[12] *Journal*, II.49; Gradin's account was written in Latin.   [13] *Letters*, I.255.

interpretations in Wesley's writings. Our quotations from Wesley have already shown that πληροφορία πίστεως is quite distinct from 'hope'. Nor is it truly represented in the statement that 'this assurance ... is given to some in a smaller ... degree', since its distinguishing feature is its *fullness* (a possible rendering of πληροφορία).

These inconsistencies appear in Wesley's early writings, the latest of which is in 1746. As in his teaching on assurance generally, the passing of the years helped to clarify his view of this aspect of the doctrine.

By 1751 we find a clear distinction drawn between πληροφορία πίστεως and πληροφορία τῆς ἐλπίδος. Wesley writes to Dr Lavington as follows: 'The full assurance of faith does not imply the full assurance of perseverance: this bears another name, being styled by St Paul "the full assurance of hope". ... Some have the full assurance of faith, a full conviction of present pardon; ... not the full assurance of hope, not a full conviction of their future perseverance.'[14]

The text in which πληροφορία τῆς ἐλπίδος appears is Hebrews 6[11], and reads thus: 'And we desire that each one of you may show the same diligence unto the fulness of hope even to the end.' In the margin of the Revised Version, πληροφορία is rendered 'full assurance', as in Wesley's version. Wesley comments in his *Notes*: 'The full assurance of faith relates to present pardon; the full measure of hope, to future glory. The former is the highest divine evidence, that God is reconciled to me in the Son of His love; the latter is the same divine evidence wrought in the soul by the Spirit of persevering grace, and of eternal glory.'[15]

Writing to Elizabeth Ritchie on 6th October 1778, Wesley carries further his definition of πληροφορία τῆς ἐλπίδος and also relates it to Christian perfection. He says: 'The plerophory (or full assurance) of hope is a divine revelation that we shall endure to the end; or, more directly, that we shall enjoy God in glory. This is by no means essential to or inseparable from perfect love.[16] It is sometimes given to those who are not perfected in love, as it was to Mr Grimshaw. And it is not given (at least not for some time) to many who are perfected in love.'[17]

[14] *Letters*, III.305.
[15] *Notes on the New Testament*, pp. 553f.
[16] cf. *Journal*, II.49.   [17] *Letters*, VI.323.

Later, in 1781, Wesley draws another sharp distinction between πληροφορία πίστεως and πληροφορία τῆς ἐλπίδος and considers also the bearing of the latter on the notion that no saint shall fall from grace. 'The plerophory (or full assurance) of faith is such a clear conviction that *I am now* in the favour of God as excludes all doubt and fear concerning it. The full assurance of hope is such clear confidence that I *shall enjoy* the glory of God as excludes all doubt and fear concerning this. And this confidence is totally different from an opinion that "no saint shall fall from grace". It has no relation to it. . . . The giving way to anything unholy . . . clouds the full assurance of hope; which cannot subsist any longer than the heart cleaves steadfastly to God.'[18]

As was noted above, πληροφορία appears only four times in the New Testament; and on each occasion it is capable of bearing the meaning of 'full assurance'. We saw that in Hebrews 10[22] it was coupled with πίστεως, in 6[11] with ἐλπίδος. It occurs also in Colossians 2[2] with συνέσεως ('understanding') and in 1 Thessalonians 1[5] it is used absolutely. Neither of the last two is a basic text in Wesley's doctrine of assurance. The former scarcely calls forth a comment in his *Notes*,[19] though in connexion with the latter Wesley writes: 'Literally, with "full assurance" and much of it; the Spirit bearing witness by shedding the love of God abroad in your hearts, which is the highest testimony given.'[20]

In reference to these three kinds of full assurance (πίστεως, ἐλπίδος, συνέσεως), Dr Pope maintains that in one sense these three are various forms of the same thing, the sure conviction of the reality of the objects personally trusted in, hoped for, and apprehended in knowledge.[21]

Commenting on Hebrews 10[22] (πληροφορία πίστεως), Dr Dods says: 'Believing not only that God is (11[6]), but that a way to His favour and fellowship is opened by the Great Priest. To engender this full assurance has been the aim of the writer throughout the Epistle.'[22]

Dr T. H. Robinson interprets the Greek as 'absolute assurance of faith, or . . . in full faith'; and this, he holds, 'is the result of having "our hearts sprinkled clean from a bad conscience, and our bodies washed in pure water"'.[23] πληροφορία τῆς

[18] *Letters*, VII.57f.   [19] *Notes on the New Testament*, p. 504.
[20] ibid., p. 509.   [21] Pope, *Prayers of St Paul*, p. 214.
[22] Dods, *Hebrews, Expositor's Greek Testament*, p. 346.
[23] Robinson, *Epistle to the Hebrews, Moffatt New Testament Commentary*, p. 143.

ἐλπίδος is taken by Dr A. B. Bruce to mean 'that your salvation may be a matter of certainty and not of charitable hope'.[24] Peake, however, believes that 'full assurance' (R.V. margin) is less probable than 'fulness' and considers that the burden of the author's message is that his readers should be as zealous in gaining a full hope and holding it fast to the end as they had been in ministering to the saints.[25]

Weiss is quoted as saying that hope is only what it ought to be when a full certainty of conviction (eine volle Ueberzeugungsgewissheit) accompanies it.[26] In a comment relating both to Hebrews 10^{22} and 6^{11}, Davidson says: 'Fulness or full assurance of faith and hope is not anything distinct from faith and hope, lying outside them and to which they may lead; it is a condition of faith and hope themselves, the perfect condition.'[27] Davidson's statement confirms Wesley's view that the difference between saving faith, the full assurance of faith and the full assurance of hope is not one of kind but of degree.

[24] Bruce, *Hebrews—the First Apology for Christianity*, p. 222.
[25] Peake, *Hebrews, Cambridge Bible*, p. 148.
[26] Quoted by Marcus Dods, *Hebrews, Expositor's Greek Testament*, p. 301.
[27] ibid., p. 301.

CHAPTER FIVE

WAS WESLEY'S EXPOSITION ADEQUATE?

A REMARKABLE statement is made by Wesley to Samuel Walker in a letter dated 19th September 1757. 'Assurance', says Wesley, 'is a word I do not use because it is not Scriptural.' How are we to interpret this? Dr R. N. Young treated it with great seriousness. He devoted an appendix of some three pages to this question in his Fernley Lecture of 1882.[1] This sentence sends him in search of interpretations offered by lexicons, versions, commentators and others. His main concern is to determine the meaning of the word πληροφορία, which, as we have already shown, is the New Testament word (together with its verbal forms) most frequently translated as signifying a high degree of assurance.

From this research, Dr Young draws the following conclusion: 'On the whole, in consideration of the fact that the etymology of the word πληροφορία does not necessarily involve the sense of assurance, and considering further that the passages in which the word occurs in Holy Scripture may be clearly interpreted without any reference to assurance, I venture to conclude that Mr Wesley was justified in his statement: "Assurance is a word I do not use, because it is not Scriptural."'

Dr Young might well say, 'I *venture* to conclude'!—for his conclusion has an unconvincing ring about it. The evidence submitted could equally well form premises for the opposite conclusion.

Apart from all this, one wonders why it apparently never occurred to Dr Young to cross the threshold of Wesley's writings and examine the question on Wesley's own ground. Did he make any other statements on this subject? If so, are they consistent or contradictory? The answer is that he did make other statements and that they are not consistent. We quote some of the evidence.

Writing to Arthur Bedford on 4th August 1738, Wesley says: 'That assurance of which alone I speak, I should not choose to call an assurance of salvation, but rather (with the Scriptures) the assurance of faith. . . . I think the Scriptural words are

[1] Young, *Witness of the Spirit* (1882), pp. 87ff.

always the best.'[2] The word 'assurance' is also used by Wesley in a letter of 20th December 1760, addressed to the Editor of the *Lloyd's Evening Post*, though he apologizes for employing the term by inserting the following words in parentheses—'if we must use the expression'.[3]

In examining Wesley's teaching on the degrees of assurance,[4] we had occasion to quote several instances of Wesley's use of the phrases 'full assurance of faith' and 'full assurance of hope'.[5] Moreover, if Dr Young had consulted the *Notes on the New Testament*, he would have found that Wesley translates πληροφορία by 'full assurance' in his rendering of Colossians 2[2]; Hebrews 6[11], 10[22], and by 'much assurance' in 1 Thessalonians 1[5].[6] Nor do Wesley's comments detract from such a translation.

And there we can leave the matter. It is plain from the above evidence that Wesley did use the word 'assurance'—despite his denial—and that he believed the term was in harmony with the meaning of the original Greek of the New Testament. Our examination leads us to the conclusion, not only that Wesley employed the word 'assurance' in rendering πληροφορία, but that he was right in so doing.

We now turn to another matter that calls for criticism. In his first sermon on 'The Witness of the Spirit' (1746), Wesley advances the view that the prefix συν of συμμαρτυρεῖ (Romans 8[16]) denotes only that the Spirit bears witness '*at the same time* that He enables us to cry, Abba, Father'.[7]

Wesley, however, corrects the interpretation he gives here when he writes his second sermon on 'The Witness of the Spirit' (1757). 'It is manifest', he says, 'here are two witnesses mentioned, who together testify the same thing; the Spirit of God and our own spirit.'[8] The large majority of scholars offer an interpretation in support of this concurrence of two witnesses.[9]

In our examination of the Greek terms bearing on assurance,[10] we saw that Paul's use of the compound verb to imply concurrent testimony is supported by other passages in the New Testament. Moreover, confirmatory evidence that the compound verb signifies concurrent testimony is traceable in

[2] *Letters*, I.255.   [3] ibid., IV.126.
[4] Part II, chs. 2 and 3, pp. 70; 76ff., *supra*; Part III, ch. 4, pp. 128ff., *supra*.
[5] *Journal*, II.49; *Letters*, III.161, 305, IV.116, V.358, IV.323, VII.57f., VIII.290.
[6] *Notes on the New Testament*, pp. 504, 553, 563, 509.
[7] *Sermons*, I.204.   [8] *Sermons*, II.346.
[9] cf R. N. Young, op. cit., pp. 85f.   [10] Part III, ch. 1, pp. 109f., *supra*.

classical writers—including Euripides,[11] Xenophon,[12] Sophocles,[13] and Thucydides.[14]

'The "concurrent witness" ', says Dr Flew, 'is Paul's way of preserving the distinction of the Spirit of God from the spirit of man. All human attempts to distinguish clearly the limits of one from the other in religious experience break down at last. But Paul does here assert that, by the Spirit's power, every believer may know that conscious communion with God as a child knows a father.[15] . . . The sense of sonship (cf. Galatians 4[7]) is the gift of the Spirit here and now.[16] Therefore the *consciousness* of the relationship is an important part of the relationship.'[17]

In considering the Biblical evidence of Wesley's teaching on the direct witness, we criticized the view that the direct witness of God's Spirit must be antecedent to the indirect witness of our own spirit.[18] We are interested here in his attempt to justify his argument in terms of Scripture. Wesley says: 'We must love God before we can be holy at all, this being the root of all holiness. Now, we cannot love God, till we know he loves us: "We love Him because He first loved us";[19] and we cannot know His love to us, till His Spirit witnesses it to our Spirit.'[20]

One wonders how Wesley failed to realize that he used the word 'know' here in two senses. The argument is invalidated by his passing from one meaning of the word to another without recognizing the distinction. The connotation of the term is plainly different in the two phrases, 'know He loves us' and 'know His love'. The one is merely *intellectual* knowledge, the other is *experiential* knowledge.[21]

What are our conclusions concerning the Biblical foundation of Wesley's doctrine of assurance? As our examination in the last three chapters has revealed, it cannot be said that Wesley's exegesis and exposition have always been in line with modern scholarship. This can scarcely be expected.

---

[11] *Hippolytus*, 286.   [12] *Hellenica*, iii.32, vii.3, 35.
[13] *Philoctetus*, 438; *Electra*, 1.224.   [14] *History*, VIII.51.
[15] Weiss, *Das Urchristentum*, p. 390, errs in regarding the consciousness of adoption as limited to the future.
[16] See Kennedy, *The Theology of the Epistles*, pp. 137ff.
[17] Flew, *The Idea of Perfection in Christian Theology* (1934), p. 64.
[18] Part II, ch. 3, pp. 76ff., *supra*.   [19] 1 John 4[19].   [20] *Sermons*, II.349.
[21] cf. Bertrand Russell, *Problems of Philosophy*, p. 69.

Admitting this, we can still allow that Wesley has given his doctrine of assurance a secure foundation in the New Testament. The advance in Biblical scholarship has not undermined the pillars on which he built his doctrine. The main Scriptural passages quoted by Wesley are sure to form an integral part of any valid Biblical doctrine of Christian certainty. No sound New Testament doctrine of assurance can fail to give a conspicuous place to the writings of Paul (especially Romans and Galatians) and the to First Epistle of John. And these sources, as we have seen, have figured prominently in Wesley's teaching.

Yet, it must be admitted that the Scriptural foundation on which he built was too narrow. He did not feel himself called upon to undertake a systematic examination of all the relevant New Testament passages. It was not Wesley's aim to construct a comprehensive doctrine from various parts of Scripture. This was doubtless due to a tendency in the eighteenth century to lean overmuch on 'proof texts'.[22] It is not surprising, therefore, that from the Biblical point of view his treatment is limited.

Wesley did not attach enough importance to the objective and historical aspects of assurance in the New Testament.[23] We are *not* saying that he did not treat adequately, in his teaching *generally*, the historical facts of the Gospel; but that he did not sufficiently relate his doctrine of assurance to these in the course of his exposition.[24]

The Biblical doctrine of assurance presupposes, as a matter of course, the believer's personal acquaintance with the saving truths of Christianity and the faith of divine revelation.[25] As Dr H. Maldwyn Hughes says: 'The New Testament contains the record of the facts which lie behind Christian experience. . . . Intuition can never produce the same authoritative conviction as an objective historical revelation.'[26]

We would supplement further the Biblical data of Wesley's doctrine by pointing out that Paul not only teaches the inner witness of the Spirit, but rests this subjective assurance on a broad basis of fact in the Person and work of Christ: 'I know Him whom I have believed, and I am persuaded (πέπεισμαι)

---

[22] See W. E. Sangster, *The Path to Perfection*, p. 44.
[23] cf. Dr Pope, *Compendium of Christian Theology*, III.113ff.
[24] Mackintosh, *The Christian Experience of Forgiveness*, p. 249.
[25] M. S. Terry, article on 'Assurance' in *Dictionary of Christ and the Gospels*, I.132.
[26] Hughes, *The Theology of Experience*, pp. 228f.

that He is able to guard that which I have committed unto him against that day' (2 Timothy 1¹²).

Paul enjoys a confidence that can withstand all the perils of present and future, of this earthly life and of the Hereafter. 'I am persuaded (πέπεισμαι) that neither death, nor life, nor angels, nor principalities, nor things present, nor things to come, nor powers, nor height, nor depth, nor any other creature, shall be able to separate us from the love of God, which is in Christ Jesus our Lord.'²⁷

No Biblical doctrine of assurance should ignore Paul's reference to the 'sealing' of believers by the Spirit of God:²⁸ 'Now He that stablisheth us with you in Christ, and anointed us, is God; who also sealed us, and gave us the earnest of the Spirit in our hearts.'²⁹ 'In whom [i.e. Christ], having also believed, ye were sealed with the Holy Spirit of promise, which is an earnest of our inheritance.'³⁰ As Dr Banks points out, 'the very purpose of a seal is to certify or give evidence. If, then, we have the Holy Spirit, as all true Christians have, we have a seal or evidence of our salvation.³¹

The use of the passive ἐσφραγίσθητε (ye were sealed) in the latter passage is significant.³² It is a defence against the charge of subjectivism to which any claim to an inner experience of certainty is vulnerable. The passive implies that while Christian assurance lies in the inner consciousness, it is initiated from without—that is, by the Holy Spirit.

We would add further to the Scriptural foundation of Wesley's doctrine by drawing attention, not only to Paul's teaching, but to the Apostle's religious experiences as reflected in the New Testament, and especially in the Acts of the Apostles.³³ However diverse may be the theories that gather round Paul's revolutionary experience at Damascus, one thing is certain: Paul had no doubt about his meeting with the Risen Christ.³⁴ He gained there an assurance of salvation which he never lost for the rest of his life.

²⁷ Romans 8.³⁸, ³⁹.
²⁸ See Basil, *De Spiritu Sancto*, in *Nicene and Post-Nicene Fathers*, VIII.9, note 10 (by Blomfield Jackson).
²⁹ 2 Corinthians 1²². ³⁰ Ephesians 1¹², ¹⁴; cf. 4³⁰.
³¹ Banks, *Manual of Christian Doctrine*, p. 223.
³² There is not likely to be any allusion here to a Jewish or heathen custom, or to the rite of baptism; Dr S. D. F. Salmon, *Ephesians, Expositor's Greek Testament*, p. 268.
³³ See Rattenbury, *Testament of Paul*, passim.
³⁴ Acts 9⁴⁻⁶, 22⁷⁻¹⁰, 26¹⁴⁻¹⁸.

Nobody suffers the deprivations and hazards to which Paul was subjected in his missionary work unless he has an unshakable confidence in God.[35] Here we have a clear instance of the reality of a personal experience of assurance though none of the usual terminology of the doctrine appears. And in this wider sense the teaching or experience of Christian certainty is traceable in nearly all the books of the New Testament. As Haering says: 'All who are in possession of this new life are represented as having a clear consciousness of it. "You know", "We know" are expressions used again and again.'[36]

There are two other important elements in the experience and teaching of the New Testament which Wesley practically ignored in presenting his doctrine of assurance. These are Pentecost and Paul's repeated use of the phrase 'in Christ' (ἐν Χριστῷ). They are of such importance that we must give a separate chapter to them.

[35] 2 Corinthians 11$^{23-33}$.
[36] Haering, *Ethics of the Christian Life* (Eng. trans., 1909), p. 199.

CHAPTER SIX

THE APOSTOLIC CHURCH

WESLEY believed that the Christian experience of the Apostolic Church was normative for Christians in all ages. Here could be seen the Christian society as it should be.[1] In worship, fellowship, and witness—this was the perfect pattern for those 'who profess and call themselves Christians'. The alleged similarity between Moravianism and the Apostolic Church is said to have been the primary cause of Wesley's association with the Moravian Brethren; who, as we have seen, were the chief human agents in preparing John Wesley for his Aldersgate Street experience.[2]

From the general tenor of Wesley's teaching on assurance, it is clear that he believed it was an experience enjoyed by the Apostolic Church. We noted in the last chapter however the slight attention Wesley gave to Pentecost and the numerous ἐν Χριστῷ phrases. These two features are vital to an understanding of the place of assurance in the lives of the early Christians.

The Crucifixion of Jesus had left the disciples in a state of bewilderment and uncertainty. Their highest hopes had been dashed to the ground. The 'communications' which oppressed the two disciples who journeyed to Emmaus on that first Easter Day express their despair: 'But we hoped that it was He who should redeem Israel.'[3] Thomas was not the only one who had doubted.[4]

The 'appearances' of Christ after His Resurrection did much to revive the spirits of His followers; but the assurance necessary for their future pioneer work was still wanting. This the Master well knew. 'I send forth the promise of My Father upon you: but tarry ye in the city, until ye be clothed with power from on high.'[5] It is true that the Risen Christ had already 'breathed on them,[6] and said unto them, Receive ye the Holy Spirit'.[7] Dr Chase interprets this as signifying that

[1] See W. F. Slater, *Methodism in the Light of the Early Church* (1885).
[2] *Journal*, I.170f.   [3] Luke 24[17, 21].
[4] Mark 16[11]; John 2[24-9]; Luke 24[11].   [5] Luke 24[49].
[6] See Dr Plummer, *St John*, in *Cambridge Greek Testament*, p. 343; cf. Harnack, *Acts of the Apostles*, pp. 175–89.
[7] John 20[22]; G. G. Findlay, *Fellowship in the Life Eternal*, p. 298.

He made them partakers of His own risen life. 'The Church henceforth lived. . . . But the divine work of renewal was not yet complete. If Easter Day was the day of the Church's birth, Pentecost was the day of the Church's unction, the Church's sealing.'[8]

While a measure of assurance is doubtless implied in the words of the Emmaus disciples—'Was not our heart burning within us, while He spake to us in the way'[9]—a deeper sense of certainty still awaits them. This need of a stronger degree of assurance is the burden of Christ's 'parting' message before His 'ascension'; 'And being assembled together with them,[10] He charged them not to depart from Jerusalem, but to wait for the promise of the Father, which, said He, ye heard from Me. For John indeed baptized with water; but ye shall be baptized with the Holy Ghost not many days hence. . . . Ye shall receive power when the Holy Ghost is come upon you.'[11]

Dr Chase holds that the activity of the Church between the Resurrection and Pentecost is the action of spiritual immaturity. After the day of Pentecost, all is changed. Henceforth, the life of the Church is the revelation of the Spirit. Before Pentecost, 'communion with the unseen Lord is not sought in an inner and spiritual presence'.[12]

It is not our purpose to trace the significance of the 'pre-Pentecostal' presence of the Holy Spirit.[13] Nor need we pause to consider the exact geographical location of the events recorded in Acts 2.[14] Scholars are not agreed on the degree of literalness to be attached to the very unusual happenings which marked this coming of the Spirit. Dr Swete is careful to point out that 'the whole was a vision . . . but a vision that corresponded to a great spiritual fact which at the same moment accomplished itself in the experience of all who were present'.[15]

Edward Grubb observes that the occurrences described in

[8] Chase, *The Credibility of the Acts of the Apostles* (London, 1902), p. 41.
[9] Luke 24^{32}.
[10] Or 'eating with them'; see Dr Knowling, *Acts of the Apostles*, in *Expositor's Greek Testament*, p. 54.
[11] Acts 1$^{4, 5, 8}$.   [12] Chase, op. cit., p. 42.
[13] See Humphries, *The Holy Spirit in Faith and Experience*, p. 163.
[14] Dr Swete favours 'the upper room' rather than 'the court of the Women in the Temple precincts'. See his *The Holy Spirit in the New Testament*, pp. 69f. But cf. Chase, op. cit., pp. 30ff.
[15] Swete, op. cit., p. 71.

Acts 2 bear resemblances to phenomena that are familiar to us in many 'revivals' of spiritual religion. The really important thing is not the outward marvels of the wind, the fire, or even the gift of tongues (whatever that may have been), but the flooding of their whole being with a new moral energy, a new hope, a new joy, a new love—with a triumphant sense of power, brought by the consciousness that the Jesus who had conquered death was not only with them, but *in* them, and working through them.[16]

Our chief concern is with the spiritual experience of which these phenomena are the means or the expression. Our brief survey leads us to the conclusion that an assurance of personal salvation, centred in a crucified and risen Christ, is a salient feature of the Pentecostal experience.

Dr J. G. Tasker points out that the first and emphatic word in the final sentence of Peter's address on the day of Pentecost is ἀσφαλῶς: 'Let all the house of Israel therefore know *of a certainty* that God hath made him both Lord and Christ, this Jesus whom ye crucified.'[17] Dr Tasker holds that the significance of Peter's argument is its appeal to various grounds of assurance. 'Religious certainty', he says, 'in the sense of the inward experience of the Holy Spirit's working, is itself regarded as witnessing to the reality of the resurrection of Christ; but that certainty may also, it is assumed, be strengthened by testimony to the objective grounds of faith, as they are found in Scripture and in history.'[18]

In the *Minutes of Conference* for 16th June 1747, the question is asked: 'But do you not know that the Apostles themselves had it [i.e. assurance] not till after the day of Pentecost?' Wesley replies: 'The Apostles themselves had not the proper Christian faith till after the day of Pentecost.'[19]

In a sermon on 'Salvation by Faith' which Wesley preached at St Mary's, Oxford, before the University, on 11th June 1738, the founder of Methodism points out that 'saving faith' was not 'that which the Apostles themselves had while Christ was yet upon earth'.[20]

This spiritual certainty is clearly revealed in the boldness and 'glad fearlessness' with which the Primitive Church proclaims the 'new faith'. 'Boldness' occurs not infrequently in Acts and is characteristic of the early Christian preaching. Luke clearly

[16] Grubb, *The Religion of Experience* (1918), p. 87. [17] Acts 2³⁶.
[18] *E.R.E.*, III.326.   [19] *Works*, VIII.291.   [20] *Sermons*, I.39.

links it with the Spirit![21] 'They were all filled with the Holy Ghost, and they spake the word of God with boldness' (μετὰ παρρησίας).[22]

Dr Pope has shown that the Greek words for 'boldness' and 'full assurance' are correlative terms.[23] This connexion is illustrated in the experience of Peter. The Peter of the Passover has become the Peter of Pentecost, whose words now show, not only the freedom of speech which was characteristic of this Apostle, but a blending of courage, wisdom, and skill which we do not associate with him as he appears in the Gospels.[24]

Another mark of the Spirit's influence at Pentecost—a mark reflected in Wesley's Aldersgate experience[25]—is the access of new power (δύναμις) for the missionary task facing the Apostles.[26] Dr Swete says that a new strength, which was not their own, marked all the sayings and deeds of the Apostolic Church. It is in this change of mental and spiritual attitude rather than in the external signs of wind and fire or in strange powers of utterance that we recognize the supreme miracle of the day of Pentecost.[27] This new sense of power—'always the characteristic creation of the Spirit'—clearly breaks into consciousness at Pentecost.[28] Such a personal experience of spiritual strength is bound up with an 'assurance of the Resurrection and the Ascension' which has its roots 'in the inner witness of the Spirit—"We are witnesses of these things; and so is the Holy Ghost".'[29]

In early chapters of this book, we saw how central was the Holy Spirit to the doctrine of the 'Witness of the Spirit'. Wesley's religious transformation at Aldersgate Street was seen to be an assurance of personal salvation centred in Christ, and wrought in the individual by the Spirit. Our study of Wesley's spiritual illumination and the story of Pentecost (as told by Luke in Acts 2) has revealed a number of significant similarities, which we summarize as follows:

[21] A. M. Hunter, *Paul and His Predecessors* (1940), p. 118.   [22] Acts 4^{31}.

[23] Pope, *Compendium of Christian Theology* (1880), III.118.

[24] Swete, op. cit., p. 76.   [25] *Journal*, I.477.

[26] Hunter, op. cit., pp. 114, 117; Acts 1^8; cf. Romans 15$^{13, 19}$; 1 Corinthians 2^4; Ephesians 3^{16}.

[27] Swete, *The Holy Spirit in the New Testament*, pp. 76f.

[28] Wheeler Robinson, *The Christian Experience of the Holy Spirit* (1940), p. 14.

[29] Chase, *The Credibility of the Acts*, pp. 152f.; *E.R.E.*, III.326.

THE APOSTOLIC CHURCH 143

(1) Neither Pentecost nor Aldersgate can be understood or explained without reference to the supernatural agency of the Spirit of God.[30]
(2) In both cases the transformation did not consist primarily in any change in the intellectual content of their Gospel.[31]
(3) The spiritual illumination was an *individual* one.[32]
(4) Both religious experiences were centred in Christ, by whose death and resurrection a sense of conscious pardon was gained.[33]
(5) For the Apostles and for Wesley, this personal assurance of salvation led to a quickened life of spiritual power and of sacrificial service for Christ and His Church.[34]
(6) In this spiritual transformation—at Aldersgate Street and especially at Pentecost—fear had been displaced by boldness (παρρησία).[35]

Our comparative analysis of Pentecost and Aldersgate finds confirmation in the words of the Rev. W. F. Slater: 'The spiritual condition of the Wesleys before their conversion was similar to that of the disciples before the day of Pentecost. They were under the teaching of the Lord, and served Him with sincere affection. They were "servants" but not "sons".'[36]

We now turn to the phrase ἐν Χριστῷ, which occurs no fewer than 164 times in Paul's letters, and which is of decisive importance in any discussion of the religion of St Paul.[37] Scholars are not agreed on the precise interpretation to be given to this conception in Pauline theology. E. F. Scott holds that it never occurred to Paul to identify the Spirit and Christ. 'His aim on the contrary is to keep them distinct, and his very phrase "the Spirit of Christ" which brings them so closely together implies an effort to distinguish.'[38] Deissmann stresses the view that Paul employed the phrase in a sense that equated the risen Christ with the Holy Spirit: 'Like the Spirit,

---

[30] *Journal*, I.476; Hunter, *Paul and His Predecessors*, pp. 114f.
[31] See Luke 24[26, 27, 45-9]; Acts 1[8]; *Journal*, I.454f.
[32] Acts 2[3]; *Journal*, I.461f., 475f.   [33] *Journal*, I.471; Acts 2[22-4, 32-9].
[34] Acts 1[8], 24[7], 5[14]; *Journal*, I.476.
[35] Pope, *Compendium of Christian Theology* (1880), III.118; Swete, *The Holy Spirit in the New Testament*, p. 76; Hunter, *Paul and His Predecessors*, p. 118.
[36] Slater, *Methodism in the Light of the Early Church* (1885), p. 32; see corrective note in the *Journal*, I.423.
[37] Flew, *The Idea of Perfection in Christian Theology* (1934), p. 48.
[38] E. F. Scott, *The Spirit in the New Testament*, pp. 182f.

He is conceived of as a Sphere or Atmosphere within which men may live and move.'[39]

While Deissmann may have carried his mystical interpretation too far, the general usage of ἐν Χριστῷ in the New Testament, and especially in Paul's Epistles, implies a mystical experience. And such an experience plainly involves an assurance of oneness with Christ or the Spirit. In the very nature of the case, this human-Divine relationship carries with it a sense of inner, spiritual certainty.[40]

In harmony with this, Dr H. Wheeler Robinson says that Paul 'traced back to the Holy Spirit of God (or Christ) . . . the assurance of sonship'.[41] This was borne out in the Apostle's own experience. 'All that he had been taught to expect as the contents of a distant salvation was already his', writes Dr C. A. A. Scott, 'peace with God, freedom from the dominion of Sin, the gift of the Spirit. . . . Of this Paul could have no doubt.'[42]

The connexion of Pentecost with ἐν Χριστῷ in Paul's religious life, as the source of an inner consciousness of salvation, is brought out by Dr Inge: 'The Damascus Road experience was identical in content with what other Apostles knew as the illapse of the Holy Spirit, but which he felt as the risen and ascended Christ.'[43] Commenting on this quotation, Dr A. M. Hunter observes: 'At all events, in Paul's Epistles, experience of Christ and experience of the Spirit are often indissolubly blended. For Paul, being "in Christ" and being "in the Spirit" stand for much the same thing; and he even goes so far in one passage as to aver: "The Lord is the Spirit." '[44] Dr Wheeler Robinson holds that if the Lord gave personality to the Spirit, the Spirit gave ubiquity to the Lord.[45] It is held that Paul in his teaching drew the Spirit and the living Christ closer together, and that he presented Christianity as the religion of the Spirit.[46]

And there we must leave our consideration of the place of assurance in the Apostolic Church. Our examination of

---

[39] C. A. A. Scott, *Christianity According to St Paul*, p. 153.
[40] cf. Underhill, *The Mystic Way* (1913), p. 173.
[41] Robinson, *The Christian Experience of the Holy Spirit* (1930), pp. 15f.
[42] C. A. A. Scott, op. cit., p. 138.
[43] Inge, *Congregational Quarterly*, October 1934, p. 504.
[44] 2 Corinthians 3^{17}; cf. 1 Corinthians 15^{45}; Hunter, *Paul and His Predecessors*, p. 119.
[45] Robinson, op. cit., p. 19.   [46] Hunter, op. cit., p. 112.

Pentecost and of Paul's conception of ἐν Χριστῷ must be supplemented by the evidence already given in previous chapters.[47] This evidence leads to the conclusion that an assurance of personal salvation centred in Christ occupies a conspicuous place, if not always in the terminology, at least in the experience of the primitive Christian society as revealed in the New Testament.

[47] If space allowed, consideration might also be given, as Dr C. Ryder Smith kindly suggested, to 'the complementary phrases "Christ in you", etc., which identify the Son and the Spirit *at this point*' (cf. John 14[16-18]).

Part Four

Assurance in the History of the Church

CHAPTER ONE

THE EARLY FATHERS

WESLEY maintained that the 'Witness of the Spirit' was traceable, not only in the New Testament and in the primitive Church, but also in the post-Apostolic Fathers[1] from whom he quoted in his *Farther Appeal to Men of Reason and Religion*.[2] In his letter to Richard Tompson on 25th July 1755, Wesley writes: 'With regard to the assurance of faith, I apprehend that the whole Christian Church in the first centuries enjoyed it. For though we have few points of doctrine explicitly taught in the small remains of the ante-Nicene Fathers, yet I think none that carefully reads Clemens Romanus, Ignatius, Polycarp, Origen, or any other of them, can doubt whether either the writer himself possessed it or all whom he mentions as real Christians.'[3] Writing again to Tompson on 5th February 1756, Wesley says: 'I believe the ancient Fathers are far from silent on our question, though none that I know have treated it professedly. But I have not leisure to wade through that sea.'[4]

Unlike Wesley, we must *find* time, if not for '*wading* through that sea', at least for the dipping of our pail into those waters in order to appreciate the historical antecedents of Wesley's doctrine. In this chapter, therefore, our brief historical survey will glean references to spiritual certainty in the post-Apostolic Church and in the Nicene and post-Nicene Fathers.

We pause, however, to observe two features characteristic of this period.

One feature is the comparatively rare appearance of that phraseology with which we became familiar as we traced assurance in the eighteenth century and in the New Testament. The other is the striking contrast between the fervent experience of spiritual certainty in the primitive Church,[5] and the less vivid expression of this experience in the post-Apostolic Fathers.

With reference to this latter feature, Dr Rainy says: 'Perhaps

---

[1] Dr J. S. Simon, *John Wesley and the Religious Societies* (1921), p. 331; *John Wesley and the Methodist Societies*, p. 50; *Sermons* I.95.

[2] 1745, *Works*, VIII.91ff.   [3] *Letters*, III.137; *Works*, XII.468.

[4] *Letters*, III.159; cf. II.100, 325.   [5] See Part III, ch. 6, pp. 139ff., *supra*.

the most needful preparation for appreciating the beliefs of the early Church is to get rid of the assumption . . . that the post-Apostolic Church started with the fullness of the Apostolic teaching as that is embodied, for instance, in the New Testament.'[6] The reason for this is that some of the Fathers wrote before the writings of the Apostles had been collected into a canon.[7] Moreover, it has to be realized that what the Apostles taught was one thing; what the Church proved able to receive is quite another.[8] With this caution in mind, we will consider the glimmerings of assurance in the early Christian centuries.

In his first *Epistle to the Corinthians*, Clement of Rome devotes a chapter to the 'Order of Ministers in the Church', in which he writes: 'Having therefore received their orders, and *being fully assured* by the Resurrection of our Lord Jesus Christ, and established in the word of God, *with full assurance of the Holy Ghost*, they went forth proclaiming that the kingdom of God was at hand.'[9]

In the same Epistle, Clement declares: 'How blessed and wonderful, beloved, are the gifts of God . . . truth in perfect confidence, faith in assurance . . . and all these fall under the cognizance of our understanding now.'[10] Later on he speaks of Christ as central to this sense of certainty: 'By Him are the eyes of our hearts opened. By Him our foolish and darkened understanding blossoms up anew towards His marvellous light. By Him the Lord has willed that we should taste of immortal knowledge.'[11]

The 'Shepherd of Hermas' calls upon his readers to turn to the Lord, and ask of Him without doubting, and they will know the multitude of His tender mercies.[12] Again, he urges: 'Keep this flesh pure and stainless, that the Spirit which inhabits it may bear witness to it, and your flesh may be justified.'[13]

Nowhere have we clearer and more glorious evidence of a Christian's assurance of salvation or certainty of God than in the records of the early martyrs. Polycarp, with death before him, refused to deny Christ and 'swear by the fortune of Caesar'.[14] The contemporary record of *The Martyrdom of*

[6] Rainy, *The Ancient Catholic Church* (1926), p. 66.
[7] Dr G. P. Fisher, *History of Christian Doctrine* (1927), p. 42.
[8] Rainy, op. cit., p. 66.   [9] Hastings, *Dictionary of the Apostolic Church*, I.108.
[10] Clement, *First Epistle to the Corinthians*, XXXV.   [11] ibid., XXXVI.
[12] Hermas, *Commandment Ninth*.   [13] Hermas, *Similitude Fifth*, VII.
[14] Eusebius, *Ecclesiastical History*, IV.15.

Polycarp says that the Proconsul urged him: 'Swear, and I will set thee at liberty; reproach Christ.' The aged Bishop replied: 'Eighty and six years have I served Him, and He never did me an injury. How then can I blaspheme my King and my Saviour?' The record goes on: 'While he spoke these . . . things, he was filled with confidence and joy, and his countenance was full of grace.'[15]

In his message to the Smyrnaeans, Ignatius speaks of their steadfast faith and their certainty of truth: 'I have observed that ye are perfected in an immovable faith, as if ye were nailed to the Cross of our Lord Jesus Christ, both in the flesh and in the Spirit, and are established in love through the blood of Christ, *being fully persuaded* in every truth.'[16] Writing to the Philadelphians, Ignatius says that the Apostles receive from God, through Jesus Christ, one and the same Holy Spirit, 'who is . . . the *Author of saving knowledge.*'[17]

Justin Martyr, in his *Dialogue with Trypho*, holds that the Gentiles who have believed in Christ and have repented of their sins 'shall receive the inheritance' and 'assuredly they shall receive the holy inheritance of God'. He would have his readers 'hasten to know in what way forgiveness of sins and a hope of inheriting the promised good things shall be yours.'[18]

With reference to the early Christians, Aristides, in his *Apology*, says that these are they who more than all the nations on the earth have found the truth. 'For they know God, . . . through the only-begotten Son and the Holy Spirit. . . . They have the commands of the Lord Jesus Christ Himself graven upon their hearts.'[19]

Tatian, in his *Address to the Greeks*, maintains that 'it becomes us now to seek . . . to unite the soul with the Holy Spirit, and to strive after union with God'. After defining the constitution of man, Tatian adds that if it is like a temple, God is pleased to dwell in it by the Spirit.[20]

Irenaeus, in *Against Heresies*, refers to those who have received the grace of the 'adoption by which we cry Abba, Father'.[21] In a subsequent section of the same work, Irenaeus says that 'this earnest, therefore, thus dwelling in us, renders us spiritual

---

[15] *The Encyclical Epistle of the Church at Smyrna—Concerning the Martyrdom of the Holy Polycarp*, IX, XII.
[16] Ignatius, *To the Smyrnaeans*, I.   [17] *Epistle of Ignatius to the Philadelphians*, V.
[18] Justin Martyr, *Dialogue with Trypho*, XXVI, XLIV, CXVI, CXXI.
[19] *Apology of Aristides*, XV.   [20] Tatian, *Address to the Greeks*, XV.
[21] Irenaeus, *Against Heresies*, III.6.

even now, and the mortal is swallowed up by immortality (2 Corinthians 5⁴). "For ye", he declares, "are not in the flesh, but in the Spirit, if so be that the Spirit of God dwelleth in you" (Romans 8⁹). This, however, does not take place by a casting away of the flesh, but by the impartation of the Spirit. For those to whom he was writing were not without flesh, but they were those who had received the Spirit of God, "by which we cry, Abba, Father" (Romans 8¹⁵).'[22]

At least two relevant statements are found in the writings of Tertullian.[23] 'That we may have the *assurance*', he writes, 'that we are children of God "He hath sent forth His Spirit into our hearts, crying Abba, Father" (Galatians 4⁶).'[24] Tertullian speaks somewhat in terms of Wesley's doctrine of the 'witness of our own spirit' when he says: 'We ought indeed to walk so holily, and with so entire substantiality of faith, as to be confident and secure in regard of our own conscience.'[25]

In *The Miscellanies*, Clement of Alexandria has a chapter headed 'The knowledge which comes through faith the surest of all', in which he says: 'Faith, therefore, and the knowledge of the truth render the soul . . . always uniform and equable. . . . The real gnostic is he that knows Him, and the Father by Him.'[26]

Clement, in *The Instructor*, refers to baptism as a means of conveying spiritual illumination and a sense of divine adoption. He says that we who are baptized, having wiped off the sins which obscure the light of the Divine Spirit, have the eye of the spirit free, unimpeded, and full of light, by which alone we contemplate the Divine, the Holy Spirit flowing down to us from above. Again, explains Clement, 'Being baptized, we are illuminated; illuminated, we become sons. . . . This work is variously called grace (χάρισμα) and illumination . . . by which that holy light of salvation is beheld, that is, by which we see God clearly.'[27]

We now consider some relevant passages in Origen's voluminous writings.[28] In his defence, *Against Celsus*, Origen says: 'Every man who . . . is no longer under fear . . . but who chooses good for its own sake, is "a son of God". . . . The words

---

[22] Irenaeus, *Against Heresies*, V.8.
[23] For a modern exposition of Tertullian's doctrine, see Dr R. E. Roberts, *The Theology of Tertullian* (1924).
[24] Tertullian, *Against Marcion*, V.4.   [25] *On Female Dress*, II.
[26] Clement, *The Miscellanies*, Bk. II, ch. XI.
[27] Clement, *The Instructor*, Bk. I, ch. VI.   [28] cf. Wesley, *Letters*, II.91, 101.

of Paul are as follows: "For ye have not received the spirit of bondage again to fear; but ye have received the Spirit of adoption, whereby we cry, Abba, Father." '[29] In the same work there is another significant statement; and this, too, is couched in the language of Scripture: 'We pray that the light of the knowledge of the glory of God may shine in our hearts, and that the Spirit of God may dwell in our imaginations and lead us to contemplate the things of God; for "as many as are led by the Spirit of God, they are the sons of God".'[30]

'Is there not hidden there also', inquires Origen, 'an inner, namely a divine sense, which is revealed by that grace alone which he had received who said, "But we have the mind of Christ, that we might know the things freely given to us of God; which things also we speak, not in the words which man's wisdom teaches, but which the Spirit teaches." '[31]

In his *De Trinitate*, Hilary refers to an inner assurance of personal salvation. He holds that John $14^{13, 14, 16, 17}$, $16^{7, 12}$, 'contain an *assurance* of the goodwill of the Giver.... They tell how ... our faith ... shall be illumined by the gift of the Holy Ghost, the Bond of union and the Source of light.' Of Romans $8^{14, 15}$, Hilary says: 'Here we have a statement of the purpose and results of the gift, and *I cannot conceive what doubt can remain*.... Let us, therefore, make use of this great benefit, and seek for personal experience of this most needful gift.' After quoting 1 Corinthians 2^{12}, Hilary adds: We receive Him, then, that we may *know*.... This gift is with us unto the end of the world ... the *assurance* ... of the hope shall be ours, the light of our minds, the sun of our souls.'[32]

Our next authority is Basil, Bishop of Caesarea in Cappadocia, one of the four great Greek Fathers.[33] Basil believes that sensitiveness to the spiritual world is the fruit of living, not after the flesh (Romans 8^{12}), but after the Spirit (Romans 8^{14}) and of being conformed to the image of God's Son (Romans 8^{29}). 'The Spirit is the eye of the soul. As is the power of seeing in the healthy eye, so is the operation of the Spirit in the purified soul. Wherefore also Paul prays for the Ephesians that they may have their "eyes enlightened" by "the Spirit of wisdom" (Ephesians $1^{17, 18}$).' Like reason in the human mind,

---

[29] Origen, *Against Celsus*, Bk. I, ch. LVII.　　[30] ibid., Bk. IV, ch. XCV.

[31] *Ante-Nicene Christian Library*, I.297f. *1 Corinthians* 2^{12ff}.

[32] Hilary, *De Trinitate*, Bk. II, secs. 33–5.

[33] See A. R. Whitham, *History of the Christian Church* (1936), pp. 239ff.

'so is the Holy Spirit as when He "beareth witness with our spirit" (Romans 8[16]) and when He "cries in our hearts, Abba, Father" (Galatians 4[6]).'[34]

Having shown that remission of sins is by the gift of the Spirit, Basil goes on to say that there is close relationship with God through the Spirit, for 'God hath sent forth the Spirit of His Son into our hearts, crying Abba, Father' (Galatians 4[6]).[35] In one of his numerous letters, Basil indicates the relationship between religious knowledge and belief: 'If you say that the believer also *knows*, he knows from what he believes; and vice versa he believes from what he knows. We know God from His power.. We, therefore, believe in Him who is known, and we worship Him who is believed in.'[36]

Gregory, Bishop of Nyssa,[37] holds that the certainty of passing from death to life depends on faith in the triune God. He writes that 'on us who have been redeemed from death, the grace of immortality is bestowed. . . . Having, then, this *full assurance*, . . . our baptism, our faith, and our ascription of praise are to the Father, and to the Son and to the Holy Ghost.'[38] A more significant passage appears in his *Against Eunomius*: 'For he who says that "the Spirit itself beareth witness with our spirit" (Romans 8[16]), signifies nothing else than the Holy Spirit comes to be in the mind of the faithful . . . on the reception by which of the communion of the Spirit the recipients attain the dignity of adoption.'[39]

Ambrose, Bishop of Milan, writing on the Holy Spirit, says: 'We are children through the Spirit, because "God sent the Spirit of His Son into our hearts, crying, Abba, Father; so that thou art now not a servant but a son" (Galatians 4[6, 7]).'[40] This idea of spiritual generation is carried a stage further later in the same work. Ambrose indicates the place of baptism and the Cross in the gaining of an inner witness of the Spirit to adoption: 'For the Spirit made us children by adoption, the water of the sacred font washed us, the blood of the Lord redeemed us. So we obtain one invisible and one visible testimony in a spiritual sacrament, for "the Spirit Himself beareth witness to our spirit" (Romans 8[16]).'[41]

[34] Basil, *De Spiritu Sancto*, ch. XXVI.
[35] Basil, *De Spiritu Sancto*, ch. XIX; cf. ch. XXIV. [36] Basil, Letter *CCXXXIV*.
[37] Foakes-Jackson, *History of the Christian Church* (1914), pp. 380ff.
[38] Gregory of Nyssa, *Letter II, To the City of Sebasteia*.
[39] Gregory, *Against Eunomius*, Bk. VII, sec. 1.
[40] Ambrose, *On the Spirit*, Bk. I, ch. V.   [41] ibid., Bk. III, ch. X.

Ambrose again quotes this important passage from Romans when he argues for the 'inseparable connexion' between the Holy Spirit and Christ. The Bishop writes: 'For how is the Holy Spirit separated from the Son, since "the Spirit Himself beareth witness with our spirit that we are sons of God"?'[42] This conscious state of 'co-heirship' with Christ is explained by Ambrose in the following terms: 'Therefore they are heirs of God . . . because the grace of Christ is conveyed to them; joint-heirs with Christ, because they are renewed into His life; heirs also of Christ, because to them is given by His death as it were the inheritance of the testator.'[43]

Writing *On the Mysteries*, Ambrose brings out the meaning of the sealing of the believer by the Holy Ghost. He urges his readers to remember that they received the seal of the Spirit; 'the spirit of wisdom and understanding . . . the spirit of knowledge and godliness . . . and preserve what you received. God the Father sealed you, Christ the Lord strengthened you, and gave the earnest of the Spirit in your heart. (2 Corinthians 5⁵).'[44]

The life and theology of Augustine have left a lasting impression on the religious thought of the succeeding centuries. Harnack makes the significant comment that 'with all his horror of sin Augustine had not experienced the horror of uncertainty of salvation'.[45] His experience of an assurance of salvation is unquestioned, as our examination of his *Confessions* reveals. On the first page we find that famous quotation: '*Fecisti nos ad te, et inquietum est cor nostrum donec requiescat in te*': 'Thou has made us for Thyself, and our heart is restless until it rests in Thee.'[46]

Augustine's debt to his mother is well known. He refers to her inner sense of God's presence and to what Wesley would call the 'indirect witness' in the form of 'the fruit of the Spirit' in her life. 'All who knew her', writes Augustine, 'praised, honoured, loved Thee in her, because she felt Thy presence in her heart, whereof the fruits of her holy conversation were the proof.'[47]

The account of his conversion is a clear instance of an inner certainty of pardon and peace. 'Why not this hour make an

---

[42] Ambrose, *On the Spirit*, Bk. II, ch. VIII.
[43] Ambrose, *Letter LXIII*, Part 10. [44] *On the Mysteries*, ch. VII, sec. 42.
[45] Harnack, *History of Dogma*, V.210.
[46] *Confessions of St Augustine*, trans. by Dr C. Bigg (Methuen & Co., 1898), Bk. I, ch. I, sec. I.
[47] ibid., Bk. IX, ch. IX, sec. 5.

end of my vileness? Thus I spoke, weeping in bitter contrition of heart, when, lo, I heard a voice from the neighbouring house. It seemed as if some boy or girl . . . was repeating in a kind of chant the words, "Take and read, take and read". . . . I stemmed the rush of tears, and rose to my feet; for I could not think but that it was a divine command to open the Bible, and to read the first passage I lighted upon. . . .[48] I ran back to the place where Alypius was sitting; for, when I quitted him, I had left the volume of the Apostle lying there. I caught it up, opened it, and read in silence the passage on which my eyes first fell: "Not in rioting and drunkenness, not in chambering and wantonness, not in strife and envying; but put ye on the Lord Jesus Christ, and make no provision for the flesh to fulfil the lusts thereof."[49] No further would I read, nor was it necessary. As I reached the end of the sentence, the light of peace seemed to shed upon my heart, and every shadow of doubt melted away. I . . . closed the volume, and with calm countenance told Alypius.'[50]

[48] This way of using the Bible was sometimes adopted by Wesley and the Moravians. See Part III, ch. 1, p. 106, *supra*.

[49] Romans 13$^{13, 14}$.   [50] *Confessions*, Bk. VIII, ch. XII, secs. 2, 3.

CHAPTER TWO

THE MEDIEVAL CHURCH

IN 1746, Wesley wrote that the Methodists were called of God to proclaim the doctrine of assurance, 'which had been for so many years well nigh lost and forgotten'.[1] These words are applicable, not only to the eighteenth century, but to the centuries preceding the Reformation.

Dr H. Wheeler Robinson points out that where the emphasis falls in the external expression of religion, as in the sacraments of Roman Catholicism, the need for an inner assurance falls into the background.[2]

'In the medieval Church', says Dr H. B. Workman, 'the individual, *qua* individual, had little or no place. His salvation was conditioned from first to last by his belonging to a corporation, in whose privileges and functions he shared; through whose sacraments his life was nourished.[3]

This reliance on external authority has had a strong appeal in every age, and to certain individuals it conveys a type of assurance. For Faber, as for others, it means an escape from 'the burden of his individuality'.[4] A possible attitude of a Christian in the medieval Church is suggested by a modern testimony: 'The Church's teaching is before me, as a glorious series of splendid certainties. . . . I have no private judgement to overcome, and no desire to exercise my private judgement. It is a greater pleasure to receive and possess truth with certainty, than to go in search of it and to be in uncertainty whether it has been found.'[5]

The extent to which individual experience and thought in the Middle Ages was dominated by Authoritarianism is estimated by Auguste Sabatier: 'A proposition of Aristotle, an utterance of Scripture, a dictum of the Fathers, a decision of a council, settled officially, and for most men quite as fitly, a

---

[1] *Works*, V.124; cf. Dr R. N. Young, *The Witness of the Spirit* (1882), pp. 3f.

[2] Robinson, *The Christian Experience of the Holy Spirit* (1940), p. 217; cf. Allen *Continuity of Christian Thought* (1895), pp. 241ff.

[3] Workman, *Christian Thought to the Reformation* (1911), p. 190.

[4] *New History of Methodism*, I.8.

[5] See M. D. Petre, *Autobiography and Life of George Tyrrell*, I.229. Compare the inertia of personal religion in the eighteenth century.

problem of physics, astronomy, or history as a problem of morals or philosophy.'⁶

In his *Earnest Appeal to Men of Reason and Religion*,⁷ Wesley admits that if number of voices is to decide the question, we must give up the doctrine of assurance at once: 'For you have on your side, not only some who desire to be Christians indeed; but ... the Romish Church, one and all. Nay, these last are so vehement in your defence, that, in the famed Council of Trent, they have decreed: "If any man hold (fiduciam) trust, confidence, or assurance of pardon, to be essential to faith, let him be accursed." '⁸

Wesley might have carried his research further and quoted a further statement made by the same Council:⁹ 'No one can know with a certainty of faith, which cannot be subject to illusion, that he has obtained the grace of God. . . . Except by special revelation, no one can know whom God has chosen unto Himself.'¹⁰ This Council denied that a Christian must have a feeling of assurance before he could be a recipient of saving grace or that this was the only meaning of faith. Assurance was not essential to salvation, nor was a claim to possess it a guarantee that one was saved. This was much in line with Wesley's later teaching.¹¹

Though such a claim to an assurance of salvation was thus discountenanced by the Council of Trent, it must not be overlooked that even the story of the Tridentine controversy reveals that thoughtful people, including Romanists, had been giving serious consideration to the subject of Christian certainty. While Dominicus da Soto, the leader of the Thomists, held that Rome taught the uncertainty of grace, Ambrosius Catherinus, an independent Dominican thinker, argued that *certitudo gratiae* was in harmony with the doctrinal pronouncements of Rome.¹²

Turning to Thomas Aquinas, we find that in his view there were three ways in which a believer could be assured of salvation:

⁶ Sabatier, *The Religions of Authority and the Religion of the Spirit* (1904), p. xxii.
⁷ Written in 1744 and addressed to Richard Smallbroke (Bishop of Lichfield and Coventry).
⁸ *Works*, VIII.23; see *Calvin's Tracts*, III.105.
⁹ 1545–7, 1551–2, 1562–3; see Fisher, *History of the Church* (1900), pp. 388ff. The Council of Trent was, of course, the Roman Church's reply to the Reformers; see next chapter.
¹⁰ *Concil. Trident.*, VI.12; cf. Schaff, *The Creeds of Christendom*, II.103.
¹¹ cf. Part II, chs. 2, 3, pp. 61ff., *supra*.   ¹² *E.R.E.*, III.326.

(1) By direct revelation from God.
(2) By himself (*certitudinaliter*).
(3) By various indications (*certitudinaliter per aliqua signa*).

Aquinas believed, however, that much uncertainty attached to these last two agencies. While he subscribed to the view that salvation was gained through the sacrament, he did not take this to imply that the communicant therefore had an inner assurance of divine acceptance. Only by a direct revelation from God can an individual enjoy a sense of inward certainty; but this immediate divine contact is very seldom vouchsafed.[13]

It follows, therefore, that according to Aquinas most Christians must forgo an individual assurance of salvation: *Revelat Deus hoc aliquando aliquibus ex speciali privilegio*.[14]

The analysis of St Thomas's teaching bearing on a certainty of salvation can be carried further.[15] Aquinas holds that we cannot be absolutely sure that we love God with a pure love, but that a measure of certitude can be gained by observing that love exemplified in our lives. In support of his reasoning here, he instances the ease with which a natural affection can be misinterpreted as spiritual or supernatural love.[16]

Thomas admits that it is possible for a person to claim a sense of forgiveness when in fact he is deceived; and that some Christians may be forgiven, though they are not conscious of it. He holds that there are four ways by which we can ascertain whether a claim to conscious pardon be genuine:

(1) Hearing the word of God with joy.[17]
(2) Readiness to do good.
(3) A firm intention of not sinning in future.
(4) Sorrow for past sins.[18]

Aquinas also points out that confession may not produce real forgiveness, if the person, believing himself truly penitent, is nevertheless not properly disposed. This would mean that one could *claim* assurance, but this would be vitiated by its not being set in a spiritual state of justification.[19]

---

[13] Hagenbach, *History of Christian Doctrine*. (Eng. trans., 1880), II.303f.

[14] Aquinas, *Summa Theologica*, II. i. qu. 112, art. 5: 'God reveals this sometimes to some in accordance with a special privilege.' *E.R.E.*, III.326.

[15] I am here greatly indebted to Professor H. Francis Davis, of Oscott College, Birmingham.

[16] Aquinas, *Sent.*, I, art. 4.   [17] cf. John 8^{47}.

[18] Aquinas, *Sent.*, IX, art. 3, qu. ii, *ad lum*.

[19] ibid., XXI, qu. 2, art. 2.

Despite the sparse reference in the medieval Church to an inner sense of certainty, most, if not all, theologians in the Middle Ages would hold the doctrine of the indwelling of the Holy Spirit in a justified Christian.[20] Thomas, for instance, refers to the Spirit's 'enlightening us internally as to what we should do'.[21] He refers to the Christian's being instructed, and his being inwardly moved, by the Spirit, as by a heavenly instinct. The Christian, however, still remains a free agent, since the Spirit operates through the will.[22]

An attitude of religious dependence on the priest could not be expected to commend itself to every member of the medieval Church; more particularly in the light of the gradual, yet distinct, growth of individual consciousness, accelerated by the Renaissance and brought to full bloom at the Reformation.[23] As time passed, there was an increasing disposition to question the validity of the premises on which the Roman Church based its uncompromising pronouncements.

This growing resistance to the corporate power of Roman Catholicism—though remaining for a considerable time inarticulate—finds partial expression in the 'pre-Reformation reformers'; yet even among their ranks there is little clear support for a doctrine of assurance as such.

Wyclif appears to have deprecated an inner certainty of salvation even more categorically than Pope Gregory. His scholastic method identified too closely 'knowing' and 'being'. 'Knowing', as interpreted by Wyclif, had no reference to spiritual assurance or consciousness, but was a purely intellectual conception. Since in Wyclif's theology 'charity' was a correlative of 'grace', he claimed that 'working by right life, ended after God's will, maketh a man God's child'.[24] He went so far as to say that no man, not even a Pope, 'wots whether he be of the Church, or whether he be a limb of the fiend'.

Dr H. Watkin-Jones says that the fact that the Hussites emerged from the Counter-Reformation to become the assurance-preaching Moravians of Wesley's day can be satisfactorily accounted for only by the increasing vitality of their own spiritual experience and a sane perception of its implications.[25]

We have already seen that Aquinas referred to the internal

---

[20] In addition to the evidence that follows, see also the Roman Missal.
[21] *Commentary on Romans*, c. viii, lect. III.   [22] *Commentary on Galatians*, c. ii.
[23] Bett, *Spirit of Methodism*, p. 142.
[24] See *New History of Methodism*, I.22.; Harnack, *History of Dogma*, V.271.
[25] Watkin-Jones, *The Holy Spirit in the Medieval Church*, p. 352 note.

guidance of the Holy Spirit; and it would appear that this activity of the Spirit in the believer was generally accepted by most churchmen in the Middle Ages, though in the earlier centuries it was treated much more objectively than it was by later, and especially by Protestant, theologians. This is partly explained by the fact that in the ancient languages it was difficult to find a word which exactly expresses what we mean by *experience*.

Despite this alleged linguistic difficulty, Dr R. Newton Flew finds the following references to personal religious experience in medieval writers:[26] Rudolf Seeberg holds that in the works of Ratherius of Verona who stresses the practical side of personal religion and the need of conversion,[27] we see the individual soul coming to its own. The account given by Othloh of St Emmeram of his religious life is not unlike that of an early Methodist Class Meeting. He has 'experienced', in his temptations, the presence and power of God.[28] Among others who claim such personal religious experiences are Ivo of Chartres and William of St Thierry.[29]

We shall be devoting two chapters of this book to the relationship of mysticism to the doctrine of assurance.[30] But we must not conclude this very brief survey of the place of Christian certainty in the medieval Church without indicating the importance of the mystics in this period. Dr J. G. Tasker points out that the experience of devout souls cannot be confined within the limits of official definitions. That before the Reformation believers attained to religious certainty cannot be doubted by those who remember how great is the debt which Roman Catholic mysticism owes to two twelfth-century saints—not to mention others—Hugo of St Victor and Bernard of Clairvaux. 'The writings of the former have "a mystical tinge", and the latter knew by experience that Jesus is the "bridegroom" of the individual soul.'[31]

Bernard's hymns, '*Jesu dulcis memoria*' and '*Jesu, dulcedo cordium*', have found their way into the hymnals of most Christian denominations. They breathe the spirit of the certainty of Christ's inner presence and of an assurance of

---

[26] Flew, *The Idea of Perfection in Christian Theology* (1934), p. 220.
[27] Seeberg, *Lehrbuch der Dogmengeschichte*, III.120.
[28] Migne, *P.L.*, 38, 146, 162, 566.
[29] For further instances of this 'experience', see Seeberg, op. cit., III.122f.
[30] Part V, chs. 4, 5, pp. 198ff., *infra*.   [31] J. G. Tasker, *E.R.E.*, III.326.

personal salvation.[32] In one of his sermons, Bernard says that God's Spirit, bearing witness, may persuade our spirits that we are the children of God. 'That which lieth hid concerning us in the heart of the Father, may by his Spirit be revealed unto us, and the same Spirit testifying unto us may persuade our spirits that we are the sons of God.'[33] 'What soul among you all', asks Bernard, 'but hath at some times felt the Spirit of His Son in his secret conscience, crying, Abba, Father?' Certainty and serenity can be found in contemplation of the Passion of our Lord. This leads to a knowledge of God's love and a sense of forgiveness.[34]

And so it was in the medieval Church, with its emphasis on externalism in religion and on the corporate authority of Rome, that a mystic experience of conscious contact with God proved to be an 'inner light' that no one could put out.

[32] See *Methodist Hymn Book* (1933), Nos. 106, 108, 109.
[33] Bernard of Clairvaux, *Sermon V, De Dedicat.*
[34] In *Cant. S.*, 43. 3, 4, 20. 2; 11. 7; 61. 4.

CHAPTER THREE

THE REFORMERS

THE Reformation was a new day in the developing self-consciousness, not only of the European States, but of the Christian believer.[1] Protestantism, according to Dr W. A. Brown, began as a reassertion of the rights of the individual. The protest against Rome took different forms. Luther emphasized justification by faith, Calvin the divine decree; the substance was the same. 'In either case, the necessity of ecclesiastical mediation was denied, and the essence of religion found in the relation between the individual soul and God.'[2]

The view that the Reformation only served to replace the infallibility of the Pope by the infallibility of the Bible[3] should be considered in the light of a statement by Auguste Sabatier: 'The Reformers were very far from that Protestant dogma of the exterior and absolute authority of the Bible which the succeeding age elaborated to rob the Christian conscience of that liberty which this age had so dearly bought.'[4] Gwatkin holds that the first principle of the Reformation was the belief that the knowledge of God is direct and personal. But if the knowledge of God is direct and personal, it must in the end be a personal experience depending on personal character, not on any action of other men.[5]

On the other hand, it must be admitted that this turn of the tide from the authoritarianism of the medieval Church to the emphasis on individual consciousness opened the flood gates to an unhealthy subjectivism characteristic of certain religious sects subsequent to the Reformation. Dr James Stalker says that some went so far as to believe themselves favoured with an illumination which left even the Bible far behind.[6] Moreover, there was also traceable in Protestantism a strong disposition to ignore the importance of the period between the closing of the canon and the Reformation.[7]

[1] See Allen, *Continuity of Christian Thought* (1895), pp. 241ff.
[2] Brown, *Christian Theology in Outline* (1907), p. 109.
[3] R. E. Davies, *The Problem of Authority in the Continental Reformers* (1946), p. 12 and *passim*.
[4] Sabatier, *The Religions of Authority and the Religion of the Spirit*, p. 160.
[5] H. M. Gwatkin, *The Knowledge of God*, II.221f.
[6] Stalker, *The Expositor*, Vol. VI, Sixth Series, p. 344.   [7] ibid., p. 345.

While welcoming the liberty inherited by the individual believer at the Reformation—a liberty without which no personal experience of assurance can long survive—we must not overlook the confusing elements that followed in its wake. Some 'turned the letter of Scripture into a more rigid law than the decretals, while others decried reason, and made the knowledge of God purely emotional—as if there could be a personal knowledge without an element of reasoning. Others again in one age turned it into a jangle of scholasticism, and in another into a wilderness of mechanical criticism—as if there could be a personal knowledge without an element of feeling. . . . New truth is always a sword of division; and when it is a far-reaching principle which leaves no human thought unaltered, we must expect the old to struggle against the new for centuries.'[8]

Wesley believed that the doctrine of assurance was taught by the Reformers. In a letter to Richard Tompson on 25th July 1755, Wesley says: 'And I really conceive, both from the *Harmonia Confessionum* and whatever else I have occasionally read, that all the Reformed Churches of Europe did once believe "Every true Christian has the divine evidence of his being in favour with God".'[9] In the following year, Wesley writes to the same correspondent: 'I know likewise that Luther, . . . and many other (if not all) of the Reformers frequently and strongly assert that every believer is conscious of his acceptance with God, and that by a supernatural evidence, which if any choose to term immediate revelation he may.'[10]

Dr Workman asks what could be nearer the Methodist doctrine of assurance than the following words of Luther: 'Faith is a living deliberate confidence in the grace of God, so certain that for it one could die a thousand deaths, and such confidence and knowledge of divine grace makes us joyous, intrepid, and cheerful towards God and all creation.'[11]

In reference to assurance, there seem to be two distinct elements in Luther's theology:

(1) One is fittingly represented in the words of Dorner. 'Christian certainty', he says, 'is the Divinely effected certainty that we are known, loved, and reconciled by God (1 Corinthians 8³; Galatians 4⁹), since He regards us in Christ. . . . The Holy Spirit . . . creates a firm because a Divine consciousness. The

[8] Gwatkin, op. cit., p. 223.   [9] *Letters*, III.137.
[10] ibid., p. 159 (5th February 1756).   [11] Workman, *N.H.M.*, I.23f.

knowledge of man is exalted to divine knowledge. It is Divine as to its contents, for it knows God and His thought of men. But it is also Divinely certain of these contents, without ceasing to be human.'[12]

(2) The other strain in Luther's teaching is the view that assurance is based, not merely on the Bible as such, but on the Scriptures as these are interpreted by the believer with the aid of the Spirit. This explains why Lutheran theologians have tended to regard the *Testimonium Spiritus Sancti* as the guarantee of Scriptural truth rather than of a personal certainty of salvation. More recent followers of Luther, however, have thought of objective certainty in terms not of the Bible itself, but of the Christ as presented in the Bible.[13]

We must be careful to distinguish the Reformers' *Testimonium Spiritus Sancti* from Wesley's doctrine of assurance. In describing the authoritative character of Scripture, 'the Reformers always insisted that its recognition was awakened in believers by that operation which they called the witness of the Holy Spirit. Just as God Himself makes us know and feel the sense of pardon in an inward experience by a faith which is His own work, so they believed that, by an operation of the same Spirit, believers were enabled to recognize that God Himself is speaking to us authoritatively in and through the words of Scripture.'[14]

The relationship obtaining between Luther's doctrine of assurance and the idea of Biblical inspiration is dealt with by Sabatier: 'Thence came a personal certainty of faith, as far above the letter of Scripture . . . as above the traditions of the Romish Church and the bulls and decrees of the Papacy. . . . The certitude of his [Luther's] faith does not rest upon a previous theory of the infallibility of Scripture; it is his theory of Scripture which rests upon the inward certitude of his faith.'[15]

Dr Mackinnon points out that Luther's conception of the assurance of salvation differs from the Nominalist view of *fiducia*, which was based on the confidence that God will ultimately accept the works of the believer as meritorious in His sight and grant him salvation accordingly. Luther, on the

---

[12] Dorner, *System of Christian Certainty* (Eng. trans., 1880), I.153ff.
[13] Robinson, *The Christian Experience of the Holy Spirit* (1940), pp. 181f.
[14] Lindsay, *The History of the Reformation*, I.461.
[15] Sabatier, *The Religions of Authority and the Religion of the Spirit*, pp. 161f.

other hand, bases it solely on faith in God's gracious promise of salvation, begetting the confident hope that He will bring to pass what we have not merited and cannot merit in any sense. An indispensable condition of its realization is self-distrust, not self-confidence (*securitas*).[16]

Luther denied that the believer must remain in a state of uncertainty concerning his salvation. 'Let us assure ourselves that God sendeth the Holy Ghost into our hearts. This I say to confute that pernicious doctrine of the Papists, which taught that no man certainly knows whether he be in the favour of God or no; whereby they utterly defaced the doctrine of faith, tormented men's consciences, banished Christ quite out of the Church, and darkened and denied all the benefits of the Holy Ghost.'[17]

Dr H. B. Workman raises the question as to why assurance did not become a real factor in the life of the Protestant Churches? The answer is not far to seek. Owing to the obscuration of Luther's primary positions through his conflict with the 'Enthusiasts' and the Anabaptists, 'his conception of faith became more and more intellectual, till at last it comprised little beyond the assent of the mind to certain articles of an orthodox creed'.[18]

As Luther grew older, his theology became almost as scholastic as the Scotists and Thomists, whom at first he had so strenuously opposed. In this respect, Melanchthon followed in his wake. When faith is thus reduced to the assent of the intellect, says Dr Workman, 'it ceases to have that guarantee or assurance which faith can have only when it is the consciousness of the soul transformed with the passion of love'.[19] Against this intellectualism of Luther, German Pietism and Schleiermacher's stress on experience would appear to be a reaction.

Calvinistic principles were held by many of John Wesley's contemporaries in the eighteenth century, and gave rise to numerous polemical writings both inside and outside the Methodist fold.[20] This is partially explained by the fact that Wesley's doctrine of assurance involved as a necessary corollary an Arminian theory of the atonement.[21] Christian certainty in the Calvinistic creed has been vitiated by its association with

[16] Mackinnon, *Luther and the Reformation*, I.197f.
[17] Luther, *Commentary on Galatians*, iv, 6.
[18] Workman, *New History of Methodism*, I.24.   [19] ibid., p. 25.
[20] Rattenbury, *Wesley's Legacy to the World*, pp. 92ff.
[21] Workman, op. cit., I.34.

the doctrine of election.[22] 'In connexion with the belief in unconditional election, the doctrine in Calvinism takes the form of assurance of final salvation.'[23] Wesley always insisted that his doctrine was not an assurance that we shall *persevere* in a state of salvation, but an assurance that we *are now* in such a state.[24]

Calvin's exposition of assurance, however, is not without relevance to our inquiry. Its positive value has been admirably summed up by Dr W. Adams Brown. 'The true significance of Christian assurance', he says, 'has been often obscured by its association with the doctrine of election. The result was to turn men's thoughts from the present to the future, and concentrate them upon final salvation. None the less, it is true that since the God with whom we have present communion through Christ is at the same time the Lord of all life, our thought reaches out inevitably to the future, and the consciousness of present acceptance and forgiveness passes imperceptibly into hope of final salvation.'[25]

Calvin's linking of assurance with election was characterized, not only by stress on a certainty of future as well as of present salvation, but also by the fact that the 'ultimate ground of certainty—the immutable Divine decree—was as external as the special revelation granted to favoured Roman Catholics'.[26]

Calvin deals at length with the assurance of being one of the elect. He holds that the enjoyment of their election is in some measure communicated when the elect are called; though election is doubtful and ineffectual till confirmed by faith. Moreover, since we are elected in Christ, we cannot find the certainty of our election in ourselves. That predestination renders assurance of salvation somewhat insecure is revealed in the two questions which Calvin admits believers are sure to ask: 'Whence our salvation but from the election of God? But what proof have we of our election?'[27]

Calvin teaches that the imputed righteousness of Christ gives us boldness to call upon God, for without this we should

[22] Westminster Confession, Art. XVIII, *De certitudine gratiae et salutis*; Schaff, *Creeds of Christendom*, III.638.
[23] Article on 'Assurance' in *The New Schaff-Herzog Encyclopaedia of Religious Knowledge*.
[24] *Letters*, I.255; cf. *Works*, VII.376f.; Church, *The Early Methodist People* (1948), p. 103.
[25] Brown, *Christian Theology in Outline*, p. 387.
[26] Dr J. G. Tasker, *E.R.E.*, III.328.
[27] Calvin, *Institutes of the Christian Religion* (Eng. trans., 1845), III.24.

have no access, Scripture teaching that we never shall be heard while in doubt and disquietude (Hebrews 11⁶; James 1⁶, ⁷). 'Therefore we hold that our sovereign good and repose consists in being assured of the forgiveness of sins, by the faith which we have in Jesus Christ, seeing that this is the key which opens the gate that leads us to God.'[28]

Another passage in Calvin's writings emphasizes the centrality of Christ in an experience of assurance. 'All hope, and the assurance of all confidence, ought to be in the precious blood of Christ, which was shed because of us and our salvation.' In Him alone we have 'the confirmation of the Holy Spirit, who bears witness with our spirit that we are the children of God'.[29]

Calvin has significant comments on three of the passages which figure prominently in the Biblical basis of Wesley's doctrine of assurance.[30]

(1) With reference to Romans 8¹⁶, Calvin writes: 'The Spirit of God gives us such a testimony that, when He is our guide and teacher, our spirit is made assured of the adoption of God; for our mind of itself, without this preceding testimony of the Spirit, could not convey to us this assurance. . . . When the Spirit testifies to us that we are the children of God, He . . . pours into our hearts such confidence that we venture to call God our Father.'

In another passage, Calvin speaks as though assurance were *essential* to salvation: 'Let this truth stand sure—that no one can be called a son of God, who does not know himself to be such; and this is called knowledge by John, in order to set forth its certainty (1 John 5¹⁹, ²⁰).'[31]

(2) Commenting on the phrase, 'And because ye are sons' in Galatians 4⁶, Calvin writes: 'This adoption must have preceded the testimony of the adoption given by the Holy Spirit; but the effect is the sign of the cause. In venturing . . . to call God your Father, you have the advice and direction of the Spirit of Christ; therefore it is certain that you are the sons of God.'[32]

---

[28] *Calvin's Tracts*, II.145f.

[29] *The Adultero-German Interim*, ch. VIII; 'Of Confidence in the Forgiveness of Sins', *Tracts*, III.201f.

[30] See Part III, pp. 103ff., *supra*.

[31] Calvin, *Commentaries on . . . Romans* (Calvin Translation Society, 1849), pp. 299f.

[32] *Commentaries on . . . Galatians*, p. 120.

(3) Calvin understands the writer[33] of Hebrews 6[11] to mean: 'As they who profess the Christian faith were distracted by various opinions, or were as yet entangled in many superstitions, he bids them to be so fixed in firm faith, as no longer to vacillate, ... suspended between alternate winds of doubts.' Calvin adds a further interpretation of this verse: 'It is a full assurance, πληροφορία, an undoubting persuasion, when the godly mind settles it with itself, that it is not right to call in question what God, who cannot deceive or lie, has spoken.'[34]

In reference to the findings of the Council of Trent on the subject of assurance, Calvin says that 'they inveigh against what they call the Vain Confidence of Heretics. This consists ... in our holding it as certain that our sins are forgiven, and resting in this certainty. But if such certainty makes heretics ... where is the peace of which Paul discourses in the fifth chapter of Romans ... where is the boldness of which Paul elsewhere speaks (Ephesians 3[12]) ... boldness, which is certainly something more than certainty? ... Faith is destroyed as soon as certainty is taken away.'[35]

Calvin places on the Council the onus of explaining 'how πληροφορία (full assurance) can be reconciled with doubt. For Paul makes it the perpetual attendant of faith. ... Were Paul in doubt, he would not exult over death and write as he does in the eighth chapter of Romans, when he boasts of being so certain of the love of God that nothing can turn him from the persuasion.'[36]

Apart from the uncertainty as to whether an individual is among the elect, the doctrine of assurance is weakened by Calvin's view that human nature involves the possibility of illusion, which leads to 'the constant struggle of the faithful with their own distrust'. Such an attenuated doctrine of Christian certainty would not commend itself to the Wesleys. These limitations led Sabatier to conclude that, in the Reformers' teaching, the 'witness of the Spirit' was not a *saving* witness so much as a witness of moral judgement.[37]

Dr W. B. Pope holds that assurance, in the Calvinistic system, both falls below and goes beyond the teaching of the Bible. The evidence which he adduces in support of this view we summarize as follows:

[33] Paul, according to Calvin.   [34] Calvin, *Commentaries on ... Hebrews*, p. 145.
[35] *Calvin's Tracts*, III.125.
[36] ibid., p. 126; cf. Schaff, *Creeds of Christendom*, II.103.
[37] Watkin-Jones, *The Holy Spirit in the Medieval Church*, p. 353.

(1) Calvinism falls short of the Biblical standard:

(*a*) By distinguishing too sharply between assurance and faith, and by emphasizing the external grounds of certainty at the cost of the internal.

(*b*) By making assurance a special privilege of the few, who through much discipline attain it as a gift of God.

(*c*) By confusing the assurance of present faith with the assurance of hope.

(2) Calvinism goes beyond the teaching of Scripture:

(*a*) By asserting that assurance is indefectible.

(*b*) By presenting certainty as an independent fruit of faith and a high attainment of the spiritual life.

(*c*) By treating assurance as a Divinely inwrought confidence of an eternal salvation.[38]

It might appear that we have given a disproportionate amount of space, not only to the significance of the Reformation, but also to the teaching of Luther and Calvin. But this is the measure of their importance both in this brief historical survey and in their relationship to the life and thought of the Wesleys.

[38] Pope, *Compendium of Christian Theology*, III.124f.

CHAPTER FOUR

THE SEVENTEENTH CENTURY

'THE course of the Reformation in England during the sixteenth century', says Dr H. Wheeler Robinson, 'was largely dominated by political considerations. It was not until the seventeenth that there was free play for the consciousness of God's direct activity in religious life. This is the feature which makes the seventeenth century more interesting than any other in the history of English religion.'[1] In this short chapter, therefore, we shall briefly consider some of the evidence for Assurance in the century which immediately preceded the age of the Wesleys.

Despite the fact that the establishing of Anglicanism as a State Church lacked the fervour of a personal founder, enjoyed by Lutheranism and Calvinism, and was in its inception political rather than religious,[2] there can be no doubt that the idea of an inner certainty of salvation was laying its hold on the minds of men.

In the *Lambeth Articles*, compiled by Dr Whittaker and approved by several bishops and the University of Cambridge, it is stated that 'a man truly faithful, that is, such an one who is endued with a justifying faith, is certain, with a full assurance of faith, of the remission of sins'.[3]

'Prompted by Hooker', says Dr H. Watkin-Jones, 'Protestant divines in England during the seventeenth century gave, on the whole, increasingly cordial approval to the doctrine of assurance.'[4] Richard Hooker wrote: 'The Spirit of God hath been given to us, to assure us that we are the sons of God, to embolden us to call upon Him as our Father.'[5]

John Smith, the Cambridge Platonist, in his *Select Discourses*, distinguishes the testimony of our own spirit from that of the Spirit of God by referring to the former as 'our continual feast' and to the latter as 'a superadded taste out of God's right hand,

---

[1] Robinson, *The Christian Experience of the Holy Spirit* (1940), p. 259.

[2] J. R. Green, *History of the English People*, II.155, 158ff.

[3] *Lambeth Articles*, VI; cf. Articles of the Church of Ireland (1615), Art. VIII; see also Hall's *Harmony of Protestant Confessions* (1842), p. 521.

[4] Watkin-Jones, *The Holy Spirit from Arminius to Wesley* (1929), p. 306.

[5] Hooker, *Sermon on Certainty of Faith*.

as it were a piece of heaven in the soul . . . like a morning light, chasing away all our dark and gloomy doubtings before it'.[6]

In tracing the evidence for Christian certainty in the seventeenth century, we cannot neglect the references in the writings of the Puritans and the Nonconformist divines.[7] It is noteworthy that some of these writers place the direct witness after the indirect witness of the believer's own spirit. Nevertheless, the general tendency is to interpret assurance as signifying an inner sense of *present* salvation, conveyed as a privilege to the Christian by the direct testimony of the Holy Spirit.[8]

The Confession of Faith issued by the Westminster Assembly of Divines shows the relationship of assurance to faith and to the Spirit of adoption. 'This certainly is not a bare conjectural and probable persuasion, but an infallible assurance of faith, founded upon the testimony of the Spirit of adoption witnessing with our spirit that we are the children of God.'[9]

Dr John Owen held that assurance can be conveyed 'from Him immediately unto them that are concerned in it'. He is careful to point out, however, that assurance is not of the *essence* of saving faith: 'It is one thing to have holiness really thriving in the soul, another for that soul to know it and to be satisfied in it; and these things may be separated.' Dr Owen also maintained that salvation is accomplished more by faith than by feeling: 'we live by faith, and not at all by sense'.[10] In his work on *Communion with God*, Owen explains that the 'Spirit worketh joy in the hearts of believers immediately by himself, without the consideration of any other acts or works of his, or the interpositions of any reasonings, or deductions, or conclusions. This does not arise from our reflex consideration of the love of God, but rather gives occasion thereunto.' On another page, he adds: 'The Comforter comes; and by a word of promise, or otherwise, overpowers the heart with a comfortable persuasion . . . that he is a child of God.'[11]

From the publication of Dr Owen's views on assurance, the doctrine of the direct witness of the Spirit was destined to

---

[6] John Smith (1618–52), *Select Discourses* (1660), pp. 449f.

[7] See Dr G. F. Nuttall, *The Holy Spirit in Puritan Faith and Experience* (1946), especially ch. III. on 'The Witness of the Spirit', pp. 48ff.

[8] Charles Prest, *An Essay on the Witness of the Holy Spirit to the Adoption of the Christian Believer* (1848), p. 55.

[9] *Confession of Faith* (third edition, 1688), article on 'Assurance'.

[10] John Owen (1616–83), *Concerning the Holy Spirit*, pp. 234, 470ff.

[11] *Communion with God* (1657), *Works* (Orme's edition), X.310, 295.

encounter a more critical reception in England, especially by Anglican theologians.[12]

We conclude our historical survey by considering the relevance of Quakerism. Dr H. B. Workman minimizes, not only the influence of Moravianism on Methodism, but also that of the Quakers.[13] He plainly errs in stating that 'Wesley never mentions Fox'.[14] It is true that there are only a *few* references to George Fox, or to Quakerism; and these few are usually unsympathetic.[15] But the principles of the Society of Friends cannot be excluded from Wesley's religious thought—any more than the influence of Darwin can be discounted in the writings of modern theologians—purely on the ground that the source of the influence is never, or seldom, mentioned.

It is clear that there are affinities between the Friends' doctrine of the 'inner light' and the doctrine of assurance. Christian certainty pervades Fox's assertion: 'I was commanded to turn people to that inner light ... by which all might know their salvation.'[16] Dr Rufus M. Jones, an eminent Quaker writer, has shown that the Quakers universalized the principle which Luther made fundamental in salvation—namely, that the final test of everything in religion is the test of experience.[17]

There is the ring of assurance in what amounts to the testimony of George Fox: 'When all my hopes ... in all men were gone, so that I had nothing outwardly to help me, nor could I tell what to do ... then I heard a voice which said, There is one, even Christ Jesus, that can speak to thy condition; and when I heard it, my heart did leap for joy.'[18]

While Quakerism has been widely condemned for its alleged rejection of the outward forms of religion,[19] the Quaker doctrine of the 'inner light' came as a relief to the theory of verbal inspiration which was held by the Puritans.[20] While the Quakers did not coin the phrase 'inner light', they have undoubtedly contributed to its content. The phrase has been defined as 'the doctrine that there is something Divine, "something of God" in the human soul'.[21] The early Quakers sought

---

[12] Watkin-Jones, op. cit., p. 309. [13] *New History of Methodism*, I.40, 54.
[14] See *Wesley's Works*, VI.263, 328.
[15] cf. Dr J. H. Whiteley, *Wesley's England* pp. 16, 18.
[16] *Journal of George Fox* (1901 ed.), I.36.
[17] Quoted by Dr J. G. Tasker in *E.R.E.*, III.328. [18] *Journal*, I.11.
[19] See Wand, *History of the Modern Church*, p. 131.
[20] *The Doctrine of the Holy Spirit* (Headingley Lectures), p. 88.
[21] Rufus Jones, *Social Law in the Spiritual World* (1923 ed.), p. 149.

to revive in their 'society' the 'spiritual immediacy' of the primitive Church. This principle is exemplified in the life and thought of representative Quakers.

At a meeting at Swannington in 1654, Isaac Penington 'felt the presence and power of the Most High. ... I have met with my God; I have met with my Saviour. ... I have felt the healings drop into my soul from under His wings. I have met with the true knowledge, the knowledge of life.' On a later page, Penington writes: 'The light of God's Spirit is a certain and infallible rule, and the eye that sees it is a certain eye.'[22]

Robert Barclay says that 'when I came into the silent assemblies of God's people, I felt a secret power among them which touched my heart, and as I gave way unto it, I found the evil weakening in me and the good raised up'. He goes on to say that the witness of God arises in the heart and the Light of Christ shines.[23]

A distinction must be drawn, however, between this 'inner light', as understood by the Quakers, and Wesley's teaching on an inner illumination effected by the direct testimony of God's Spirit. 'The Witness of the Spirit', says Dr H. Maldwyn Hughes, 'is conceived of as operating *ab extra*, the inner light *ab intra*. The former is a development of Christian experience, the latter is a presupposition. The inner light has been compared with the Stoic σπερματικὸς λόγος and *anima mundi*.'[24]

'By this Seed, Grace, and Word of God', Barclay explains, 'we understand a Spiritual, Heavenly, and Invisible Principle, in which God as Father, Son, and Spirit dwells: a measure of which Divine and Glorious Life is in all men, as a seed which of its own nature draws, invites, and inclines to God.'[25] The reference here is not to the general idea of the indwelling Christ, but only that Christ is present in the Seed.[26] Nor is this light within to be identified with conscience or reason. A man must wait for it till it works powerfully in the soul and then he will come to know salvation.[27]

In a letter to the Editor of the *London Magazine* on 12th December 1760, Wesley distinguishes between the interpretation attached to the inner light by the Quakers and by the Methodists. He points out that the Methodists allow no inward

---

[22] *Works of Isaac Penington* (1861), I.37f., 67.
[23] Barclay (1648–90), 'Apology' in *Works* (1831), II.355ff.   [24] *E.R.E.*, V.633.
[25] Barclay, *Apology* (1736), pp. 137f.   [26] ibid., p. 143.   [27] ibid., pp. 141f.

light but what is subservient to the written Word and to be judged thereby,[28]

The criticism is sometimes advanced that the Quakers undervalued the objective and historical aspects of Christianity, and that their doctrine of the 'inner light' lent itself to unbridled individualism and to the depreciation of the intellect.[29] This charge has been countered by leading writers on Quakerism. 'The early Friends', says Dr Rufus Jones, 'did not minimize the importance of the Scriptures, or of the historic Christ and His work for human redemption. . . . One of the great fruits of the Incarnation and Passion, according to their view, was the permanent presence of Christ among men in an inward and spiritual manner, bringing to effect *within* what His *outward life* had made possible.'[30] Edward Grubb holds that the Holy Spirit is a present possession of the Church, and concludes that in the unity of the Christian consciousness there is an authority, not absolute and final, but real and living, which has its place in correcting the vagaries of individual illumination.[31]

[28] *Letters*, IV.123f.
[29] Dr H. M. Hughes, *The Theology of Experience*, pp. 120ff.
[30] Rufus Jones, op. cit., pp. 167f.
[31] Grubb, *Authority and the Light Within* (1909), p. 25.

Part Five
Assurance and its Validity

CHAPTER ONE

THE CHARGE OF 'ENTHUSIASM'

THE Methodist claim to an inner sense of certainty was assailed from many quarters. Wesley, however, was a well-informed and vigorous defender of his teaching on the Spirit's witness. But these attacks and Wesley's defence can be appreciated only when they are viewed in relation to the climate of thought prevalent in the eighteenth century.

Deism was the dominant creed of the time; and it is not difficult to detect elements in this school of thought which would militate against any doctrine or experience of assurance.

The more important contributory causes of this current thought include John Toland's *Christianity not Mysterious*, Shaftesbury's *Characteristics*, Antony Collin's *Discourse of Freethinking* (1713), *Grounds and Reasons of Christian Religion* (1724), and *Scheme of Literal Prophecy* (1726); and Matthew Tindal's *Christianity as Old as Creation* (1730).

The sub-title of Toland's work is significant: 'A Discourse showing that there is nothing in the Gospel contrary to Reason, nor above it, and that no Christian doctrine can be properly called a mystery'. Moreover, it could be argued that John Locke's *Essay on the Human Understanding* (1690) and the *Reasonableness of Christianity* supplied the Deists with philosophical principles, though this was far from being Locke's design. 'Locke repudiated Toland as his disciple', says Dr Plummer, 'but Toland claimed Locke as his teacher.'[1]

This gives support to the view that Deism is best understood in relation to the development of philosophical, rather than of religious, ideas.[2] In some limited degree, the Deistic writers expressed views somewhat in line with Wesley's own thought, as, for instance, Shaftesbury's emphasis on an intuitive moral faculty, and also the Deists' stress on an appeal to human reason or on common sense.[3] On the other hand, the Deists' support of Biblical criticism and their deprecation of all supernatural elements in religion were directed against the foundation on which Wesley's doctrine of assurance was built.

[1] Plummer, *The Church of England in the Eighteenth Century*, p. 99.
[2] *E.R.E.*, IV.537.   [3] Whiteley, *Wesley's Anglican Contemporaries*, p. 52.

As Dr W. R. Cannon has pointed out, men no longer started with the premises of revealed religion, but, treating their own discoveries as basic, called into question the primary assumptions of the faith.[4]

In such a sphere of thought, we can understand why so many people looked with great disfavour upon the appeals to the feelings and upon every form of 'enthusiasm'.[5] This so called 'enthusiasm' has been defined by Dr Whiteley as 'something akin to fanaticism and nastiness, something abnormal and common, something allied to buffoonery, something that was exaggerated, simulated feeling or uncurbed, false eccentricity'.[6]

Dr Sugden finds three causes for this charge of 'enthusiasm' against the doctrine of assurance:

(1) The extravagant claims of many of the Puritans to special divine illumination.[7]
(2) The horror of anything approaching presumption in religion.[8]
(3) The unspiritual character of the period, and its passion for cold correctness and good form.[9]

This antipathy was reinforced by two other causes—one political, the other temperamental:

(1) 'The staunch Toryism of the age,' says Dr Workman, 'felt that there was danger to the constitution in the presumption of ignorant underlings to a knowledge denied their betters.'[10] Confirmation of this is found in a letter written by the Duchess of Buckingham to the Countess of Huntingdon.[11]
(2) The opposition of the English to a new idea. Never before in the history of the Church since the writings of St Paul had the doctrine of assurance been so clearly enunciated.[12]

No charge was levelled against the Methodists as frequently

[4] Cannon, *The Theology of John Wesley*, p. 16.
[5] Lecky, *History of England in the Eighteenth Century*, III.3f.
[6] Whiteley, *Wesley's Anglican Contemporaries*, p. 59; cf. Augustine Birrell, *John Wesley: Some Aspects of the Eighteenth Century in England*, pp. 8ff.
[7] See W. H. Carnegie, *Anglicanism*, pp. 115ff.
[8] cf. Susanna Wesley, *Journal*, II.267.
[9] Sugden, *Standard Sermons*, I.201f.; cf. Simon, *John Wesley and the Religious Societies*, I.257.
[10] *New History of Methodism*, I.20.
[11] Tyerman, *Life of the Rev. George Whitefield* (London, 1890), I.160f.
[12] cf. Pope, *Compendium of Christian Theology*, III.128f.

THE CHARGE OF 'ENTHUSIASM'

as the charge of enthusiasm.[13] It is not our purpose to attempt a detailed examination of these numerous attacks. Dr Sugden gives a representative list in his Standard Edition of Wesley's *Sermons*.[14] An almost complete list appears in Richard Green's *Anti-Methodist Publications*.[15] We limit ourselves to those attacks that have an important bearing on the doctrine of assurance.

In his *Dissertation on Enthusiasm*, Thomas Green, an Anglican vicar, held that assurance was an 'extraordinary gift of the Spirit' which ceased when the canon of Scripture was closed. 'When persons affirm, that they are absolutely sure of their own salvation in particular, and look on others, who fall short of their confidence, as in a dangerous way—this is a mark of spiritual pride; a persuasion rather proceeding from the spirit of delusion than the infallible Spirit of God.'[16]

Writing in 1757, Theophilus Evans says: 'The presumptuous doctrine of the assurance of pardon, present and future, and the certainty of salvation (whereof the two champions[17] do make such a rant in their Journals) does naturally fill the head with spiritual pride, and induces a false and fatal security, and the neglect of future endeavours.'[18]

Evans paints a somewhat gruesome picture depicting the way in which the Methodist preachers played on the feelings of their hearers. 'The manner of the itinerants' holding-forth is generally very boisterous and shocking, and adapted to the best of their skill to alarm the imagination, and to raise a ferment in the passions, often attended with screaming and trembling of the body.'[19]

The Bishop of Lichfield argues that the Methodists' claim to a 'testimony of the Spirit' as a privilege Christians can enjoy now is a misapplication by 'enthusiasts' of a Scriptural passage which refers only to the early Church.[20]

It is significant that the Fellows of St Mary Magdalen College, Oxford, would grant Charles Graves a testimonial in 1740 only on condition that he signed a document in which the

---

[13] cf. Bishop George Lavington's *Enthusiasm of Methodists and Papists compared* (London, 1749–51); *New History of Methodism*, I.19ff.

[14] Sugden, op. cit., II.341f. [15] London, 1902.

[16] Lomas Green, *Dissertation on Enthusiasm* (London, 1755), pp. 1, 2, 138.

[17] viz., *John Wesley and George Whitefield*.

[18] Theophilus Evans, *History of Modern Enthusiasm* (London, 1757), p. 117.

[19] ibid., p. 119. [20] *Works*, VIII.83f.

182   THE DOCTRINE OF ASSURANCE

Methodists and 'their pretensions to an extraordinary and inward feeling of the Holy Spirit' were renounced.[21]

Dr Gibson, Bishop of London, maintained that 'enthusiasm' in Wesley's time was a failure to distinguish the ordinary from the extraordinary gifts of the Holy Spirit—the latter being enjoyed exclusively by the primitive Church. By reference to Whitefield's *Journal*, the Bishop asserted that the Methodists claimed 'more than ordinary assurances of a special Presence with them'.[22] In an interview with Wesley on 18th August 1739, Bishop Butler said: 'Sir, the pretending to extraordinary revelations and gifts of the Holy Ghost is a horrid thing—a very horrid thing!'[23]

Bishop William Warburton interprets the work of Wesley in terms of the 'abuses of fanaticism'; and holds that his teaching concerning 'the direct witness of the Spirit', though couched in Biblical language, is neither truly Scriptural nor historical.[24]

It would be easy to quote further charges of 'enthusiasm' against the doctrine of assurance.[25] But the foregoing should suffice. Our next question concerns the extent to which the early Methodists merit the condemnation levelled against them.

It must be admitted that in the early days of the Revival there were scenes which could only be a disservice to the Methodist cause and which provided critics with data for a charge of 'enthusiasm'. Both the preaching and the singing appear to have contributed to an exaggerated and undesirable emotionalism.[26]

An instance of this is given by Wesley himself on 15th June 1739, when he was preaching on the 'full assurance of faith' (Hebrews 10[22]). Wesley writes in his *Journal*: 'While I was earnestly inviting all sinners to "enter into the holiest" by this

[21] *Journal*, III.40.
[22] *The Bishop of London's Pastoral Letter to the People of His Diocese*, Second ed. (London, 1739), pp. 45f.
[23] *Journal*, II.257; Simon, *John Wesley and the Religious Societies*, p. 314.
[24] Warburton, *The Doctrine of Grace; or the Office and Operations of the Holy Spirit Vindicated from the Insults of Infidelity, and the Abuses of Fanaticism* ... (London, 1763); *Works*, VIII.237–455; see Wesley's Correspondence with Bishop Warburton, *Works*, IX.117–73.
[25] 'Assurance as the privilege of *all* believers was denied by "most of the serious dissenters" '.—*Minutes* (1747); Watkin-Jones, *The Holy Spirit from Arminius to Wesley*, p. 317.
[26] Note the comparison drawn by W. H. Carnegie between eighteenth-century Methodism and Rousseauism, *Anglicanism* (1925), pp. 63f.

"new and living way" many of those that heard began to call upon God with strong cries and tears. Some sank down, and there remained no strength in them; others exceedingly trembled and quaked; some were torn with a kind of convulsive motion in every part of their bodies, and that so violently that often four or five persons could not hold one of them.'[27]

A scene savouring even more of what modern psychologists would doubtless call 'hysteria' is recorded by John Cennick in a letter addressed to Wesley and dated 12th September 1739: 'On Monday night, I was preaching at the school, on the forgiveness of sins, when numbers cried out with a loud and bitter cry. Indeed, it seemed that the devil and the powers of darkness were come among us. My mouth was stopped. The cries were terrifying. . . . The hurry and confusion cannot be expressed. The whole place seemed to resemble the habitation of apostate spirits; many raving up and down, and crying "The devil will have me. . . . I am gone, gone for ever!" . . . I came to all that desired me. Then they spurned me with all their strength, grinding their teeth, and expressing all the fury that heart can conceive. Their eyes were staring and their faces swollen, and several have since told me that when I drew near, they felt fresh rage, and longed to tear me in pieces.'[28]

It is plain that the clergy of Wesley's day could easily point to such excesses in support of their attack on the Methodists for an 'enthusiastic' expression of assurance. Wesley, however, did not deny the evidence—as we have seen, he produced some —but he would not have agreed that such 'enthusiasm' was necessarily or usually associated with an experience of the Spirit's witness. Nor would he have allowed that such emotionalism was typical of the Methodist services generally.

Dr W. Lawson Jones would regard this 'behaviour' as a sign of intense mental conflict and as not in itself invalidating the experience.[29] Wesley sometimes views such 'enthusiasm' as Satan's opposition to the work of God.[30] In his sermon on 'The Nature of Enthusiasm', however, he urges his followers to avoid those enthusiastic excesses which their critics were ready to quote against the Methodist cause.[31] It is significant that there is little trace of such scenes after 1739.[32]

[27] *Journal*, II.221.
[28] Tyerman, *Life and Times of John Wesley*, I.263; cf. pp. 255ff.
[29] W. L. Jones, *Psychological Study of Religious Conversion*, p. 45f.
[30] *Journal*, III.69, IV.359.   [31] *Sermons*, II.94f.
[32] Tyerman, op. cit., 1.263.

In answer to a tract by John Downes on *Methodism Examined and Exposed*, Wesley sent a letter, dated 17th November 1759: 'For "reason", you say, "cannot do much with an enthusiast, whose first principle is, to have nothing to do with reason, but resolve all his religious opinions and notions into immediate inspiration". Then, by your own account, I am no enthusiast; for I resolve none of my notions into immediate inspiration. . . . I am ready to give up every opinion which I cannot by calm, clear reason defend.'³³

In his *Farther Appeal to Men of Reason and Religion*, Wesley offers an explanation for the frequent use of the term 'enthusiast' against one who holds the Methodist doctrine: 'To object enthusiasm to any person or doctrine is but a decent method of begging the question. It generally spares the objector the trouble of reasoning, and is a shorter and easier way of carrying his cause.' On a later page, Wesley continues: 'I believe, thinking men mean by enthusiasm, a sort of religious madness; a false imagination of being inspired by God. And by an enthusiast, one that fancies himself under the influence of the Holy Ghost, when, in fact, he is not. Let him prove me guilty of this who can.'³⁴

³³ *Works*, IX.105.

³⁴ ibid., VIII.105f. Wesley records in his *Journal* two occasions when he met people who were 'properly enthusiasts': *Journal*, II.130, 136; cf. Charles Wesley's condemnation of the 'French Prophets' in his *Journal*, I.152f.; Simon, I.241

CHAPTER TWO

THE INDICTMENT OF 'HERESY'

WE have considered the climate of thought in the eighteenth century—with Deism as its dominant philosophy—out of which arose the charges of 'enthusiasm' against the doctrine of assurance. Another related product of this intellectual background was the indictment of heresy with which Wesley was confronted in many religious quarters—especially in his contacts with his fellow clergymen.

Dr J. H. Whiteley points out that throughout the century divinity slumbered in the Church. 'Most of the leaders were . . . deeply rooted in the philosophy of the Deists.' Wesley's 'deep consciousness of the witness of the Spirit . . . would perplex and offend an age of deistic thought'.[1] This view is endorsed by Dr Watkin-Jones: 'There was . . . within the Church of England comparatively little sense of God as vitally concerned in the religion of the individual. For this the subtle influence of Deism was doubtless responsible in some measure.'[2]

While we must not jump to the conclusion that the Anglican Church accepted Deistic principles as such—indeed, leading clergymen, including Bishop Butler, did much to destroy this philosophy—the fact is that the drift even of Christian thought is towards the elimination of the supernatural from religion, and the depreciation, if not the denial, of the doctrine of the direct interposition of God in the affairs of human life. Few people in the eighteenth century would deny the claim of orthodoxy to Locke, Berkeley, Bentley, Clarke, Butler, Waterland, or Warburton; but it would appear that 'rationalism had penetrated the ranks of orthodoxy'.[3]

The impulse to pour scorn on the spiritual blindness of Wesley's Anglican contemporaries is curbed when we realize that Wesley himself, prior to Aldersgate, was not impervious to this trend of current thought. As we saw in earlier chapters, when the doctrine of the Spirit's witness was presented by the

---

[1] Whiteley, *Wesley's Anglican Contemporaries*, p. 30.

[2] Watkin-Jones, *The Holy Spirit from Arminius to Wesley*, p. 317.

[3] Dr W. R. Cannon, *The Theology of John Wesley*, p. 19.

Moravians, the Wesleys were 'quite amazed, and looked upon it as a new gospel'.[4]

Though John Wesley's father could testify on his death-bed, 'the inward witness, son, the inward witness—this is the proof, the strongest proof, of Christianity',[5] there is no evidence that it figured as an orthodox feature of his life's ministry. Susanna Wesley 'had scarce heard such a thing mentioned as the having forgiveness of sins now, or God's Spirit bearing witness with our spirit; much less did she imagine that this was the common privilege of all true believers. "Therefore", said she, "I never durst ask it for myself"'.[6]

Wesley asked his mother whether her father (Dr Annesley) had embraced the doctrine of assurance. 'She answered that he had it himself; and declared, a little before his death, that for more than forty years he had no darkness, no fear, no doubt at all of his being "accepted in the beloved". But that, nevertheless, she did not remember to have heard him preach—no, not once—explicitly upon it; whence she supposed he also looked upon it as the peculiar blessing of a few, not as promised to all the people of God.'[7]

In studying the relationship between Wesley and the Moravians, we saw how the founder of Methodism took it for granted that he need only consult the Anglican standards in order to find official refutation of the Moravians' claim to an inner sense of certainty. In this, however, it was Wesley, not the Moravians, for whom there was disillusionment. The more he scrutinized the doctrinal statements of Anglicanism, the more confirmation he found for this 'new gospel',[8] though it cannot be said that he found assurance clearly defined. There was little trace of the Moravians' phraseology.

The entry in the *Journal* for 13th September 1739 reads: 'A serious clergyman[9] desired to know in what points we differed from the Church of England. I answered, "To the best of my knowledge, in none. The doctrines we preach are the doctrines of the Church of England; indeed, the fundamental doctrines of the Church, clearly laid down, both in her

---

[4] Part I, ch. 3, pp. 20ff., *supra*; Part II, ch. 1, pp. 53ff., *supra*; *Journal*, I.471; cf. p. 442.
[5] *New History of Methodism*, I.168; *Letters*, II.135.   [6] *Journal*, II.267.
[7] ibid., II.268; see extract from Dr Annesley's *Sermons* (1661), quoted by Tyerman: *Life and Times of John Wesley*, I.285.
[8] *Works*, VIII.102ff.
[9] Probably 'courteous Mr Howard'; cf. *Charles Wesley's Journal*, 6th July 1739.

THE INDICTMENT OF 'HERESY'   187

Prayers, Articles, and Homilies." '[10] Writing on 1st December 1760 to the Editor of the *Lloyd's Evening Post*, Wesley maintains: 'I do not defend or espouse any other principles ... than those which are plainly contained in the Bible as well as in the Homilies and Book of Common Prayer.'[11]

In 1807, Joseph Nightingale could write: 'Mr. Wesley's chief aim has been to prove that the religious opinions of the Methodists are the same as those taught in the articles and homilies of the Church of England.'[12] The same note is re-echoed nine years later by George Cubitt when he expresses the view that 'the leading doctrines of the people called Methodists' are based on 'the principles of the Reformation, the fundamental doctrines of the Establishment'.[13]

We will assume that Wesley's quotations from the doctrinal standards of the Church prove that his teaching on the Spirit's witness is truly orthodox. How then do we account for the fact that so many of his Anglican contemporaries continued to regard his doctrine of assurance as unorthodox?

The most probable reason would appear to be the widespread ignorance of these doctrinal standards. With reference to Thomas Broughton, Dr Simon writes: 'On one occasion when the Book of Homilies was mentioned, he confessed it was a work he had never read. As he became Secretary of the Society for the Promotion of Christian Knowledge, we presume that he formed an acquaintance with this standard of his own Church.'[14]

That the doctrine of assurance had suffered concealment for a considerable time is made plain by Wesley himself.[15] Dr W. H. Fitchett holds that the doctrine of the Spirit's witness was, in Wesley's day, one of the lost doctrines of Christianity: 'It was in the Thirty-nine Articles, but it had faded out of human memory. It was no longer realized, nor even expected, in human experience. It had become a mere incredibility.'[16]

---

[10] *Journal*, II.274f.; cf. p. 335.

[11] *Letters*, IV.115; see Conference of 1744, when serious consideration was given to the relationship of Methodism to Anglicanism; Simon, *John Wesley and the Methodist Societies*, pp. 210ff.

[12] Nightingale, *Portraiture of Methodism* (London, 1807), p. 443.

[13] Cubitt, *A Brief Defence of the People called Methodists* (1816), p. 11; cf. *Works*, VII.423.

[14] Simon, *John Wesley and the Religious Societies*, p. 186.

[15] Sermon No. 11; *The Doctrine of the Holy Spirit* (Headingly Lectures, 1937), pp. 102f.

[16] Fitchett, *Wesley and His Century*, p. 428; Hastings, *The Christian Doctrine of Faith*, p. 286.

In his *Farther Appeal to Men of Reason and Religion*, Wesley argued by quotations from the Scriptures, the Articles and the Homilies of the Church of England that his teaching was in harmony with the word of God and the standards of the Church.[17] But in that day, comments Dr Simon, 'few people were acquainted with the contents of the Articles and the Homilies, and the readers of this section of the "Appeal" must have doubted the accuracy of Wesley's statements.'[18]

Reference has already been made to the insidious and pervading influence of Deism, with its rationalistic interpretation of Christianity. In such a Deistic and irreligious atmosphere, one could expect that the Articles and Homilies, even if they were known, would be variously interpreted. It follows, therefore, that the Churchmen of the eighteenth century, while unable to deny the accuracy of Wesley's quotations from the doctrinal standards, would not feel committed to his conclusions.

[17] *Works*, VIII.46ff.   [18] Simon, op. cit., p. 155.

CHAPTER THREE

WAS WESLEY'S DOCTRINE ORTHODOX?

THE last two chapters have cleared the ground for our consideration here of the evidence, drawn by Wesley from various sources of Anglican dogma, in support of his constant claim that the doctrine of assurance was confirmed by the doctrinal standards of the Church of England.

We turn to those passages from the 'Daily Service', the 'Collects', the 'Offices', and the 'Homilies', quoted by Wesley in his *Farther Appeal to Men of Reason and Religion*.[1]

'In her Daily Service', writes Wesley, 'she teaches us all to beseech God:

(1) 'To grant us His Holy Spirit, that those things may please Him which we do at this present, and that the rest of our life may be pure and holy.
(2) 'To pray for ... the King that God would "replenish him with the grace of His holy Spirit"; for all the royal family that they may be "endued with His holy Spirit, and enriched with His heavenly grace".
(3) 'For all the clergy and people, that He would "send down upon them the healthful Spirit of His grace".
(4) 'For "the Catholic Church, that it may be guided and governed by His good Spirit"; and for all therein who at any time "make their common supplication unto Him", that "the fellowship" or communication "of the Holy Ghost may be with them all evermore".'[2]

Wesley then quotes the following extracts from the Collects of the Church of England:

(1) 'Grant that we may daily be renewed by Thy Holy Spirit.'[3]
(2) 'Grant that in all our sufferings here, for the testimony of Thy truth, we may by faith behold the glory that shall be revealed, and, "being filled with the Holy Ghost" may love and bless our persecutors.'[4]

---
[1] Published, 1745; *Works*, VIII.102ff.; *Journal*, III.225.   [2] *Works*, VIII.102.
[3] Collect for Christmas Day.   [4] St Stephen's Day.

(3) 'Send Thy Holy Ghost, and pour into our hearts that most excellent gift of charity.'[5]
(4) 'O Lord, from whom all good things do come, grant to us, Thy humble servants, that by Thy holy inspiration we may think those things that are good, and by Thy merciful guidance may perform the same.'[6]
(5) 'We beseech Thee, leave us not comfortless, but send us the Holy Ghost to comfort us.'[7]
(6) 'Grant us by the same Spirit to have a right judgement in all things and evermore to rejoice in His holy comfort.'[8]
(7) 'Grant us, Lord, we beseech Thee, the Spirit, to think and do always such things as be rightful.'[9]
(8) 'O God, forasmuch as without Thee we are not able to please Thee, mercifully grant that Thy Holy Spirit may in all things direct and rule our hearts.'[10]

Wesley adds to the above evidence two quotations from the Offices of the Anglican Church:

(1) 'Cleanse the thoughts of our hearts by the inspiration of Thy Holy Spirit, that we may perfectly love Thee, and worthily magnify Thy holy name.'[11]
(2) 'Almighty God, who hast vouchsafed to regenerate these persons by water and the Holy Ghost, strengthen them with the Holy Ghost and Comforter, and daily increase in them the manifold gifts of Thy grace.'[12]

From the point of view of establishing the doctrine of assurance, these passages do not carry much weight. There is sparse reference, if any, to the experience of an inner certainty of personal salvation. While there is frequent allusion to the indwelling of the Holy Spirit, there is no clear teaching regarding the *consciousness* of the Spirit's operations in the individual, which is plainly implied in Wesley's doctrine of 'the witness of the Spirit'.[13]

Wesley himself appears to recognize the inadequacy of these quotations when he comments as follows: 'From these passages it may sufficiently appear, for what purposes every Christian, according to the doctrine of the Church of England, does now

[5] Quinquagesima Sunday. [6] Fifth Sunday after Easter.
[7] Sunday after Ascension Day. [8] Whit-Sunday.
[9] Ninth Sunday after Trinity. [10] Nineteenth Sunday after Trinity.
[11] Communion Office. [12] Office of Confirmation.
[13] *Sermons*, 10, 11, 45; *Standard Sermons*, I.199ff., 219ff., II.341ff.

"receive the Holy Ghost". But this will be still more clear from those that follow, wherein the reader may likewise observe a plain, rational sense of God's *revealing* Himself to us, of the *inspiration* of the Holy Ghost, and of a believer's *feeling* in himself 'the mighty working' of the Spirit of Christ.'[14]

Wesley now turns to the Homilies of the Church of England, and presents the following extracts:

(1) 'God gave them of old grace to be His children, as He doth us now. But now, by the coming of our Saviour Christ, we have received more abundantly the Spirit of God in our hearts.'[15]
(2) 'He died to destroy the rule of the devil in us; and he rose again to send down His Holy Spirit, to "rule in our hearts".'[16]
(3) 'We have the Holy Spirit in our hearts, as a seal and pledge of our everlasting inheritance.'[17]
(4) 'The Holy Ghost sat upon each of them, like as it had been cloven tongues of fire; to teach, that it is he which giveth eloquence and utterance in preaching the Gospel, which engendereth a burning zeal towards God's word, and giveth all men a tongue, yea, a fiery tongue.'[18]

Wesley adds a significant comment to this last quotation: 'Whatever occurs in any of the *Journals* of God's "giving me utterance", or "enabling me to speak with power", cannot therefore be quoted as *enthusiasm*, without wounding the Church through my side.'[19] Turning again to the Homilies, Wesley quotes as follows:

(5) 'So that if any man be a dumb Christian, not professing his faith openly, he giveth men occasion to doubt lest he have not the grace of the Holy Ghost within him.'[20]
(6) 'It is the office of the Holy Ghost to sanctify; which the more it is hid from our understanding, the more it ought to move all men to wonder at the secret and mighty workings of God's Holy Spirit which is within us. For it is the Holy Ghost that doth quicken the minds of men, *stirring up* godly motions in their hearts. Neither doth he think it

---

[14] *Works*, VIII.103.   [15] Homily on Faith, Part II.
[16] Homily on the Resurrection.   [17] ibid.
[18] Homily on Whit-Sunday, Part I. See Part III, ch. 6, pp. 139ff., *supra*.
[19] *Works*, VIII.103; see ch. 1, pp. 179ff., *supra*.
[20] Homily on Whit-Sunday, Part I.

sufficient inwardly to work the new birth of man, unless he do also dwell and abide in him. "Know ye not", saith St Paul, "that ye are the temple of God, and that His Spirit dwelleth in you? Know ye not that your bodies are the temple of the Holy Ghost, which is in you?"[21] Again he saith, "ye are not in the flesh, but in the spirit".[22] For why? "The Spirit of God dwelleth in you." To this agreeth St John: "The anointing which ye have received abideth in you."[23] And St Peter saith the same: "The spirit of glory and of God resteth upon you."[24] O what comfort is this to the heart of a true Christian, to think that the Holy Ghost dwelleth in him. . . . He doth instruct the hearts of the simple in the knowledge of God and His word, and therefore he is justly termed "the Spirit of truth".'[25]

With reference to the above citation, Wesley writes, 'From this passage, I learn:

(1) 'First, that every true Christian now "receives the Holy Ghost as the Paraclete or Comforter promised by our Lord".'[26]
(2) 'Secondly, that every Christian receives him as "the Spirit of Truth", to "teach him all things".'[27]
(3) 'And, thirdly, that "the anointing", mentioned in the First Epistle of John, "abides in every Christian".'[28]

Wesley turns again to the Homilies:

(7) 'In reading of God's word, he profiteth most that is most *inspired* with the Holy Ghost.'[29]
(8) 'Make him know and *feel* that there is no other name under heaven given unto men, whereby we can be saved.'[30]
(9) 'If we *feel* our conscience at peace with God, through remission of our sins,—all is of God.'[31]
(10) 'If you *feel* such a faith in you, rejoice in it, and let it be daily increasing by well-working.'[32]

---

[21] 1 Corinthians 3^{16}. For an examination of the Biblical basis of Assurance, see Part III, pp. 103ff., *supra*.
[22] Romans 8^9. [23] 1 John 2^{27}. [24] 1 Peter 4^{14}.
[25] John 16^{13}; Homily on Whit-Sunday, Part I. [26] John 14^{16}.
[27] John 16, *passim*. [28] 1 John 2^{27}; *Works*, VIII.104.
[29] Homily on Reading the Scripture, Part I.
[30] Homily on Rogation Week, Part III. [31] ibid.
[32] Homily on Faith, Part III.

WAS WESLEY'S DOCTRINE ORTHODOX? 193

(11) 'The faithful may *feel* wrought tranquillity of conscience, the increase of faith and hope, with many other graces of God.'[33]

(12) 'Godly men *feel* inwardly God's Holy Spirit, inflaming their hearts with love.'[34]

(13) 'God give us grace to know these things, and to *feel* them in our hearts! This knowledge and *feeling* is not of ourselves. Let us therefore meekly call upon the bountiful Spirit, the Holy Ghost, to *inspire* us with His presence, that we may be able to hear the goodness of God to our salvation. For without His lively inspiration, can we not so so much as speak the name of the Mediator. . . . In the power of the Holy Ghost resteth all ability to *know* God, and to *please* Him. . . . He *enlighteneth* the heart, to conceive worthy thoughts of Almighty God. . . .'[35]

Wesley holds that these 'operations of the Holy Ghost' are 'common to all Christians in all ages' and are 'clearly maintained by our own Church'.[36]

On a later page, Wesley considers the charge that 'none but enthusiasts suppose either that promise of the Comforter,[37] or the witness of the Spirit,[38] or that unutterable prayer,[39] or the "unction from the Holy One",[40] to belong in common to all Christians'.[41]

Wesley continues: 'O my Lord,[42] how deeply have you condemned the generation of God's children! Whom have you represented as rank, dreaming enthusiasts, as either deluded or designing men? Not only Bishop Pearson, a man hitherto accounted both sound in heart, and of good understanding; but likewise Archbishop Cranmer, Bishop Ridley, Bishop Latimer, Bishop Hooper; and all the venerable compilers of our Liturgy and Homilies; all the members of both the Houses of Convocation, by whom they were revised and approved; yea, King Edward, and all his Lords and Commons together, by whose authority they were established; and, with these modern

---

[33] Homily on the Sacrament, Part I.
[34] Homily on Certain Places of Scripture, Part I.
[35] Homily for Rogation Week, Part III.
[36] *Works*, VIII.105; cf. p. 465.   [37] John $14^{16, 26}$, 16^{13}.   [38] Romans $8^{15, 16}$.
[39] Romans $8^{26, 27}$.   [40] 1 John $2^{20, 27}$.   [41] *Works*, VIII.110.
[42] Wesley is addressing the Bishop of Lichfield and Coventry (Richard Smallbroke). *Letters*, II.100; *Sermons*, I.203; Simon, *John Wesley and The Methodist Societies*, 296–301.

enthusiasts, Origen, Chrysostom, and Athanasius are comprehended in the same censure!'[43]

Wesley has already, in the *Farther Appeal*, quoted at length from Bishop Pearson:

'It is also the office of the Holy Ghost to "assure us of the adoption of sons", to create in us a sense of the paternal love of God towards us, to give us an earnest of our everlasting inheritance.' Bishop Pearson substantiates this statement by quoting from Romans 8[15, 16], and also from Galatians 4[6]—texts which, as we have seen, are basic to Wesley's doctrine of assurance. Pearson continues: 'As, therefore, we are born again by His Spirit, and receive from Him our regeneration, so we are also, by the same Spirit, "assured of our adoption". Because, being "sons, we are also heirs, heirs of God, and joint-heirs with Christ", by the same Spirit we have the pledge, or rather the "earnest, of our inheritance".[44] For "he which establisheth us in Christ, and hath anointed us, is God; who hath also sealed us, and hath given us the earnest of His Spirit in our hearts".[45] So that "we are sealed with that Holy Spirit of promise, which is the earnest of our inheritance".'[46]

We recall Wesley's contact with Peter Böhler and an entry in the *Journal* which reads: 'I had now no objection to what he said of the nature of faith; namely, that it is (to use the words of our Church) "a sure trust and confidence which a man hath in God, that through the merits of Christ his sins are forgiven and he reconciled to the favour of God".'[47]

Charles Wesley, in a sermon preached on 4th April 1742 in Oxford University, says: 'Our own excellent Church . . . speaks plainly of "feeling the Spirit of Christ", of being "moved by the Holy Ghost" and knowing and "feeling there is no other name than that of Jesus", whereby we can receive life and salvation. She teaches us all to pray for the "inspiration of the Holy Ghost". Nay, and every Presbyter of hers professes to receive the Holy Ghost by the imposition of hands. Therefore, to deny any of these, is, in effect, to renounce the Church of England, as well as the whole Christian revelation.'[48]

---

[43] *Works*, VIII.110.   [44] Ephesians 1[14].   [45] 2 Corinthians 1[22].
[46] *Works*, VIII.101; Wesley quotes from Pearson's *Exposition of the Creed*, Art. viii, 'I believe in the Holy Ghost'.
[47] Homily 'Of Salvation'; *Journal*, I.454; cf. *Works*, VIII.23f.; *Letters*, IV.126. Quoted by Wesley in his remarkable interview with Bishop Butler on 18th August 1739. *Journal*, II.257.
[48] *Sermons*, I.83.

Full quotations and references here alluded to by Charles Wesley, are as follows: [49]

(1) The doctrine of Election is full of comfort 'to godly persons, and such as feel in themselves the working of the Spirit of Christ'.[50]
(2) Do you trust that you are inwardly moved by the Holy Ghost to take upon you this office and ministration?'[51]
(3) 'The Almighty Lord . . . make thee know and feel that there is none other Name under heaven given to men, in whom, and through whom, thou mayest receive health and salvation, but only the Name of our Lord Jesus.'[52]
(4) 'Cleanse the thoughts of our hearts by the inspiration of Thy Holy Spirit.'[53]
(5) 'Strengthen them . . . with the Holy Ghost the Comforter.'[54]
(6) 'Receive the Holy Ghost for the office and work of a priest in the Church of God, now committed unto thee by the Imposition of our hands.'[55]

In a letter dated 20th December 1760 to the Editor of *Lloyd's Evening Post*, John Wesley considers his correspondent's assertion that 'No Protestant divine ever taught your doctrine of assurance'. In reply, Wesley says, 'I hope you know better; but it is strange you should not. Did you never see Bishop Hall's Works? Was not he a Protestant divine? Was not Mr Perkins, Bolton, Dr Sibbs, Dr Preston, Archbishop Leighton? Inquire a little farther; and do not run thus hand over head, asserting you know not what.'[56]

Wesley does not cite passages from the authorities he quotes. We therefore quote the following evidence from these writers bearing on the subject of assurance:[57]

Referring to Romans 8[16], Perkins says: 'In these words are two testimonies of our adoption set down: the first is the Spirit of God dwelling in us, and testifying unto us that we are God's children. The Holy Ghost gives testimony, by applying the promise of remission of sins, and life everlasting by Christ, to

---

[49] ibid., Dr Sugden's Notes; cf. Lawson, *Notes of Wesley's Forty-four Sermons*, p. 21.
[50] Article XVII.
[51] Office for Ordering of Deacons.   [52] Order for Visitation of Sick.
[53] Order for Holy Communion.   [54] Order for Confirmation.
[55] Office for Ordering of Priests.   [56] *Letters*, IV.126.
[57] Quoted from Charles Prest, *The Witness of the Spirit* (1848), p. 54.

the heart. The second testimony of our adoption is our spirit, that is, our conscience sanctified and renewed by the Holy Ghost.'[58]

'What an heaven do I feel in myself, when . . . I find in my heart a feeling possession of my God—when my soul hath caught fast and sensible hold of my Saviour, and can and dare secretly vouch, I know whom I have believed.'[59]

'That you may know the voice of the Spirit of God from the carnal confidence of our own spirits, inquire what went before, what accompanieth it, what followeth after this ravishing joy.'[60]

'The witness of the Spirit . . . is a certain divine expression of light, a certain inexpressible assurance that we are the sons of God, a certain secret manifestation that God hath received us, and put away our sins: no man knows it, but they that have it. . . . If there were not some Christians that did feel it, and know it, you might believe there were no such thing, that it were but fancy and enthusiasm; but it is certain there are a generation of men that know what this seal of the Lord is.'[61]

This, then, represents the major portion of the evidence adduced by Wesley in his attempt to justify his doctrine of assurance at the bar of Anglicanism. In considering the validity of his claim to orthodoxy, we have to take into account, not only the quotations from Anglican sources presented in this chapter, but also the Biblical and historical sources of the doctrine examined in Parts III and IV, pp. 105ff., 149ff., *supra*. More particularly must we bear in mind the claim made by Wesley that assurance was a Scriptural doctrine, that it was a living experience in the early Church and that the doctrine was taught by the Reformers. If this claim be allowed, then it is to be expected that assurance should occupy a rightful place in Anglican theology, since it is on these Biblical and historical foundations that the doctrine of the Church of England is said to be based.[62] All this, therefore, is supplementary to the evidence presented in this chapter, and must be considered in deciding the issue whether Wesley's doctrine of assurance was orthodox.

A closer look, however, at the quotations submitted here from the doctrinal *standards* of the Anglican Church reveals the fact

[58] *Perkins' Works*, II.18f.; cf. I.564.
[59] Bishop Hall (1633–1710), *Decad.*, II, epist. 1.
[60] Richard Sibbs, *Works*, V.443.
[61] Preston *The New Covenant* (1630), p. 400.
[62] Garbett, *The Claims of the Church of England*, chs. 1 and 2.

WAS WESLEY'S DOCTRINE ORTHODOX? 197

that the phrases 'the witness of the Spirit' or 'assurance of salvation' seldom, if ever, appear—though, as we have seen, this phraseology is not wanting in certain Anglican *writers*.

This point is touched upon by George Cubitt in 1816 when he says: 'After looking over the Book of Common Prayer and the Homilies, I can find nothing that contradicts this statement of Mr Wesley[63]—very much that confirms it. I admit . . . that I do not find the *term* "witness of the Spirit", but expressions abound, which signify the *thing* itself.'[64]

Our conclusion is in line with the findings of George Cubitt. In the light of our examination of the Biblical evidence; the testimony of the Early Church and of subsequent centuries; and of Anglican authorities in this, and previous, chapters, our view is:

(1) That 'special and particular assurance was never condemned for heresy before the Council of Trent condemned it'.[65]

(2) That, while the Methodist *terminology* is not found in the doctrinal *standards* of the Church of England, the idea and experience of a personal assurance of salvation are certainly implied, and, in some Anglican *writers*, explicitly stated.

[63] Concerning the nature of assurance in Sermon No. 45, *Sermons*, II.344f.
[64] Cubitt, *A Brief Defence of the People Called Methodists* (1816), p. 29.
[65] *Perkins' Works*, I.540.

CHAPTER FOUR

THE DANGERS OF 'STILLNESS'

A SUBJECTIVE element is involved in every genuine claim to an inner experience of Christian certainty. It follows that no examination of assurance can ignore Wesley's relationship to Mysticism. We shall therefore need to consider the principal features of Wesley's struggle against the plausible arguments and pernicious influence of Molther's doctrine of 'stillness'.

On Wesley's arrival in London from Bristol on 1st November 1739, the first person he met was a Mrs Turner, whom he had left strong in faith and zealous of good works. 'But she now told me Mr Molther had fully convinced her she never had faith at all, and had advised her, till she received faith, to be "still", ceasing from outward works; which she had accordingly done, and did not doubt but in a short time she would find the advantage of it.'[1]

Philip Henry Molther[2] had arrived in London on 18th October 1739, and was introduced by James Hutton to the Fetter Lane Society—a Society which, on Böhler's embarkation for Carolina, had been left in the hands of John and Charles Wesley.[3] Molther persuaded many members to accept his doctrine of 'stillness' or 'quietism', a kind of Moravian mysticism.[4] This doctrine was an exaggerated interpretation of Luther's teaching on 'salvation by faith alone', and was held by certain Moravians as the only way to an assurance of sins forgiven. It deprecated, among other things, the use of the 'means of grace' and the doing of good works.

Wesley tells us that 'Bray[5] also was highly commending the being "still" before the Lord. He likewise spoke largely of the great danger that attended the doing of outward works, and of the folly of people that keep running about to Church and sacrament, "as I", said he, "did till very lately".'[6]

[1] *Journal*, II.312.
[2] Educated at Jena University and ordained a Moravian Minister by Zinzendorf.
[3] Tyerman, *Life and Times of John Wesley*, I.297.
[4] Dr J. S. Simon holds that there was a tendency in this direction at Fetter Lane even before Molther arrived: *John Wesley and the Religious Societies*, p. 323.
[5] For Bray's influence on Charles Wesley, see pp. 41f., *supra*.
[6] *Journal*, II.312.

THE DANGERS OF 'STILLNESS'

Spangenberg,[7] who had reached London from Savannah on 24th October 1739, now comes into the picture. 'Our society', writes Wesley, 'met at seven in the morning and continued silent till eight. One [Spangenberg] then spoke of looking unto Jesus, and exhorted us to lie still in His hand.'[8]

Wesley goes on to say: 'In the evening I met the women of our society at Fetter Lane, where some of our brethren strongly intimated that none of them had any true faith, and then asserted, in plain terms:

(1) 'that, till they had true faith, they ought to be "still"; that is (as they themselves explained) to abstain from the means of grace, as they are called—the Lord's Supper in particular;

(2) 'that the ordinances are not means of grace, there being no other means than Christ.'[9]

In reference to these quietistic elements, Wesley has a long conference with Spangenberg, about which he says: 'I could not agree either that none has any faith so long as he is liable to any doubt or fear; or that, till we have it, we ought to abstain from the Lord's Supper or the other ordinances of God.'[10] Regarding a society meeting on 7th November, Wesley writes: 'We sat an hour without speaking. The rest of the time was spent in dispute', as to whether one ought to receive the Lord's Supper without the full assurance of faith.[11]

On 31st December 1739, Wesley has a long and particular conversation with Mr Molther himself. 'I weighed all his words with the utmost care; desired him to explain what I did not understand. . . . I then wrote down what I conceived to be the difference between us in the following words:

'As to faith, you believe:

(1) 'There are no degrees of faith, and that no man has any degree of it before all things in him are become new, before he has the full assurance of faith, the abiding witness of the Spirit, or the clear perception that Christ dwelleth in him.

(2) 'Accordingly you believe there is no justifying faith, or state of justification, short of this. . . .

(3) 'And, in general, that that gift of God which many received

---

[7] See pp. 21f., *supra*. [8] *Journal*, II.313.
[9] ibid. [10] ibid., p. 314. [11] ibid.

since Peter Böhler came into England—viz. "a sure confidence of the love of God to them"—was not justifying faith.[12]

(4) 'And that the joy and love attending it were from animal spirits, from nature, or imagination; not "joy in the Holy Ghost", and the real "love of God shed abroad in their hearts".'[13]

Wesley then indicates his own belief by re-stating these points in the affirmative.

He further distinguishes his views from those of Molther, by adding:

'As to the way to faith, you believe:

'That the way to attain it is to wait for Christ, and be still —that is,

'Not to use (what we term) the means of grace;

'Not to go to church;[14]

'Not to communicate;

'Not to fast;

'Not to use so much private prayer;

'Not to read the Scripture; . . .

'Not to do temporal good;

'Not to attempt spiritual good.'[15]

Again Wesley expresses his own belief by repeating the above sentences without the negative. Molther's doctrine was based on an unbalanced exposition of a few Bible passages. It spread so swiftly and dangerously in the Fetter Lane Society because it was presented fervently to somewhat credulous folk by one commissioned by the great Zinzendorf. It is doubtful, however, whether he was commissioned to teach these troublesome tenets.

Charles Wesley printed his fine hymn on the 'means of grace' and circulated it as an antidote to stillness.[16] Despite his resistance to this quietism, Charles himself fell a victim to its seductive influence on 22nd January 1741,[17] for which Jackson holds Böhler, Gambold, and Hall responsible.[18] The Countess

[12] See Part I, ch. 3, pp. 25ff., *supra*, and Part II, ch. 1, pp. 53ff., *supra*.
[13] *Journal*, II.328f.
[14] For the relationship of the Fetter Lane Society to the Church of England, see Telford, *Life of Wesley* (1886), p. 148; *Journal of Charles Wesley*, I.153; *Journal of George Whitefield*, 20th May 1739.
[15] *Journal*, II.329f. [16] *Journal of Charles Wesley*, I.221.
[17] Sugden, *Standard Sermons*, I.236; *Journal*, II.418.
[18] Jackson, *Life of Charles Wesley*, I.273, 278.

of Huntingdon, however, rescued him from the fascination of 'stillness'. His lapse lasted only three weeks.[19]

Answering the Moravian assertion that 'weak faith is no faith', Wesley states that weak faith is associated with fear, or doubt, or a life not fully purified. And this, observes Wesley, is the type of faith of almost all Christians within a short time after they have first peace with God. After quoting the New Testament in support of his interpretation of weak faith, Wesley sums up by saying: 'Therefore, there are degrees in faith;[20] and weak faith may yet be true faith.'[21]

In reply to the quietistic claim that there is but one commandment in the New Testament, viz. 'to believe', Wesley shows, by copious texts, 'how gross, palpable a contradiction is this to the whole tenor of the New Testament'.[22] Wesley next considers the disparagement of all 'the means of grace' by the doctrine of stillness. While admitting that it is not a Biblical phrase, he holds that the sense of it undeniably is.[23] Wesley maintains that both believers and unbelievers are commanded to search the Scriptures. Preaching on 'Do this in remembrance of me', he argues that experience shows the gross falsehood of that assertion that the Lord's Supper is not a converting ordinance.[24]

The situation moved more to a climax when Wesley read at Fetter Lane an extract from the *Mystic Divinity* of Dionysius 'full of the same "super-essential darkness"'. This citation claimed that it would be deadly poison and destructive for one not born of God to read the Scriptures or to pray or to communicate, or to do any outward work. Wesley put the test question: 'My brethren, is this right, or is it wrong?' Bell replied: 'It is right . . . to this we must all come, or we never can come to Christ.'[25]

The final separation of Methodism from Moravianism took place on 20th July 1740. The historic entry in the *Journal* reads: 'In the evening I went with Mr Seward to the lovefeast in Fetter Lane; at the conclusion of which . . . I read a paper, the substance whereof was as follows:

'About nine months ago certain of you began to speak

---

[19] *Journal*, II.424.

[20] For Wesley's teaching on degrees of faith, see Part II, chs. 2, 3, pp. 70, 77ff., *supra*, and Part III, ch. 4, pp. 128ff., *supra*.

[21] *Journal*, II.355.   [22] See Part III, pp. 103ff., *supra*.

[23] *Journal*, II. 360.   [24] ibid., p. 361.   [25] ibid., p. 366.

contrary to the doctrine we had till then received. The sum of what you asserted is this:

(1) 'That there is no such thing as weak faith. That there is no justifying faith where there is any doubt or fear, or where there is not, in the full sense, a new, a clean heart.
(2) 'That a man ought not to use those ordinances of God which our Church[26] terms "means of grace", before he has such a faith as excludes all doubt and fear and implies a new, a clean heart.'

'You have often affirmed that to search the Scriptures, to pray, or to communicate before we have this faith is to seek salvation by works; and that till these works are laid aside no man can receive faith.

'I believe these assertions to be flatly contrary to the word of God. I have warned you hereof again and again and have besought you to turn back to the law and the testimony. I have borne with you long, hoping that you would turn. But as I find you more and more confirmed in the error of your ways, nothing now remains but that I should give you up to God. You that are of the same judgement, follow me.

'I then, without saying more, withdrew, as did eighteen or nineteen of the Society.'[27]

On 8th August 1740, Wesley wrote a long letter to the Moravian Church at Herrnhut, vindicating the steps he had taken. It deprecates the various aspects of stillness, with which we are now quite familiar. Wesley goes on to condemn the quietistic Moravians because they receive not the ancient but the modern mystics as the best interpreters of Scripture; and that, 'in conformity to the mystics, you likewise greatly check joy in the Holy Ghost'. Wesley adds another stricture on the ground that they undervalue good works, and concludes by saying: 'I have now delivered my own soul.'[28]

This criticism, however, must not be regarded as a condemnation of the Moravian Church as such. For the mischievous effects of the doctrine of 'stillness'—effects which troubled him for many years—he never held Moravianism as a whole responsible; but only such representatives as Molther, Spangenberg and certain other Moravians in London.[29] We

[26] i.e. The Church of England.   [27] *Journal*, II.370.   [28] ibid., pp. 350f.
[29] Tyerman, *Life and Times of John Wesley*, I.308; *Letters*, II.83, 215ff.

have already assessed, in earlier chapters, Wesley's indebtedness to the Moravians in Georgia, in England and in Germany.[30] But the Moravians had no further contribution to make to Wesley's religious life and thought.

Three further matters call for comment:

(1) It must be admitted that Molther's disparagement of the 'means of grace' and of 'good works' might seem to be supported by Wesley's earlier depreciation of his pre-Aldersgate ritualistic practices and Christian service. We recall how Wesley termed these a 'refined way of trusting to my own works and my own righteousness'.[31]

(2) Wesley had already turned his back on mysticism; and 'stillness' was a kind of Moravian mysticism.[32] His practical mind saved him from imagining that there could be any genuine 'witness of the Spirit' which did not issue in the 'fruit of the Spirit' in the form of Christian service.

(3) Wesley was defending his teaching on assurance against an antinomian interpretation of Luther's doctrine of justification by faith. After reading 'that celebrated book, Martin Luther's *Comment on the Epistle to the Galatians*', Wesley says: 'I was utterly ashamed. . . . He is deeply tinctured with mysticism throughout and hence often dangerously wrong. . . . Here [I apprehend] is the real spring of the grand error of the Moravians. They follow Luther, for better for worse. Hence their "No works; no law; no commandment".'[33]

This separation from the Moravians cost Wesley many a pang. He often cast a longing glance back to the time when they worshipped and worked together. Wesley wrote: 'Surely the time will return when there shall be again "Union of mind, as in us all one soul".'[34] But, as far as the early Methodists and Moravians were concerned, it was not to be.

[30] Part I, chs. 3, 4, pp. 20ff., *supra*; Part II, ch. 1, pp. 53ff., *supra*.
[31] *Journal*, I.469.   [32] Dr G. C. Cell, *Rediscovery of John Wesley*, p. 123.
[33] *Journal*, II.467.
[34] Misquoted from Milton, *Paradise Lost*, VII.705; *Journal*, II.451.

CHAPTER FIVE

THE RELEVANCE OF MYSTICISM

MYSTICISM cannot be disposed of as summarily as many of Wesley's adverse criticisms might be taken to imply. An inner consciousness of the Spirit's witness involves, in the very nature of the case, some kind of mystic experience.

Wesley's attacks on mysticism, especially on Moravian 'stillness', served to protect his doctrine of assurance against the charges of 'enthusiasm' and individual excesses. They made it clear that Wesley would not tolerate any theory of an inner witness of the Spirit unless this testimony was based on such objective facts as the Scriptures, the ordinances of the Church and the corporate experience of the Christian society.

Dr. H. B. Workman offers a comprehensive list of the main causes of Wesley's antagonism, which we summarize as follows:

(1) The extravagances of Molther's doctrine of 'stillness' disgusted his logical common sense and energetic spirit.
(2) Much current mysticism lent itself to Antinomianism.
(3) Wesley's *Letters* and *Journal* reveal that he believed that mysticism advocated a union with God which robbed man of his personality.
(4) He deprecated the mystics' exclusion of reason for an appeal to feeling.
(5) He hated the 'fondling, amorous', irreverent language and symbolism which some mystics used.
(6) He lived in an age which vehemently suspected anything savouring of 'inner light'.
(7) The philosophy of Locke was fatal to all forms of transcendental or mystical thought.[1]

As early as 23rd November 1736, Wesley could write from Savannah to his brother Samuel: 'I think the rock on which I had nearest made shipwreck of the faith was the writings of the mystics; under which term I comprehend all, and only those, who slight any of the means of grace.'[2]

After reading 'Mr Hartley's ingenious defence of the Mystic Writers', Wesley criticizes mysticism in general under the date

[1] Workman, *New History of Methodism*, I.54f.   [2] *Letters*, I.207.

5th February 1764 in the *Journal*. The main points of Wesley's condemnation are as follows:

(1) The mystics have no conception of church communion.
(2) They disparage, not only works of piety and the ordinances of God, but even works of mercy.
(3) They cherish many unscriptural speculations.
(4) They are of a dark, shy, reserved, unsociable temper.
(5) They are apt to despise all who differ from them.
(6) Mysticism is both unscriptural and affectedly mysterious.
(7) St John speaks as high and as deep things as Jacob Behmen. Why then does not Jacob speak as plainly as he?[3]

Professor William James holds that mystic experience is distinguished by having 'four marks', viz. ineffability, noetic quality, transiency, and passivity.[4] This last element, 'passivity', in James's analysis would certainly not commend itself to Wesley. As Dr Workman puts it, 'the negative passivity, which makes Eckhart and Tauler use language curiously similar to that of Hegel, is not a doctrine of Methodism'.[5]

Wesley, as we have seen, strongly resented the non-social tendency of mysticism. He never forgot the advice 'a serious man' gave him in his early days:[6] 'You cannot serve Him alone. You must therefore find companions or make them; the Bible knows nothing of solitary religion'.[7] Wesley had painful and convincing evidence of the fact that isolationism is not conducive to the true culture of the soul, but paves the way to subjective delusions and individual excesses.

Another reason for Wesley's antipathy to the 'mystic way' is said to be the importance attached by mysticism to the subconscious. 'Suso, Tauler, Eckhart . . . in a Methodist Class-meeting would be worse than dumb; they would be unintelligible.'[8] Some of the mystics discounted the value of the outer ordinances of the Church—ordinances which Wesley could never allow himself nor his followers to neglect. In view of this perilous introvertive tendency of mysticism, we can appreciate Wesley's refusal to recognize the genuineness of any claim to the inner witness of the Spirit unless that inner testimony were confirmed by 'the fruit of the Spirit' or 'the indirect witness'.[9]

---

[3] *Journal*, V.46.   [4] James, *Varieties of Religious Experience* (1904), pp. 380f.
[5] Workman, *New History of Methodism*, I.59.   [6] Probably in 1729.
[7] Henry Moore, *Life of Wesley*, I.162.   [8] *New History of Methodism*, I.60f.
[9] See Part II, ch. 3, pp. 79f., *supra*, and Part III, ch. 3, pp. 111ff., *supra*.

That the teaching of certain mystics was opposed to the doctrine of assurance is brought out by Dr Pope: 'The extravagant mystics of the Illuminist and Quietist types erred exceedingly: the former, forgetting the conditions of assurance, repentance and faith; the latter making the perfection of religion to consist in an absolute indifference to assurance and evidence and feeling of every kind.'[10]

Moreover, there were elements in mysticism generally—as well as in Moravian 'quietism' in particular—which not only paid slight attention to the 'means of grace' and the historicity of Christianity, but also neglected the redeeming work of Christ for the salvation of man. This plainly cut at the root of Wesley's doctrine of assurance, for, as we have seen, it was based on an inner certainty of personal salvation, imparted by the Spirit of God, and centred in a crucified Christ.[11]

In the light of the evidence submitted here and in the previous chapter, it is not surprising that some scholars have drawn the conclusion that Wesley was in no sense a mystic.[12] Other scholars, however, hold that mystical elements are traceable in Wesley's religious life and thought.[13]

It is difficult to deny that Wesley was in some measure indebted to mysticism. It was mainly the influence of Thomas à Kempis's *Christian Pattern* on the youthful Wesley[14] which led him in 1738 to write: 'I began to see that true religion was seated in the heart, and that God's law extended to all our thoughts as well as words and actions'.[15] William Law's *Christian Perfection* and *Serious Call* convinced him more than ever of the exceeding height and breadth and depth of the law of God. Wesley adds: 'The light flowed in so mightily upon my soul that everything appeared in a new light'.[16]

Moreover, if Wesley deemed much mystical teaching as 'sublime nonsense', he did not fail to see that the 'gold' of mystic writers was well represented in his 'Christian Library'.[17]

Dr Bett believes that, apart from Law and Byrom and their devotion to Boehme, there was little knowledge of the mystic writers in Wesley's century. It might be seriously argued that

[10] Pope, *Compendium of Christian Theology*, III.123f.
[11] See Part II, ch. 1, pp. 53ff., *supra*.
[12] Tyerman, *Life and Times of Wesley*, I.54.
[13] Cell, *Rediscovery of John Wesley*, pp. 94, 97f.
[14] In 1725, when he was twenty-two years old.
[15] *Journal*, I.466. Six editions of this book were issued between 1741 and 1788.
[16] ibid., p. 467.
[17] *Works*, XIV.290f.; fifty volumes, 1749-55; Bett, *Spirit of Methodism*, pp. 61ff.

Wesley stood almost alone in his age for his knowledge of some of the great mystics, and for his appreciation of what was best in them.[18]

Dr G. C. Cell observes that the 'mellower judgement of the mature Wesley receded far enough from his first total veto of mysticism to appraise it for its positive values as well as a valuable corrective to the Church system which prevailed in the day and generation of the great mystics'.[19] As we have seen, it was mysticism as divorced from the means of grace and historical Christianity against which Wesley levelled his bitterest attacks.[20] While Wesley expressed a preference for the ancient as opposed to the modern mystics, his verse translations convey some of the finest sentiments of the German mystics.[21] Though Wesley disapproved of certain mystic elements in his brother's 1749 hymnal, later editions show many ineradicable traces of mysticism.[22]

Dr Bett draws the conclusion that Wesley and early Methodism were considerably influenced, directly and indirectly, by the mystics, 'at some points by the study of great mystical books, and at others by the strain of mystical teaching which reached them through the Moravians and the Pietists, and thus linked the religious revival in England with an evangelical succession of doctrine and experience reaching far back into the past'.[23]

Evelyn Underhill represents the mystical ladder of assent as having five rungs:

(1) Awakening.
(2) Purgation by discipline.
(3) Illumination or vision.
(4) Mystic death or mortification.
(5) Union or absorption in the Infinite.[24]

Commenting on this, Dr Dimond says that Wesley characteristically stopped short of the mystic ecstasy, and neither mystic death nor union can be said to describe any experience in Wesley's life. Dr Dimond admits that the first three stages

---

[18] Bett, op. cit., p. 62.   [19] Cell, *Rediscovery of John Wesley*, p. 111.
[20] Dimond, op. cit., pp. 85, 87; see letter to Samuel Wesley, 23rd November 1736; *Works*, XII.27f.
[21] Part II, ch. 4, pp. 82ff., *supra*; Bett, *Hymns of Methodism*, pp. 116ff.
[22] Rattenbury, *Evangelical Doctrines of Charles Wesley's Hymns*, p. 63; Part II, ch. 5, p. 98, *supra*; cf. Leger, *La Jeunesse de Wesley*, p. 191.
[23] Bett, *Spirit of Methodism*, p. 63.   [24] Underhill, *The Mystic Way*, p. 54.

correspond to the main lines of Wesley's religious development.[25] 'Awakening' can, therefore, be taken to represent the vows of 1725, 'purgation' the years leading up to 1738, and 'illumination' as typical of the Aldersgate experience. It has been said of Charles Wesley that in the period preceding 21st May 1738 he was passing through that time of darkness and suspense which in the annals of the mystics has often been known to precede a great spiritual illumination.[26]

Dr Rufus Jones, however, says that 'mystical states are not knowledge-states, but feeling-states. The mystic has an inward perception, but he cannot put it into the common language of thought.'[27] But are we justified in separating 'knowing' and 'feeling' so rigidly? Psychology has familiarized us with the view that consciousness is never purely 'cognitive' or 'affective', but an experience in which both these elements are involved.[28] Moreover, is knowledge to be determined by the extent to which it is communicable? Bergson has told us that whilst our reason explains reality to us, it is by intuition and not by reason that we grasp the existence of reality at all.[29]

The immediate and inexpressible element in mystical experience is summed up by James in the word 'ineffability'. This term means that such immediate experience must to a large extent remain 'private'. James says that 'no adequate report of its contents can be given in words . . . it cannot be imparted or transferred to others'.[30] As a twelfth-century mystic expresses it:

'The love of Jesus, what it is
None but His loved ones know.'[31]

This inadequacy of human language was appreciated by Wesley in his attempt to define his doctrine of assurance. He admits that 'it is hard to find words in the language of men to explain "the deep things of God". Indeed, there are none that will adequately express what the children of God experience.'

[25] Dimond, *Psychology of the Methodist Revival*, pp. 77, 78.
[26] Jones, *Charles Wesley*, p. 65; see pp. 40ff., *supra*.
[27] Rufus Jones, *Social Law in the Spiritual World*, p. 129.
[28] See, for instance, Stout, *Manual of Psychology* (1938), pp. 10ff., Montague, *The Ways of Knowing*, *passim*.
[29] Dr E. S. Waterhouse, *Psychology and Religion* (1930), p. 146.
[30] James, *Varieties of Religious Experience*, pp. 380f.
[31] Bernard of Clairvaux (1091–1153); *M.H.B.* (1933), No. 108, verse 4.

He invites 'any who are taught of God to correct, to soften, or strengthen the expression' which he gives to 'the testimony of the Spirit'.[32]

But the 'four marks' by which William James distinguishes the mystic experience include, not only 'ineffability', but also what he calls the 'noetic quality'. He defines this characteristic as follows: 'Although so similar to states of feeling, mystical states seem to those who experience them to be also states of knowledge. They are states of insight into depths unplumbed by the discursive intellect.[33]

This 'noetic quality' is very significant from the point of view of Wesley's doctrine of assurance. This inner sense of Christian certainty is meaningless and worthless if the believer cannot regard the direct testimony of the Spirit as true knowledge. In order to substantiate such a claim, Wesley, as we have seen, was careful to indicate the criteria—Scripture, communal testimony and the indirect witness—by which such an inner consciousness of salvation could be checked and certified.

'Mysticism and Methodism', says Dr Workman, 'both build upon the same foundation, not of argument or observation, but of conscious spiritual experience. The doctrine of assurance is not far removed from a belief in the "inner light". Hence mystics and Methodists are one in their claim for spiritual certainty, though the claim is stated by the mystic in more unguarded language than by the Methodist.'[34]

Even the individualism of some of the mystics must not be dismissed too summarily, since a repetition of an experience in other people's lives, while generally a safeguard against subjectivism, is not in itself an infallible guarantee of its truth. It would seem that a prophet's certainty of God is sometimes intensified and deepened by his very isolation. The 'heretic' is on occasion a 'Joan of Arc'.

If mysticism be defined, not in terms of philosophy or theosophy, but of experience—as the doctrine, for instance, that a man may live in conscious fellowship with God—then Christianity is mystical. Some now hold that *this* is the true definition. Under it, as this book shows, Wesley at last gave the mysticism of experience its right place in Christian doctrine.[35]

[32] *Sermons*, I.207f.   [33] James, op. cit., pp. 380f.
[34] Workman, *N.H.M.*, I.55f.; cf. Watkin-Jones, *The Holy Spirit from Arminius to Wesley*, pp. 314f.
[35] I am indebted here to the Rev. Dr C. Ryder Smith.

CHAPTER SIX

THE VALIDITY OF AN INNER SENSE OF CERTAINTY

IN THE light of this inquiry, it is clear that Wesley spared no effort to safeguard his doctrine of assurance from the charge of subjectivism. He insisted on basing this inner sense of certainty on the objective and historical facts of the Christian religion. His bulwarks of defence included the teaching of Scriptures, the history of the Church, the doctrinal standards of Anglicanism, and the corrective influences of corporate fellowship. Moreover, he maintained that no claim to an assurance of salvation could be accepted as genuine unless it expressed itself in the form of Christian graces and 'good works'. The direct witness must be confirmed by the indirect witness. The 'testimony of the Spirit' must issue in the 'fruit of the Spirit'.

Despite all these safeguards, however, the scheme is not as impregnable as it might at first appear. In his maturer years, Wesley taught that assurance was not an essential accompaniment of a state of salvation, but was a privilege which all Christians should seek. Our examination of Wesley's Aldersgate experience revealed the fact that its distinctive feature was an inner sense of personal salvation centred in Christ. In Wesley's case, some of the outward 'marks' of the inner witness ante-dated Aldersgate. We saw that even before 24th May 1738 he had based his faith on the Bible as the oracles of God, his feet had already traversed the path to perfection, and he was already full of 'good works'.

In a word, while the inner witness cannot long survive without expressing itself in the outward 'fruit' of the Spirit, the outward 'fruit' is not an infallible guarantee of an inner consciousness of salvation.

In the last analysis, therefore, it is not easy to see how anybody can *prove* that he has the witness of the Spirit. To the experient, of course, it is self-evident and needs no proof.[1] But, as we saw in our treatment of mysticism, the 'noetic element' characteristic of an inner certainty has the quality

[1] *Sermons*, II.355f.; cf. p. 349.

VALIDITY OF AN INNER SENSE OF CERTAINTY 211

of 'ineffability', which makes it incommunicable.[2] Wesley admits that he who has the witness of the Spirit 'cannot explain it to one who has it not; nor indeed is it to be expected that he should'.[3]

Personal experience is 'private', and probably will always remain so. We have no *immediate* knowledge of what goes on in another person's mind.[4] Our conclusions about their feelings are always inferential and are deductions based on a study of their 'behaviour'. The accuracy of our knowledge of another's inner experience, therefore, depends on the accuracy of our interpretation of the outward expression of that experience; and, at best, this knowledge can be only approximate.[5]

This is a difficulty which we must pause briefly to consider. In doing so, we shall have to look more closely at the psychological and philosophical implications of assurance, to which some reference has already been made in earlier chapters. Or, to raise a prior question, to what extent was Wesley a philosopher? Like the interpretation of the Aldersgate experience, this is a question which has given rise to some controversy.

Let us look at some of the facts. In many ways Wesley was a child of his age. The strict discipline and the cultural training of the Epworth Rectory left a life-long impression on his mind and heart. He appears in some matters to have been surprisingly credulous,[6] though Wesley disowned his brother's charge of credulity.[7] Wesley, however, once wrote that the giving up witchcraft is, in effect, giving up the Bible.[8]

There are traces in Wesley's writings of his reluctance to pursue speculative thinking.[9] 'I am convinced', he once said, 'I could not study, to any degree of perfection, either mathematics, arithmetic, or algebra, without being a deist, if not an atheist.'[10] In the Preface to his *Sermons* (1746), Wesley asserted: 'I desire plain truth for plain people; therefore . . . I abstain from all nice and philosophical speculations; from all perplexed and intricate reasonings.'[11] Lecky deplored the fact that Wesley based 'the whole weight of religious proof upon what he termed "a new class of senses opened in the soul to be the

---

[2] James, *Varieties of Religious Experience* (1904), pp. 380f.   [3] *Sermons*, I.217.
[4] Dr Hastings Rashdall, *Philosophy and Religion* (1931 ed.), pp. 110f.
[5] Dr W. T. Stace, *The Theory of Knowledge and Existence* (1932), pp. 169ff.
[6] Piette, *John Wesley in the Evolution of Protestantism*, pp. 235f.
[7] *Letters*, VIII.272; see Hampson, *Life of Wesley*, II.138.   [8] *Journal*, V.265f.
[9] *Works*, VI.356.   [10] ibid., p. 128.   [11] *Sermons*, I.30.

avenues of the invisible world, the evidences of things not seen, as the bodily senses are of visible things".'[12]

There is much, however, to be said on the other side. It would appear that Wesley was dogmatic only on the *essentials* of religion.[13] In his writings are many traces of critical power and independent judgement. He was often content to 'think and let think'.[14] We quote two passages from Wesley's pen that exemplify his 'philosophic temper'. 'In spite of all my logic *I cannot so prove* any one point in the whole compass of philosophy or Divinity as not to leave room for strong objections, and probably such as I could not answer.'[15] In his later years, Wesley wrote: 'When I was young I was *sure* of everything. In a few years ... I was not half so sure of most things as before. At present, I am hardly sure of anything, but what God has revealed to man.'[16]

Wesley held that to renounce reason is to renounce religion.[17] In 1745, he wrote: 'I believe and reason too. For I find no inconsistency between them.'[18] Wesley felt the necessity of drawing up a *Philosophy* of five volumes with the title, *A Survey of the Wisdom of God in Creation; or, a Compendium of Natural Philosophy*. In this work, Wesley is held to have anticipated in some degree Darwin's theory of evolution.[19] Fifty pages of Vol. V are devoted to mental philosophy, which Wesley introduces by saying: 'I now intend to speak particularly of the human understanding chiefly on the plan of the pious and learned Dr Peter Browne, late Bishop of Cork, in Ireland.'[20]

Dr Workman maintains that Methodism was profoundly influenced by the drift of philosophy in England, and that in any survey of English thought the place of Wesley cannot be neglected.[21] It is well at this point that we should sketch very briefly the relevant features of this 'drift of philosophy', in

---

[12] Lecky, *History of England in the Eighteenth Century*, III.137. Regarding a sixth sense for spiritual apprehension, see Dr W. B. Selbie, *Christianity and the New Psychology* (1939), p. 41.

[13] See Part III, ch. 1, pp. 105ff., *supra*, ch. 2, pp. 185ff., *supra*.

[14] See Shepherd, *Methodism and the Literature of the Eighteenth Century*, ch. VI.

[15] *Letters*, IV.181.

[16] Eayrs, *Wesley, Christian Philosopher and Church Founder*, p. 80.

[17] *Works*, XIX.354.   [18] ibid., X.267.

[19] Wesley's *Philosophy*, IV.58, 73, 102, 109, 129f.

[20] Browne's work is *The Procedure, Extent, and Limits of the Human Understanding* (1728); see W. R. Sorley, *History of English Philosophy* (1930), pp. 136f., 342.

[21] Workman, *New History of Methodism*, I.17f.

addition to what has been said on earlier pages about Deism in the eighteenth century.

Reference has already been made to the similarity between Wesley's teaching on the inner consciousness of salvation and Descartes' philosophical method. Descartes attempted to formulate a theory of knowledge on the principle, *cogito ergo sum*.[22] He could doubt everything else, including God and His world, but he could not doubt the fact that he doubted.[23] The irreducible minimum was his own self-consciousness.

Locke, rejecting the notion of 'innate ideas', held the view that the mind could be likened to a *tabula rasa*[24] on which the external world made its impressions. Locke's empirical interpretation of knowledge, therefore, was that all our ideas, however abstract, were derived from experience.[25]

Berkeley inherited elements from Locke's empiricism and also made central to his epistemology Descartes' first idea, i.e. thinking mind. His basic principle is summed up in the phrase: *esse est percipi*.[26] This idealistic philosophy held that mind or spirit was the only reality; and that the external world could be held to exist only as it is perceived by some mind, either man's or God's.

It only remained for Hume's acute intellect to carry this trend of thought to its logical conclusion.[27] Having confirmed Berkeley's denial of the reality of matter, he proceeded to deny on the same ground the reality of spirit. His unswerving application of these empirical principles led to the reduction of the self to a mere bundle or flux of impressions.[28]

'In its relation to the philosophy of the age', says Dr Dimond, 'Methodism is at once a reflexion and a reaction. It reflects the individualism and reacts from the rationalism of the century.'[29] In earlier chapters, we dealt with the reaction of Methodism to the deistic philosophy of the time. We now consider the extent to which Wesley's teaching was a reflexion

---

[22] 'I think, therefore I am'; Descartes (1596–1650), *Method* (1636).

[23] Waterhouse, *Philosophical Approach to Religion* (1933), p. 4.

[24] 'White paper'; Locke (1632–1704), *Essay Concerning Human Understanding* (1690), Bk. II, ii, 1.

[25] Galloway, *Philosophy of Religion* (1935), pp. 274f.

[26] 'To exist is to be perceived'; Berkeley (1685–1753), *A Treatise Concerning the Principles of Human Knowledge* (1710).

[27] Sorley, *History of English Philosophy*, pp. 171ff.

[28] Hume (1711–76), *A Treatise of Human Nature* (1739); *An Essay Concerning Human Understanding* (1758).

[29] Dimond, *The Psychology of the Methodist Revival* (1926), p. 224.

of the philosophical thought which we have just outlined.

It does not appear that Wesley seriously attempted to indicate the relationship of his doctrine of assurance to this trend of philosophy. Wesley seems to have laid greater store by the writings of Dr Peter Browne than by the philosophy of Locke;[30] though, says Duncan Coomer, 'Wesley was an empiricist and not a systematic theologian'.[31] Wesley's consistent appeal to experience is reminiscent of Locke's patient examination of particular facts.[32]

The influence of Descartes and Locke is traceable in Wesley's sermon on 'The Discoveries of Faith', dated 11th June 1788: 'For many years, it has been allowed by sensible men, Nihil est in intellectu quod non fuit prius in sensu....[33] All the knowledge which we naturally have is originally derived from the senses.... Some indeed have, of late years, endeavoured to prove that we have innate ideas, not derived from any of the senses, but co-eval with the understanding. But this point has now been thoroughly discussed by men of the most eminent learning; and it is agreed ... that although some things are so plain ... that we can very hardly avoid knowing them as soon as we come to the use of our understanding; yet the knowledge even to those is not innate, but derived from some of our senses.' But God, continues Wesley, has 'appointed faith to supply the defect of sense.... Sense is the evidence of things that are seen. ... Faith ... is the "evidence of things not seen".'[34]

The foundation of faith, says Balmforth, 'is to give that assurance which philosophy by its own nature can never give'.[35] Söderblom believes that faith possesses a more certain assurance of its object than does other knowledge.[36] Dr Galloway holds that there is in faith a cognitive element, which involves a claim to know. He goes on to argue that 'empiricism ... cannot meet the demands of the religious consciousness' since 'spiritual Reality lies beyond all presentations of sense.... Even the

---

[30] *Works*, XIII.416ff.; *Journal*, IV.192; *Letters*, VII.227f.

[31] Coomer, *English Dissent under the Early Hanoverians* (1946), p. 122.

[32] Dimond, op. cit., p. 227.

[33] 'There is nothing in the mind which is not first in the senses'; see Dr Tennant, *Philosophical Theology*, ch. III.

[34] *Works*, VII.231f. For the theory of a special organ of spiritual knowledge, see Dr T. H. Hughes, *The Philosophic Basis of Mysticism* (1937), pp. 98ff.

[35] Balmforth, *Is Christian Experience an Illusion?* (1923), pp. 2of.

[36] Söderblom, *The Nature of Revelation*, p. 115.

witness of God in spiritual life involves a movement of faith beyond what is given.'[37]

Wesley appears to have paid more attention to Berkeley than to any other philosopher. 'Wesley's idealism', comments Dr Eayrs, 'is that of Berkeley, Christianized.'[38] Wesley, however, criticized Berkeley's use of the words 'idea' and 'sensation' and levelled against his empiricism the charge of tautology.[39] It is not surprising that the impasse into which Hume's critical thought had brought philosophy drew from Wesley a charge of 'despiser of truth' and an enemy of 'all that is sacred and valuable upon earth'.[40] He considered that Hume knew the heart of man 'no more than a worm or a beetle does'.[41] Harald Lindström says that 'the Enlightenment led to the scepticism of Hume, but it was surmounted in Wesley by means of an irrationalism which naturally looked like enthusiasm to Locke, Butler, and Hume'.[42]

Wesley clearly has Hutcheson in mind when he refers to those writers who speak of conscience in terms of a 'moral sense'.[43] This phrase means for Hutcheson a special capacity of the soul by which moral distinctions are directly apprehended; and, therefore, has affinities with Wesley's inner sense of certainty.[44]

This inquiry leaves us in no doubt that Wesley believed that he had an inner spiritual assurance of God. Or, in philosophical terms, by an empirical method he was confident of contact with Ultimate Reality. Wesley speaks of 'God's breathing into the soul, and the soul's breathing back what it first received from God; a continual action of God upon the soul, and a reaction of the soul upon God'.[45] It has been said that the emphasis placed by Wesley upon experience is in accord with the best scientific thought of the times.[46]

Lindström points out that the obvious foundation to which he always referred was Scripture, but that this was interpreted in the light of experience.[47] Dr Cell maintains that in a century which turned radically from all speculation to investigation and poured its best thought into scientific research,

[37] Galloway, *Philosophy of Religion*, pp. 271, 275.
[38] Eayrs, *Wesley, Christian Philosopher and Church Founder*, p. 84.
[39] *Letters*, I.25.   [40] *Journal*, V.303, 458.   [41] *Works*, VIII.342.
[42] Lindström, *Wesley and Sanctification*, p. 2.   [43] *Sermons*, I.223.
[44] Lord Shaftesbury (1671–1713), *Inquiry Concerning Virtue* (1699), i, 3, 1; Hutcheson (1694–1747), *Essay on the Nature and Conduct of the Passions and Affections, with Illustrations on the Moral Sense* (1728), *System of Moral Philosophy* (1755).
[45] *Sermons*, I.311.   [46] *New History of Methodism*, I.27.
[47] Lindström, *Wesley and Sanctification*, p. 9.

Wesley, in active sympathy with the new science, has the distinction of introducing the experimental method of reasoning into religious subjects.[48]

There is little trace in Wesley's writings of any excursion into the psychological territory of his times, beyond a reference to 'what Mr Locke calls "the association of ideas",'[49] and a somewhat unscientific use of the words 'introversion' and 'extraversion'.[50] The psychological significance, however, of a claim to an inner assurance is manifest. In preceding chapters, especially in our treatment of mysticism, the psychological features of our study frequently presented themselves.

It is important to observe that, whereas contemporary thought directed its attention almost exclusively to intellectual factors, Wesley claimed a place in the content of the mind for spiritual phenomena. In so doing, Wesley was blazing the trail of a pioneer cause, for his introspective work in the realm of the Spirit has helped to establish the validity of an inner sense of certainty. Psychology is now generally disposed to recognize that religious experience has as good a claim to a respectful hearing as any of the other manifold experiences of man's inner life.[51]

There is, after all, a subjective element, not only in religious knowledge, but in *all* knowledge; and, partly for this reason, the theory of knowledge is one of the problems of philosophy.[52] Wesley's assurance of salvation involved what the psychologist might call a feeling of 'otherness'. Dr Valentine says, 'The religious consciousness must have a religious metaphysic. It must know that the object of its worship is true, and that it is truth . . . about ultimate reality. . . . In particular it may be urged that no object which is unsatisfactory to philosophy can be satisfactory to religion.'[53]

Wesley's doctrine of assurance can be seriously imperilled only by a psychological theory which questions the *possibility* whether a sense of certainty may be inwardly experienced. Any attempt on the part of psychology to deny the objective side of an inner assurance of salvation, on the ground of its being a purely subjective experience, can be ignored. In making such

[48] Cell, op. cit., p. 9.   [49] *Journal*, II.179.   [50] *Works*, VI.451.
[51] Dr H. Maldwyn Hughes, *Theology of Experience*, p. 50.
[52] Montague, *The Ways of Knowing*; Dr Oman, *The Natural and the Supernatural*, p. 151.
[53] C. H. Valentine, *Modern Psychology and the Validity of Christian Experience* (1926), p. 38.

a denial, the psychologist is overstepping the boundary of his science and invading the territory of metaphysics. Leuba, for instance, errs in stating a metaphysical, rather than a scientific, judgement when he contends that, 'in religious lives accessible to psychological investigation, nothing requiring the admission of superhuman influence has been found'.[54]

Dr Sugden points out that recent studies in the psychology of the spiritual life confirm Wesley's teaching, though they do not always use his language. They agree in holding that in some way there must be a direct communication of the Divine to the human spirit for the full development of the higher life.[55]

The development of philosophy and psychology has revealed the ill-defined distinction that has sometimes been drawn between 'material' and 'non-material' things. There was once a tendency to regard only the former as 'facts'. Such a distinction is losing its meaning today. 'Thoughts' and 'emotions' are now seen to be as 'factual' as 'bricks and mortar'. With the passing of the centuries, the connotation of 'science', which began by including the inanimate world only, and later added the biological realm, now embraces the intangible sphere of mind.

'It is true', says Balmforth, 'that experience of the spiritual is a more delicate and subtle thing than experience of the material world, and much less verifiable by external and peremptory tests; but every advance from the merely mechanical levels of reality is necessarily accompanied by such an increased difficulty of apprehension. . . . We know nothing exhaustively, least of all the Supreme Reality.'[56]

If theology is to be rejected because it leaves certain mysteries in religious experience unexplained, then other sciences must suffer the same fate. The differences between physicists regarding the nature of 'light' do not render astronomy useless. Biologists are still baffled by the secret of 'life', but this has not destroyed botany and zoology. And while psychologists continue to grope for a definition of 'mind', their science grows apace.

Our line of thought here is finely expressed by Dr C. Ryder Smith: 'As the "ordinary" man, through all the changes in optical science, has stood by the assertion, "I do see, and there is a sun"; or, as through all the history of medicine and chemistry he has maintained, "I do hunger, and there is such a

[54] Leuba, *A Psychological Study of Religion*, p. 272.
[55] Sugden, *Standard Sermons*, I.202.   [56] Balmforth, op. cit., pp. 61, 99.

thing as food"; or, as through all the gropings of psychology he still maintains, "I do love, and there is such a thing as home"; or, as amid all the revolutions of metaphysics he does not abate the claim, "I do think, and things do exist that answer to my thoughts"; so he may say confidently, "I do worship, and there is such a one as God".... The "ordinary" Christian may make a similar ground for his particular claim . . . that he not only "knows God" but "knows Christ".'[57]

No necessity, therefore, is laid upon us to jettison our doctrine of assurance merely because, in the last analysis of Christian experience, there is an inexplicable residuum, or mystery, which admits of no final explanation. Wesley himself confesses that to require a 'philosophical account . . . of the criteria or intrinsic marks whereby we know the voice of God, is to make a demand which can never be answered; no, not by one who has the deepest knowledge of God'.[58]

[57] C. Ryder Smith, *The Christian Experience* (1926), p. 307.   [58] *Sermons*, I.216.

POSTSCRIPT

I WISH in this Postscript to write in a more direct and personal strain. This book is being published, not only on account of the academic interest of the subject, but because an experience of assurance is so greatly needed by all who would 'profess and call themselves Christians'.

The widespread urge for certainty in religion partly explains why some converts have been attracted to 'Fundamentalism' on the one hand or to 'Roman Catholicism' on the other. Generally speaking, the sure guide in the former is the infallible Bible, while in the latter it is the infallibe Church. In neither direction, however, can some of us hope to gain a firm ground of personal assurance. Merely to pay lip service to such creeds, while it may appear a sound confession of faith to others, carries no conviction or certainty for the person who makes it. Intellectual dishonesty can never be a secure foundation for an assurance of salvation.

There is another way—a way which I trust this book has helped to make clear. Its reality is in the realm of the Spirit. It is the certainty which comes when, as Paul says, the 'Spirit Himself beareth witness with our spirit that we are children of God'. If this seems too unrealistic, let me approach it from the human angle.

What is the *essence* of human fellowship? One does not need to be a psychologist to see that real friendship is not a physical entity. It is an affinity of spirits. We fail to 'get on' with some people, not because they have a long nose or double chin (or both!), but for one reason only: our spirit or personality is not in tune with theirs. Harmony on the human level, therefore, is a blending of *spirits*.

Moreover, this interaction of personalities can be neither adequately explained nor demonstrated to the onlooker. But the onlooker can cultivate human fellowship for himself, and then he will know in his own consciousness that 'such harmony is in immortal souls'. And, if such communion is possible between men, we need not doubt that the Spirit of God can bear an inner witness to our place in His family. As the hymn puts it:

'O strangely art Thou with us, Lord,
 Neither in height nor depth to seek:
In nearness shall Thy voice be heard;
 Spirit to spirit Thou dost speak.'

Some readers may be inclined to ask whether 'feeling' occupies too large a place in the Doctrine of Assurance. While this book has shown how Wesley safeguarded the doctrine from excessive emotionalism, I see no reason to depreciate religious feeling as such. 'An intellectual love of God' can satisfy only a Spinoza. I am not among those who seem anxious to squeeze all 'feeling' out of Christianity.

If personality includes not only 'thinking' and 'willing' but also 'feeling', how can we exclude this element from a personal experience of God? Nobody in his right mind would try to banish emotion from the enjoyment of sport, or the appreciation of music, or from falling in love. How anyone can have a personal assurance of salvation—an experience of the pardon and peace of God—without feeling it, I cannot imagine. Nor could Wesley: 'I well saw that nobody could, in the nature of things, have a sense of forgiveness and not *feel* it.' Describing his Aldersgate experience, he said: 'I *felt* my heart strangely warmed. I *felt* I did trust in Christ, in Christ alone for salvation.'

There is no doubt that religion is 'caught' rather than taught, and that 'one loving heart sets another on fire'. It was for this reason that the Methodist Revival spread so rapidly in the eighteenth century. I have tried to show that the Doctrine of Assurance is well founded in Scripture and in the history of the Church, and that it can claim validity. But how much more important it is that we should have experimental proof in our own hearts!

An experience of assurance lives on what it produces. The meaning of this has been seen in Wesley's life and work. The certainty he found at Aldersgate made him the inspired leader of one of the greatest revivals since Apostolic times and the founder of world Methodism. And it was the doing of this great work which, in turn, stimulated the inner witness of the Spirit. By becoming less attentive to his feelings and more concerned with the tasks before him, Wesley's initial experience of assurance was sustained throughout his long life.

We do well to keep this fact always before us, especially when the heart is heavy and the vision is dim. Sluggishness of spirit seldom calls for prolonged spiritual introspection, but rather for the outward exercise of our powers in Christian work. A time of refreshing from the presence of the Lord will come the more rapidly as we spend ourselves in His service. In the light of this we can understand why Wesley was so ready to quote his brother's hymn:

> 'Jesus, confirm my heart's desire
> To work, and speak, and think for Thee;
> Still let me guard the holy fire,
> And still stir up Thy gift in me.'

How zealous are we in our search for certainty? If we really want to be sure of God we shall spare no effort to gain this experience. Are we prepared to go as far as Wesley went in order to get it? He prayed strenuously and sincerely until assurance was his. He welcomed the guidance of fellow Christians. He shared in the worship and fellowship of the Church. He feasted his soul on the Bible and at the Sacrament of the Lord's Supper.

How revealing is the page in Wesley's *Journal* that tells how he spent 24th May 1738! The morning hours found him on his knees poring over the Book of God. In the afternoon he was in St Paul's Cathedral. Yet the 'Witness of the Spirit' came to him in a simple evening service in an ordinary building—just a society meeting in Aldersgate Street. His heart was 'strangely warmed' while somebody—we are not sure who—was reading Luther's Preface to the Epistle to the Romans. God can also kindle the same flame on the mean altar of *our* hearts—whoever we are, wherever we live or work.

If it be true that the pulpit has lost its note of certainty and the pew its power of personal testimony, here is the remedy—an assurance of salvation. This experience is a privilege for which we should all strive. We need it. Methodism needs it. The universal Church needs it.

My highest hope for these pages will be fulfilled if, as the reader closes the book, he is able prayerfully to say with Charles Wesley:

> 'My God! I know, I feel Thee mine,
> And will not quit my claim,
> Till all I have is lost in Thine
> And all renewed I am.'

BIBLIOGRAPHY

I. Early Methodist Writings

Journal of the Rev. John Wesley, 8 vols., ed. Curnock, Standard Edition (1909-16).
Letters of the Rev. John Wesley, 8 vols., ed. Telford, Standard Edition (1931).
Standard Sermons of John Wesley, 2 vols., ed. E. H. Sugden (1935).
Works of the Rev. John Wesley, 14 vols., ed. Jackson (1829-31).
Lives of the Early Methodist Preachers: Chiefly written by Themselves, 6 vols., ed. Jackson (1865).
Wesley: *Explanatory Notes upon the New Testament* (1755).
Wesley: *An Earnest Appeal to Men of Reason and Religion* (1743).
Journal of the Rev. Charles Wesley, 2 vols., ed. Jackson (1849).
Journal of George Whitefield (1738, 1741, 1744).
The Arminian Magazine (1779-1800).

II. The Eighteenth Century

Abbey, C. J., and Overton, J. H.: *The English Church in the Eighteenth Century*, 2 vols. (1896).
Birrell, Augustine: *John Wesley, Some Aspects of the Eighteenth Century*.
Edwards, Maldwyn: *John Wesley and the Eighteenth Century*.
Evans, Theophilus: *The History of Modern Enthusiasm from the Reformation to the Present Time* (1756).
Fitchett, W. H.: *Wesley and His Century* (1906).
Green, J. R.: *A Short History of the English People*.
Green, Lomas: *Dissertation on Enthusiasm* (1755).
Lavington, George: *Enthusiasm of Methodists and Papists Compared* (1749-51).
Lecky, W. E. H.: *History of England in the Eighteenth Century*, 7 vols. (1872).
Overton and Relton: *History of the English Church, 1714-1800* (1906).
Plummer: *The Church of England in the Eighteenth Century*.
Shepherd, T. B.: *Methodism and the Literature of the Eighteenth Century* (1940).
Stephen: *English Thought in the Eighteenth Century*.
Whiteley, J. H.: *Wesley's England; Wesley's Anglican Contemporaries*.

III. General Methodist Literature

Bett, Henry: *The Spirit of Methodism* (1937).
Cannon, W. R.: *Theology of John Wesley* (1946).
Cell, G. C.: *Rediscovery of John Wesley* (1935).
Church, L. F.: *The Early Methodist People* (1948).
Cubit, G.: *A Brief Defence of the People Called Methodists* (1816).
Green, Richard: *John Wesley, Evangelist.*
Harrison, A. W.: *The Evangelical Revival and Christian Reunion.*
Lee, Umphrey: *John Wesley and Modern Religion* (1936).
Nightingale J.: *Portraiture of Methodism* (1807).
Piette, Maximin: *John Wesley in the Evolution of Protestantism.* Eng. trans. by J. B. Howard (1938).
Proceedings of the Wesley Historical Society.
Rattenbury, J. E.: *Conversion of the Wesleys* (1938); *Wesley's Legacy to the World* (1928).
Rigg, J. H.: *The Living Wesley* (1891).
Sangster, W. E.: *The Path to Perfection* (1943).
Simon, J. S.: *John Wesley and the Religious Societies* (1921); *John Wesley the Master Builder* (1927); *John Wesley and the Methodist Societies* (1923).
Southey, R.: *The Life of John Wesley* (1820).
Townsend, Workman and Eayrs: *New History of Methodism,* 2 vols. (1909).
Tyerman, L.: *Life and Times of John Wesley,* 3 vols. (1890); *Life of the Rev. George Whitefield* (1890).

IV. Theological

Beet, J. A.: *A Manual of Theology.*
Carnegy, P. C. A.: *Assurance of God* (1940).
Dorner: *System of Christian Certainty* (Eng. trans., 1880).
Flew, R. N.: *The Idea of Perfection in Christian Theology* (1934).
Garbett, Cyril: *The Claims of the Church of England* (1947).
Hastings, J.: *The Doctrine of Faith* (1919).
Howells: *Roman and Anglican Claims* (1933).
Humphries, A. L.: *The Holy Spirit in Faith and Experience* (1911).
Kirk, K. E.: *The Vision of God* (1931).
Lindstrom, Harald: *Wesley and Sanctification* (1946).
Mackintosh, H. R.: *The Christian Experience of Forgiveness* (1927).
Otto, Rudolf: *The Idea of the Holy* (1926).
Pope, W. B.: *Compendium of Christian Theology,* 3 vols. (1880).

Prest, Charles: *An Essay on the Witness of the Spirit to the adoption of the Christian Believer* (1848).
Robinson, H. Wheeler: *The Christian Experience of the Holy Spirit* (1928).
Scougal, H.: *The Life of God in the Soul of Man* (1702).
Smith, C. Ryder: *The Christian Experience* (1926).
Stalker, James: *The Basis of Christian Certainty*; *The Expositor*, vol. VI, Sixth Series.
Watkin-Jones, H.: *The Holy Spirit from Arminius to Wesley* (1929).
Young, R. N.: *Witness of the Spirit* (1882).
Article on Assurance in the *New Schaff-Herzog Encyclopaedia of Religious Knowledge*.
Encyclopaedia of Religion and Ethics, 13 vols., ed. James Hastings.

V. Biblical

Ball, W. E. B.: *St Paul and the Roman Law*.
Chase, F. H.: *The Credibility of the Acts of the Apostles* (1902).
Dodd, C. H.: 'Romans' in *Moffatt N.T. Commentary*.
Findlay, G. G.: *Fellowship in the Life Eternal*.
Garvie, A. E.: 'Romans' in the *Century Bible*.
Hastings, J.: *Dictionary of the Bible*, 5 vols.; *Dictionary of Christ and the Gospels*, 2 vols.; *Dictionary of the Apostolic Church*, 2 vols.
Hunter, A. M.: *Paul and His Predecessors* (1940).
Kennedy: *The Theology of the Epistles*.
Rattenbury, J. E.: *Testament of Paul*.
Scott, C. A. A.: *Christianity According to St Paul*.
Scott, E. F.: *The Spirit in the New Testament*.
Stevens, G. B.: *Theology of the New Testament*.
Swete, H. B.: *The Holy Spirit in the New Testament*.
The Cambridge Greek Testament.
The Expositor's Greek Testament.
Commentary on the Revised Version, 1882 (ed. Humphrey).
The International Critical Commentary.

VI. Hymnology

Baker, Frank: *Charles Wesley as Revealed by His Letters* (1948).
Bett, Henry: *The Hymns of Methodism*.
Gillman, F. J.: *Evolution of the English Hymn*.
Jackson, Thomas: *Life of Charles Wesley*, 2 vols.
Jones, D. M.: *Charles Wesley—A Study*.

Julian, J.: *Dictionary of Hymnology.*
Manning, B. L.: *Hymns of Wesley and Watts.*
Osborn, G.: *Poetical Works of John and Charles Wesley*, 13 vols. (1872).
Rattenbury, J. E.: *The Evangelical Doctrines of Charles Wesley's Hymns.*
Stevenson, G. J.: *The Methodist Hymn Book and Its Associations* (1870).
Wesley, Charles: *Short Hymns on Select Passages of the Holy Scriptures*, 2 vols. (1762).
Wiseman, F. L.: *Charles Wesley, Evangelist and Poet.*
A Collection of Hymns for the use of the People called Methodists (1780).

VII. Historical Theology

Allen, V. C.: *The Continuity of Christian Thought* (1884).
Calvin: *Institutes of the Christian Religion* (Eng. trans. 1845); *Tracts* (Eng. trans. 1851); *Commentaries.*
Davies, R. E., *The Problem of Authority in the Continental Reformers* (1946).
Fisher, G. P.: *History of the Church* (1900); *History of Christian Doctrine.*
Foakes-Jackson, F. J.: *History of the Christian Church* (1914).
Hagenbach: *History of Christian Doctrine* (Eng. trans. 1880).
Harnack, A.: *History of Dogma*, Eng. trans., M'Gilchrist. 7 vols.
Hastie: *Theology of the Reformed Church* (1904).
Lightfoot and Harmer: *The Apostolic Fathers.*
Lindsay: *History of the Reformation*, 2 vols.
Mackinnon: *Luther and the Reformation*, 2 vols. (1925).
Rainy: *Ancient Catholic Church* (1926).
Slater, W. F.: *Methodism in the Light of the Early Church* (1885).
Swete, H. B.: *The Holy Spirit in the Ancient Church.*
Wand, J. C. W.: *History of the Modern Church* (1930).
Watkin-Jones, H.: *The Holy Spirit in the Medieval Church* (1922).
Whitham, A. R.: *History of the Christian Church* (1936).
Workman, H. B.: *Christian Thought to the Reformation* (1911); *Dawn of the Reformation* (1901).
The Ante-Nicene Christian Library.
The Nicene and Post-Nicene Christian Library.
Concise Dictionary of National Biography (1917).
Dictionary of Christian Biography and Literature (first six centuries), ed. H. Wace and W. C. Piercy (1911).

VIII. Mysticism and Quakerism

Barclay, Robert: *Apology* (1736) in *Works*, vol. II (1831).
Journal of George Fox, 2 vols. (1901).
Green, J. B.: *John Wesley and William Law* (1945).
Grubb, Edward: *The Religion of Experience; Authority and the Light Within* (1909).
Hughes, H. M.: *Theology of Experience* (1915).
Hughes, T. H.: *The Philosophic Basis of Mysticism* (1937).
Inge, W. R.: *Christian Mysticism* (1933).
Jones, Rufus: *Social Law in the Spiritual World* (1904); *Studies in Mystical Religion* (1909).
Leuba, J. H.: *The Psychology of Religious Mysticism* (1925).
Nuttall, G. F.: *The Holy Spirit in Puritan Faith and Experience*.
Penington, Isaac: *Works* (1861).
Sabatier, Auguste: *The Religions of Authority and the Religion of the Spirit* (1904).
Underhill, E.: *The Mystic Way* (1913); *Mysticism* (1911); *The Life of the Spirit and the Life of Today* (1922).

IX. Philosophy and Psychology

Balmforth, H.: *Is Christian Experience an Illusion?*
Berkeley: *Treatise Concerning the Principles of Human Knowledge*.
Caldecott, A.: *The Religious Sentiment* (1909); *The Psychology of Religion* (1907).
Descartes: *Philosophical Works*, ed. Haldane and Ross, 2 vols. (1912).
Dimond, S. G.: *Heart and Mind* (1945); *Psychology of the Methodist Revival* (1926).
Eayrs, G.: *John Wesley: Christian Philosopher and Church Founder* (1926).
Galloway: A.: *Philosophy of Religion* (1914).
Hume: *Treatise on Human Nature* (1739).
James, Wm.: *Varieties of Religious Experience* (1902).
Kant: *Critique of Pure Reason; Critique of Practical Reason*.
Leuba, J. H.: *A Psychological Study of Religion* (1912).
Locke: *Concerning Human Understanding*.
McDougall, Wm.: *An Outline of Psychology* (1923).
Montague: *The Ways of Knowing*.
Oman, John: *Grace and Personality* (1917).
Rashdall, Hastings: *Philosophy and Religion* (1931).

Russell, Bertrand: *Problems of Philosophy*.
Selbie, W. B.: *Christianity and the New Psychology* (1939); *The Validity of Christian Experience* (1939).
Sorley, W. R.: *Moral Values and the Idea of God* (1916); *History of English Philosophy* (1920).
Stace, W. T.: *Critical History of Greek Philosophy*; *Theory of Knowledge and Existence* (1932).
Stout: *Manual of Psychology*.
Tennant, F. R.: *Philosophical Theology*.
Valentine, C. H.: *Modern Psychology and the Validity of Christian Experience* (1926).
Waterhouse, E. S.: *Philosophical Approach to Religion* (1933); *Psychology and Religion* (1930).

INDEX OF NAMES

ADENAY, W. F., 123
Ambrose, 154f.
Annesley, Dr, 186
Apollos, 43
Aquila, 43
Aquinas, Thomas, 158f., 161
Aristides, 151
Aristotle, 157
Arnold, M., 48
Asbury, F., 49
Athanasius, 194
Augustine, 86, 155f.

BAKER, F., 13
Balmforth, H., 214, 217
Banks, Dr, 137
Barclay, R., 174
Basil, 153f.
Baxter, R., 17
Bedford, A., 61, 129, 133
Beet, J. A., 82, 111f., 113
Behmen, J., 205
Bell, R., 201
Benham, 31f.
Bennett, W. H., 119
Benson, J., 73
Bentley, R., 185
Bengel, J. A., 109, 134
Berkeley, 185, 213, 215
Bergson, 208
Bernard, Dr J. H., 122
Bernard of Clairvaux, St, 68, 161f.
Bett, H., 5, 20, 206f.
Beveridge, W., 55
Black, W., 43
Boehme, J., 206
Böhler, P., 9, 10, 21, 25ff., 29ff., 32, 35, 37, 41f., 53ff., 89, 105, 115, 194, 198, 200
Bolton, R., 195
Bourignon, A., 85
Bray, of Little Britain, 42f., 86, 198
Brigden, T. E., 14
Broughton, T., 187
Brown, W. A., 163, 167
Browne, P., 212, 214
Bruce, A. B., 132
Buckingham, Duchess of, 180
Bull, Bishop G., 62
Bunyan, J., 86
Burton, Dr J., 13
Butler, Bishop, 182, 185, 215
Byrom, J., 206

CALDECOTT, DR, 44, 49
Calvin, 163

Cannon, W. R., 4, 9, 14, 56, 58, 180
Catharinus, Ambrosius, 158
Cell, G. C., 5, 9ff., 18, 58, 79, 207, 215
Cennick, J., 183
Chase, Dr, 139f.
Church, Dr L. F., 45, 47, 49
Church, T., 64
Chrysostom, 68, 194
Clarke, S., 185
Clemens Romanus, 54
Clement of Alexandria, 152
Cockburn, Dr, 41
Collin, A., 179
Coomer, D., 214
Cownley, J., 46
Cranmer, Archbishop, 193
Cubitt, G., 187, 197

DARWIN, 173, 212
David, C., 33f.
Davidson, 132
Deissmann, 143
Delamotte, C., 40, 57
Demuth, C., 37
Descartes, 213f.
Dimond, S. G., 3, 208, 213
Dodd, C. H., 112, 124, 127
Dods, M., 128, 131f.
Dominicus da Soto, 158
Dorner, I. A., 164
Downes, J., 44, 184

EAYRS, G., 6, 13, 215
Eckhart, 205
Edwards, 116
Euripides, 135
Evans, Theophilus, 181
Evans, T. S., 116

FABER, 157
Feder, A. T., 36
Findlay, G. G., 119, 123f., 126
Fisher, G. P., 81
Fitchett, W. H., 187
Flew, R. N., 135, 161
Fox, G., 173f.
Francke, A. H., 29

GALLOWAY, G., 214
Gambold, J., 200
Garvis, A. E., 112
Gaulter, J., 46
Gerhardt, P., 83f.
Gibson (Bishop), E., 182
Gifford, E. H., 134
Gradin, A., 129

Graves, C., 181
Gregory (Bishop), 154
Gregory (Pope), 160
Green, R., 181
Green, T., 181
Greenfield, E., 46
Grimshaw, W., 130
Grubb, E., 141, 175
Gwatkin, H. M., 163

HAERING, T. VON, 138
Hagenbach, 21
Haliburton, J., 54
Hall (Bishop), 195, 200
Hall, Wesley, 50
Harnack, A., 155
Hartley, Rev. T., 204
Harvey, J., 106
Heinrici, 116
Hegel, G. W. F., 205
Hilary, of Poictiers, 153
Holland, W., 56
Hooker, R., 171
Hooper (Bishop), 193
Hopkey, Sophia, 7, 23
Hughes, H. M., 136
Hugo of St Victor, 161
Hume, 213, 215
Hunter, A. M., 144
Huntingdon, Countess of, 180, 200
Hutcheson, F., 215

IGNATIUS, L., 54, 149, 151
Inge, W. R., 144
Ingham, B., 31f., 40
Irenaeus, 151
Ivo of Chartres, 161

JACKSON, T., 200
Jacob, 88, 91
James, W., 48, 77, 80, 205, 208f.
Jenyns, S., 106
Jeremiah, 124
Jesus, 18, 31, 48, 89, 96f., 108, 139ff., 151, 192 (see "Christ" in Subject Index).
Joan of Arc, 209
John the Apostle, 123ff., 205
John the Baptist, 140
Johnson, Dr Samuel, 6
Jones, R. M., 173, 175, 208
Jones, W. L., 183
Justin Martyr, 151

KEMPIS, THOMAS À, 6, 54, 206
Kirby, J., 49

LATIMER (BISHOP), 193
Lavington, G., 77, 130
Law, W., 6, 107, 206

Lawson, J., 11
Lecky, W. E. H., 211
Lee, U., 3, 15f., 19, 54
Léger, A., 3, 7
Leighton (Archbishop), 195
Leuba, J. N., 217
Lightfoot, J. B., 116
Lindström, H., 79, 215
Linner, M., 34f.
Locke, J., 179, 185, 204, 213, 214, 215
Luke, St, 141
Luther, M., 42, 53, 56, 115, 163, 170, 171, 173, 198, 203

MACKINNON, 165
Maskew, J., 46
Massie, J., 116, 118
Mather, A., 44
Melanchthon, P., 166
Meyer, E., 116, 134
Middleton, Dr C., 107
Milton, J., 99
Mitchell, T., 45
Moffatt, J., 127
Molther, P. H., 99, 198f., 202, 204
Montgomery, J., 90
Moule (Bishop), 134
Murlin, J., 44

NEISSER, A., 36
Nelson, J., 44, 49
Nelson, R. W., 55
Newton, J., 18, 105
Nightingale, J., 187
Nitschmann, D., 35f., 40

OEMLER, M. C., 7
Oglethorpe, Gen., 40
Origen, 68, 149, 152f., 194
Othloh of St Emmeram, 161
Owen, J., 172f.

PAUL, THE APOSTLE, 18, 28, 31, 48, 58, 70, 111, 114, 117, 121, 123, 125, 130, 136, 138, 143, 153, 156, 169, 180
Payne, T., 44
Peake, A. S., 132
Pearson (Bishop), 193f.
Penington, I., 174
Perkins, W., 195f.
Peter, St, 87, 141, 142
Piette, M., 3, 5, 15, 18, 53
Plato, 124
Plummer, 117, 118, 179
Polycarp, 54, 149, 150
Pope, W. B., 114, 131, 134, 142, 169, 206
Preston, J., 195
Priscilla, 43

INDEX OF NAMES

Rainy, R., 149f.
Rendall, F., 122
Ratherius of Verona, 161
Rattenbury, J. E., 5, 7, 114
Ridley (Bishop), 193
Ritchie, E., 130
Robinson, J., 43
Robinson, H. Wheeler, 144, 171
Robinson, T. H., 131
Rogers, J., 46
Rothe, J. A., 35, 84
Rutherforth, T., 18, 70, 129

Sabatier, A., 157, 163, 165, 169
Sanday, 134
Sangster, W. E., 4, 5
Schleiermacher, F. D. E., 166
Schneider, D., 36
Schwedler, Pastor, 33
Scougal, H., 6, 39
Scott, C. A. A., 144
Scott, E. F., 143
Seeberg, R., 161
Seward, B., 201
Shadford, G., 45
Shaftesbury, Lord, 179
Shepherd, T. B., 39
Sibbs, R., 195
Simon, J. S., 187f.
Slater, W. F., 143
Smallbroke, R. (Bishop of Lichfield and Coventry), 181, 193
Smith, C. R., 217
Smith, D., 119
"Smith, John," 10, 19, 39, 64, 66, 68
Smith, J., 171f.
Söderblom, 214
Sophocles, 135
Spangenberg, A. G., 21, 37, 57, 59, 84, 89, 199, 202
Stace, W. T., 73
Stalker, J., 163
Staniforth, S., 48
Stevens, G. B., 114
Sugden, E. H., 111, 121, 184, 217
Suso, H., 205
Swete, H. B., 112, 114, 140, 142

Tasker, J. G., 141, 161
Tatian, 151
Tauler, J., 205
Taylor, J., 6, 12, 55, 59, 107
Taylor, T., 46
Tersteegen, G., 83
Tertullian, 152
Thomas, St, 139
Thucydides, 135
Tindal, M., 179
Toland, J., 179
Told, S., 48
Toltschig, J., 31
Tompson, R., 69f., 72, 78, 105, 121, 149, 164

Turner, Mrs., 198, 42f.
Tyerman, 8.

Underhill, E., 207

Vaughan, Dr, 134

Walker, S., 133
Warburton, W., 182, 185
Waterland, 185
Watkin-Jones, H., 11, 160, 171, 185
Watts, I, 88
Webb, Capt., 46
Weiss, 132, 143
Wesley, Charles, 14, 16f., 26, 28, 39, 45, 55f., 58, 67, 82f., 85, 91ff., 115, 170, 194f., 200, 207, 208, 211
Wesley, John, childhood, 7, 80, 105, 211; problem of a career, 4, 5, 7; Anglican ministry, 3f., 5, 32, 40; and Anglicanism, 185ff., 189f., 195f., 210; and Methodism, 3f., 8f., 11, 17, 25, 29, 38f., 43f., 49, 71f., 75, 90, 97, 105, 108, 157, 174, 179, 186f., 201f., 205, 207, 209, 212; missionary journeys, 7ff., 15, 20f., 23f., 40f., 54, 83; preaching, 5, 26, 43ff., 55, 59, 61, 72, 105, 141, 182f.; religious life, 3f., 12f., 20ff., 31ff., 39ff., 53ff., 60, 62ff., 77ff., 83ff., 90, 92, 95ff., 105f., 113ff., 129ff., 139, 142ff., 170, 184, 190f., 198f., 204ff., 210ff.; scholarship, 5, 26, 40, 82f., 86, 105, 108f., 136, 179, 206f., 211ff., 215f.; thought and theology, 4ff., 9f., 12f., 18f., 20, 32f., 37ff., 43ff., 53ff., 61ff., 72, 77, 82ff., 91ff., 105ff., 111ff., 122, 128ff., 133ff., 139ff., 149f., 157f., 164ff., 170, 173ff., 179ff., 184, 185f., 189f., 198f., 202f., 204ff., 210ff.
Wesley, Samuel, 8, 22, 59
Wesley, Samuel, Junr, 19, 61f., 204
Wesley, Susanna, 7, 12, 31, 50, 59
Whatcoat, R., 45
Whitefield, G., 23, 39f., 181
Whiteley, J. H., 82, 180, 185
Whittaker, 171
William of St Thierry, 161
Winchester, 9
Wiseman, F. Luke, 43, 82
Wohlenberg, 126
Wordsworth, Bishop, 134
Workman, H. B., 20, 81, 157, 164, 166, 173, 180, 204, 205, 209, 212
Wyclif, 160

Xenophon, 135

Young, R. N., 114, 133f.

Zinzendorf, Count, 21ff., 25, 31ff., 38, 57, 200

INDEX OF SUBJECTS

ABIDING WITNESS, 32, 192, 199
Acceptance with God, 14, 16, 35, 65, 70, 72, 74, 80, 89, 91, 95, 113, 121, 159, 164, 167, 186, 196
Adoption, 95f., 151ff., 168; assurance of, 74, 96, 168, 172, 194ff.; Spirit of, 44, 95, 111f., 116f., 153, 172
Advocate, 36, 45, 49
Aldersgate Street Experience, 3f, 27, 29f., 31ff., 39, 43, 56f., 59f., 64, 79f., 83, 86, 90, 97, 105, 115, 129, 139, 203, 208, 210f.; what it was not, 5ff.; Wesley's own account, 11, 14ff., 35, 60, 90, 95, 113; and Pentecost, 142f.
America, 23, 30, 46f.
Amusement, love of, 44
Angels, 88, 91, 106, 137
Anglicanism, 5, 7, 19, 28, 32, 39f., 58, 61, 74, 171ff., 181ff., 185ff., 189ff., 210. (Cf. Church.)
Anniversary Hymn (Charles Wesley's), 88ff.
Anointing, 137, 192
Antinomianism, 80, 203, 204
Apostles, 28, 38, 60, 73, 123, 129, 151
Apostolic Church, 139f.; post-Apostolic, 149f.
Arminianism, 81, 166
Articles of faith, 56, 166, 171, 187f.
Ascension, 140, 142, 144
Aspiration, 85, 92, 124
Assurance (Consult 'Contents', 'Summary' and various aspects elsewhere in this Index).
Atonement, 60, 63, 78, 81, 89, 92, 166
Authority, 136, 157, 160, 162, 163ff., 175, 193, 197

BAPTISM OF JESUS, 18; with water, 131, 140, 152, 154; with fire, 95; with Holy Ghost, 140; of infants, 62
Behaviour, 20, 22, 38, 122, 183, 211
Being, and knowing, 160; *esse est percipi*, 213
Belief, 16, 19, 24f., 28, 33, 35, 42ff., 50, 54, 57ff., 62f., 65, 70, 78, 87, 89, 119f., 125, 131, 137, 151, 154, 196, 201, 212
Believers, 17, 34, 36f., 44, 46, 61, 64, 66, 69f., 74, 79ff., 84, 92ff., 96, 100, 114, 118, 122, 135, 137, 154f., 158, 161, 163ff., 172, 186, 201, 209
Bible, in life and thought of Wesley, 27f., 45, 54, 105ff., 210f., 215; of Charles Wesley, 42, 55f.; the basis of Assurance, 13, 17, 27f., 37, 50, 56f., 61f., 67f., 71, 72ff., 80, 105f., 109f., 111ff., 121ff., 128ff., 133ff., 139ff., 164f., 168ff., 175, 179, 181f., 187f., 191f., 195ff., 201, 204f., 209, 210; in the experience of assurance, 42f., 45, 48f., 75, 156; reading of, 105, 192, 200ff.; interpretation, 107f., 165, 215; fortuitous opening, 106, 156; infallibility, 106, 157, 163, 165; in Charles Wesley's hymnal, 86, 98; in Quakerism, 175; in Mysticism, 202, 204f.; Moravian interpretation, 202; criticism, 107f., 179; the canon, 150, 163, 181; 'Bible Christianity', 86, 105
Blessing, 31, 87f., 186, 189
Blindness, 66, 101
Bliss, 85, 101
Blood of Christ, 29f., 34, 36, 46, 49f., 53, 60, 63, 84, 89, 91ff., 97, 129, 151, 154, 168
Boldness, 59, 96, 118, 141ff., 167ff.
Bondage, 113; of sin, 46; night of, 87; spirit of, 112, 153
Brethren, the, 123, 125

CALM, 21, 44, 76, 156
Calvary, 46, 93
Calvinism, 44, 55, 166ff., 171
Carolina, 30, 198
Certainty, 11, 12, 14, 16, 28, 36, 41, 43ff., 47, 50, 63, 69f., 72, 80, 83, 86f., 90, 91, 97, 100f., 109, 117f., 124, 127, 132, 136ff., 141, 144, 149ff., 152 154f., 157ff., 164ff., 171ff., 181, 186, 190, 194, 206, 209, 210, 212, 214ff. (See Conviction.)
Charity, 190; the correlative of grace, 160; charitable hope, 132
Cheerfulness, 164
Childlikeness, 38, 117
Child of God, 11, 13f., 16f., 22, 28, 33f., 37, 39, 43ff., 62f., 66ff., 71, 72f., 76f., 79f., 91, 95f., 107, 111ff., 122f., 126f., 135, 143, 152ff., 160, 162, 168, 171f., 191, 195, 208; marks of, 122f.
Child, of wrath, 15, 71, 87; of grace, 98
Christ, 11, 12f., 16, 19, 20ff., 27ff., 31ff., 40ff., 45f., 49f., 53f., 56ff., 61, 63ff., 67, 69, 73, 75ff., 82ff., 92ff., 100f., 114ff., 119f., 122ff., 128ff., 137., 139ff., 143ff., 150f., 153ff., 161f., 164ff., 173ff., 191, 194ff., 199ff., 206, 210, 218. (See also Jesus.)
Christianity, 6ff., 16ff., 22, 36ff., 43, 53, 55f., 59, 62ff., 67, 70, 72, 77, 79ff., 83, 86, 100, 105f., 109, 116, 118, 121ff.,

Christianity—*cont.*
  130, 136f., 139, 141, 149f., 157ff., 163ff., 171ff., 179, 181, 185ff., 190ff., 196, 198, 204, 206f., 209, 210, 215, 218
Christlikeness, 73, 153
Chronology, double system of, 5, 18
Church, 112, 175, 180, 198, 200, 204f., 210; Anglican, 19, 28, 32, 39ff., 56, 171, 185ff., 202; Moravian, 21f., 34f., 38, 202; Dissenting, 39; Reformed, 164, 166; Methodist Episcopal of America, 47; Early, 68, 123, 139ff., 149f., 174, 181f., 196f.; Mediaeval, 157ff., 163, 165, 207
Claims to Assurance, 101, 137, 158f., 180ff., 205, 209, 210, 214ff., 216, 218. (Cf. Presumption.)
Clarity, of assurance, etc., 64ff., 92, 96, 119, 131, 138, 152, 172, 199
Class Meetings, 49, 161, 205
Clergy, 19, 39, 183, 185f., 194f.
Collects, the, 189ff.
Comfort, to the soul, 36, 42f., 69, 97, 172, 190
Comforter, 95, 172, 190, 192f., 195
Commands of God, 53ff., 75, 107, 123ff., 151, 156, 173, 201, 203
Communication, of election, 167; of Holy Ghost, 172, 189, 217; of knowledge, 208, 211
Communion, with God, 24, 135, 162, 167, 172, 215; with the unseen Lord, 140; of the Spirit, 154. (See also Holy Communion.)
Concurrence of witnesses, 111, 134f.
Condemnation, 43, 64, 67f., 72, 107; of our heart, 126
Confession, Westminster, 172
Confessions of St Augustine, 86, 155f.
Confidence, 13, 21, 27f., 43, 58, 63, 88, 95f., 100, 109f., 128, 150f., 158, 164ff., 168f., 181; filial, 114; in God, 129, 138, 194; in Christ, 137; of our own spirit, 196; of love of God, 200, 215, 218
Conflict, spiritual, 88; mental, 183
Conscience, testimony of, 63, 73, 76, 79, 97, 117, 121, 126, 131, 152, 162, 192f., 196; liberty of, 163; tormented, 166; a 'moral sense', 215; distinguished from the Quaker 'inner light', 174
Consciousness, of pardon, 66, 91, 143, 159, 167; of acceptance, 70, 72, 80, 121, 164, 167; of salvation, 144, 209f., 213; of sonship, 73, 114; testimony of our own, 73, 79, 112, 119, 122f.; of new life, 100, 138; of God's love, 122; of power, 142; of His risen presence, 141; of contact with God, 135, 162, 171, 209; of co-heirship, 155; of the Holy Spirit, 190, 204; the Christian, 123, 175; inner, 137, 213; spiritual, 162; firm and divine, 164; the religious, 214, 216; psychologically defined, 208; Christian unity of, 175; individual, 160, 163, 213; of sin, 79; of fruit of the Spirit, 79
Contact with God, 83; with Spirit, 117; with ultimate reality, 215
Contemplation of the Incarnation, 120; of things of God, 153; of the Passion, 162; of the love of God, 172
Contrition, 69, 156, 159
Conversation, edifying, 24; trifling, 38; our c. in the world, 121; holy, 155
Conversion, 3ff., 10f., 15, 18, 23, 28, 48, 54, 57, 100, 143, 155f., 161, 201
Conversion Hymns, 86ff.
Conviction, 27f., 34, 45, 55, 63, 69f., 77f., 84, 112, 115, 119, 123, 128ff., 136; of unbelief, 24, 26
Corporate experience, 204
Corporate fellowship, corrective influence, 49, 210
Council of Trent, 158
Counter-Reformation, 160
Courage, 47, 142, 164. (See Fearlessness.)
Credulity, 37, 200, 211
Creed, an orthodox, 166
Cross, 48, 93f., 151, 154
Crucifixion, 33, 46, 58, 60, 139, 141, 168, 206. (See Calvary.)
Curacy, Wesley's, 7, 40. (See Wroote.)

'DAILY SERVICE' (C. OF E.), 189
Damascus Road, 18, 31, 48, 137f., 144
Darkness, 28, 63, 74, 150, 172, 186, 201, 208; powers of, 183
Death, 11, 21, 24, 26, 46, 60, 67, 137, 141, 164, 169; of infants, 62; spiritual 125; mystic, 207; of Samuel Wesley, 22, 186; of Dr Annesley, 186; of Polycarp, 150
Deeds, 17, 34, 84, 101, 110, 121ff., 140, 142, 160, 190. (See Works.)
Degrees, of assurance, 64, 72, 77f., 101f., 128ff., 133f.; of faith, 199ff.
Deism, 179f., 185, 188, 211, 213
Deliverance, 33, 43, 48, 60, 87, 91, 100; from spirit of world, 116; from flesh, 129
Delusion, 74, 159, 181, 184, 193, 205
Despair, 139, 173; penitential, 88
Destiny, sense of, 7f.
Devil, 43, 71, 160, 183, 191; devils, 58, 60, 106f.
Devotions, 6f., 21
Diligence, 119, 130
Direct Witness. (See Holy Spirit.)
Discernment, spiritual, 41, 100, 117
Discipline, 5ff., 17, 124, 170, 207, 211

INDEX OF SUBJECTS

Divinity, 55, 82, 185, 212. (See Theology.)
Doctrine, Methodist, 3, 11, 65f., 71, 72, 82f., 93, 157f., 164, 173f., 186ff., 197; a new, 9, 26f., 45f., 53ff., 186; of Spirit's witness, 13f., 111ff., 121ff., 149; of salvation by faith, 18, 26, 53ff., 71, 198; Moravian, 20ff., 26ff., 32ff., 41, 56ff.; of assurance, 43, 53, 59f., 61ff., 72ff., 91ff., 149, 164f., 173, 186ff., 189ff.; Wesley's, 13f., 43, 53ff., 61ff., 72ff., 82f., 95f., 100ff., 105f., 109, 111ff., 121ff., 128ff., 133ff., 139, 141, 149, 164ff., 179f., 189ff.; Anglican, 58, 185ff., 189ff. (See further aspects under separate headings.)
Dogma, 70, 97, 163, 189, 212
Doubt, 4, 14, 16f., 32, 34ff., 43f., 63f., 66, 70, 74, 77f., 84, 87, 107f., 129, 131, 137, 139, 144, 150, 153, 156, 167ff., 172, 186, 199, 201f., 213
Duty, 79, 107, 118, 122

EARNEST OF THE SPIRIT, 137, 151, 155, 194
Ecstasy, 207
Election, 86, 158; doctrine of, 167, 169f., 195
Emmaus, 139f.
Emotions, 44f., 49, 164, 181ff., 217
Empiricism, 213ff.
Enemies, 24, 38
England, 23ff., 31, 37f., 41, 54, 82, 171, 203, 207, 212
English, language, 41, 83; temperament, 180
Enlightenment, 28, 39, 55, 153, 160, 193; the, 215. (See Illumination.)
Enthusiasm, 21, 69, 99, 166, 180ff., 185, 191, 193, 196, 204, 215
Enjoyment, of God, 130f.
Epworth Rectory, 8, 80, 211; Fire of, 7
Error, 86, 106, 108, 202f.
"Esse est percipi", 213
Eternal, salvation, 128, 170; inheritance, 191, 194
Eternity, 16, 107, 124, 130
Ethics, 124f.
Evangelism, 29, 72, 81, 82, 86, 207
Evidence, 57, 69, 75, 78ff., 84, 105, 115, 117, 119, 123f., 127, 128ff., 137, 164, 206, 210, 214
Evil, 106f., 116, 174
Evolution, 173, 212
Excesses, individual, 49, 98, 183, 204f.; drunkenness, etc., 156
Existence, of God, 35, 131, 218; of reality, 208; of external world, 213, 218. (See Being.)
Experience, 3ff., 15, 17ff., 25ff., 29f., 33ff., 39f., 43ff., 53ff., 59f., 62, 64f., 67f., 72, 74, 77, 79ff., 84, 86, 89f., 92f., 96f., 99f., 102, 106, 108, 113, 115, 118ff., 124f., 135ff., 139ff., 149, 153, 155, 157, 160ff., 163ff., 168, 173f., 179, 183, 187, 190, 196f., 198, 201, 204, 207ff., 210f., 213ff. (See also separate headings.)
Externalism, 157ff., 162f.
Extravagance, 99, 180, 204, 206

FACT, 68, 74, 109, 136f., 140, 204, 210, 213, 217
Faith, 4, 9f., 12, 14, 16f., 20ff., 24f., 31ff., 41ff., 53ff., 61ff., 65ff., 72, 77ff., 81, 84, 89, 91, 96, 101, 106, 110, 113, 115, 119, 122f., 125f., 128ff., 133f., 136, 141, 149ff., 158, 163ff., 171f., 182, 189, 191ff., 198ff., 206, 210, 214f.; assurance of, 128ff., 133f., 149
Faithful, the, 154, 169, 171, 193
Faithfulness, 16, 80, 95, 122
Fasting, 46, 200
Fathers, the Early, 105, 109, 123, 149ff., 157
Favour of God, 28, 46, 63, 65, 70, 81, 91f., 129, 131, 153, 164ff., 194
Fear, 12, 16, 21, 29, 32, 34f., 42, 45, 49, 62, 64, 70, 77f., 84, 96f., 112f., 118f., 129, 131, 143, 152f., 186, 199, 201f.
Fear of God, 16, 70f., 81, 86, 97
Fearlessness, 96, 141, 164
Feeling, 24, 27, 29, 32f., 34f., 37, 41ff., 49, 58, 66, 80, 87, 89, 92ff., 112, 115, 158, 162, 164f., 172, 174, 180ff., 191ff., 204, 206, 208ff., 211. (See Sense, Emotions, Postscript.)
Fellowship with God, 124, 131, 209; corporate, 49, 139, 210
Fetter Lane, 198ff., 201
Fiducia, 158, 165
Firmness, 95, 110, 159, 164, 169

GENTLENESS, 23, 80, 122
Georgia, 7, 8, 14f., 20ff., 37, 40f., 54, 57, 83, 203
German language, 20, 82f.; hymns, 29, 82; mystics, 207; people, 55; country, 31ff., 203; Pietism, 166
Gifts of God, 42, 53, 73, 79, 116f., 150, 153, 199f.; of Charity, 190; of Tongues, 141; of Grace, 190, 199; of Assurance, 168f.; of Holy Ghost, 61, 116, 123, 134, 139, 144, 151ff., 184, 189f., 194f., 215
Gloom, 62, 90, 172
Gnosticism, 124, 152
God, of Heaven, 66; Things of, 74, 78, 108, 128, 153, 208; Face of, 91; of Truth, 106; of Love, 83; Lord of Life,

God—*cont.*
167; Maker, 94; Giver, 153; Grace of, 84; In Jesus, 108; His Knowledge, 126; Cheerfulness towards, 164; Greatness of, 85; Most High, 174; In Individual Soul, 92, 155, 171ff., 185, 194f., 215; Power of, 85, 174; Contact with, 83, 162; Communion with, 124, 131, 135, 174, 209; Mystic Union with, 204, 207f.; Knowledge of, 93, 125, 164, 218; Faith in, 57; Goodness of, 87, 93, 189, 193; The Father, 36, 49, 87, 95, 107, 111ff., 134, 139, 151, 153ff., 162, 168; Triune, 154, 174.
Godliness, 155, 168
Goodness. (See Holiness.)
Gospel, the 13, 44, 60, 65, 97, 118, 136, 143, 179, 191; a new, 27, 53ff., 185f.
Grace, 12, 16f., 55, 79, 84, 91, 93, 97ff., 121ff., 130, 151ff., 158, 160, 164f., 174, 190f.; the means of, 23, 54, 198f., 200ff., 207
'Grace Abounding', 86
Graces, Christian, 80, 193, 210
Growth of Assurance, 33, 36, 64
Guarantee, 199f., 209; of Scriptural Truth, 165f.; of Inner Certainty, 210
Guidance through Scriptures, 106
Guilt, 43, 45f., 48f., 58, 84, 91

HANDS, LAYING ON OF, 194
Happiness, 28f., 63, 85, 97f.
Healing, 42, 17ff.
Heathen, 13, 16, 60
Heaven, 87, 96f., 98, 101, 172
Heirs of God. (See Inheritance.)
Hell, 84, 107, 118; child of, 87
Hellenism, 124
Heresy, 169, 185f., 197, 209; Irenæus against, 151f.
Herrnhut, 24, 31, 33f., 202
Holiness, 5f., 14, 19, 28f., 65, 74, 77, 79, 86, 101, 113, 121f., 135, 152, 155, 172. (See Righteousness.)
Holy Club, 7, 17, 39f., 105
Holy Communion, 6, 12, 23, 32, 34, 36, 49f., 98, 159, 198; Hymns on, 93, 98
Holy Spirit, 12, 42, 89; Personality of, 111; Rule of, in Church, 190; in individual, 190ff., The light of, 160, 173f., 189; Identified with Christ, 143f., 155, 162; Fruit of, 16, 34, 47, 69, 79f., 100, 121ff., 153, 155, 203, 205, 210; Indwelling of, 100, 117, 123, 150f., 153f., 174, 190f., 195; Seal of, 17, 46, 48, 93, 96, 137, 140, 155, 191, 194, 196; Witness of, 11ff., 17, 22, 28, 32ff., 36f., 39, 43, 46f., 57, 59, 61, 63f., 66, 68, 72, 78, 83, 91,

136, 149, 160ff., 165f., 168f., 171, 174, 181, 185, 187f., 190, 199, 203ff., 210f., 215; Leading of, 13, 35, 112, 122, 153; Sermons on, 72, 106f., 111f., 121f., 131, 134
Homilies, 187f., 190f., 197
Hope, 36, 41f., 63, 65, 70
Humility, 12, 20, 23f., 74, 99, 118, 190
Hussites, 160
Hymns, 29, 40, 42; Methodist, 48, 82ff., 91ff., 200, 207; St Bernard's, 161f., 208

IDEALISM, 213ff.
Ignorance, 39, 41, 62f., 65, 70, 180, 187f.
Illumination, 29, 31, 39, 46, 90, 92, 142, 152, 163, 174, 180, 207. (See Enlightenment, Light.)
Imagination, 64, 72, 153, 181, 184, 196, 200
Immediacy, of assurance, 68, 79, 113 159, 164, 172f., 184, 208f.; of knowledge, 211
Impression, on the soul, 74, 79, 115; on the mind, 213
Incarnation, 114, 120, 175
Indirect Witness, 76, 79, 100, 119, 121ff., 135, 155, 172, 205, 209
Individualism, 65, 93, 100, 157, 159, 163, 175, 185, 204f., 209, 213. (See Personal.)
Indwelling, of Christ, 122, 174, 199; of Holy Spirit. (See Holy Spirit.)
Ineffability, 205, 208, 211, 217
Infallibility, of Assurance, 64, 170, 172f., 210; of Scripture, 106, 108, 163, 165; of the Pope, 163; of Experience, 174, 209
Inheritance, 96, 113f., 137, 151, 155, 191, 194
Inner sense, or feeling, 12, 24, 63, 76, 80, 83, 85, 91, 115, 136f., 141, 144, 153, 155, 159f., 172, 182, 193, 208ff., 213, 215f.
Inspiration, 65, 79, 91, 95, 106, 115, 173, 184, 190, 194
Instantaneousness, 28, 32ff., 45f., 57, 62ff., 113
Intellect, 9, 16, 18, 32, 54ff., 60, 78, 124, 135, 143, 153ff., 160, 166, 174, 184f., 211f., 213f., 216f. (See Reason.)
Intention, Divine, 41; of not sinning, 159
Intercession, 45, 91, 193
Introspection, 49, 78, 216
Intuition, 75, 86, 136, 208; moral, 179
Irrationalism, 215
Irreligion, 188
Isolation, 205, 209

INDEX OF SUBJECTS

Joy, 12, 16, 28, 32, 36, 40, 42f., 44f., 47, 58, 64, 73f., 80, 84, 87, 90, 95, 97, 122, 141, 151, 159, 164, 172f., 190, 196, 200, 202f.
Judgement, 109, 126; individual, 157; moral, 169; by written word, 174f.; a right, 190
Justification, 10, 14, 18, 20, 25, 32f., 44, 47, 53f., 58f., 61, 63, 66, 72, 79, 89, 95, 115, 117, 129, 150, 159, 163, 199, 202f.

Knowledge, 18f., 22, 33, 41, 43, 46, 48, 63, 66, 69, 71, 79f., 85, 87, 89, 91f., 96, 98f., 107, 113, 116f., 122ff., 131, 135ff., 150ff., 160, 162ff., 166, 168, 172ff., 180, 194f., 208, 211ff., 216ff.

Lambeth Articles, 171
Law, the, 14, 27, 57, 105, 113, 122; of God, 124, 202f., 206; of sin and death, 60, 87
'Legal Night', 87f.
Life, Christian, 57, 79f., 138ff., 143, 209; Eternal, 13f., 30, 39, 129, 137, 140, 194f., 209; in Christ, 75, 83, 87, 92f., 95, 99, 143f., 154ff.; of Christ, 60, 73, 101, 119, 125, 168; of Faith, 58; New, 10, 77, 84, 92
Light, 28, 66, 74, 87, 90, 96, 150, 152f., 172; of God's spirit, 174, 196, 206; inner, 162, 173f., 204, 209
Lincoln College, 26, 40, 108
Living witnesses, 29, 31, 57
Lloyd's Evening Post, 78, 115, 119, 134, 187, 195
Logic, 204, 212f.
London, 25, 27, 29, 37, 39, 57, 198f., 202
Longsuffering, 79, 122
Lord's Supper. (See Holy Communion.)
Lord, the, 89, 94, 124, 141, 144, 155, 167, 198
Love, 13, 16, 19ff., 30, 33, 38f., 41, 43ff., 53, 58, 60, 63, 65, 67f., 73f., 78f., 83, 88, 94, 96, 99, 101, 113, 115, 118, 121f., 124, 127f., 130, 135, 137, 141, 143, 150f., 159, 162, 164, 169, 172, 189, 193, 199, 209, 217
Lutheranism, 25, 54, 171. (See Luther in Index of Names.)

Madness, religious. (See Enthusiasm).
Manifestation, divine, 44, 58, 64, 73, 111ff., 119, 195f. (See Revelation.)
Marienborn, 31f., 37f.

Marks, of child of God, 122, 125f., of Spirit, 142; of mystic experience, 205, 209f.
Marriage, 7, 23, 85
Martyrs, 150f.
Materialism, 73, 213, 217
Means of grace, 198f., 200, 202, 204, 206f
Mediation, 79, 193; ecclesiastical, 163; of Witness to believer, 75
Meekness, 20f., 38, 80, 122, 193
Mercy, 36, 43ff., 48, 69, 84, 89, 126, 150, 190; works of, 205
Merit, 55, 166
Merits of Christ, 58, 60, 63, 92, 94, 194
Metaphysics, 217f.
Methodism, Oxford, 17; American, 47, 108; and Moravianism, 20ff., 31ff., 53ff.; and Mysticism, 198ff., 204ff.; and Quakerism, 173f.
Methodist Conference, 63, 65, 67ff., 72, 115, 117, 141; doctrine (see Doctrine); Episcopal Church, 47, *Hymn Book* (see Hymns); Preachers (see Preaching) Revival, 17, 38, 78, 89, 97, 182
Methodists, early, 39ff., 90, 97. (See Heresy, Stillness, Enthusiasm.)
Mind. (See Intellect.)
Ministry, 9, 39, 132, 150, 186, 195. (See Wesley.)
Miracles, 62, 68, 142
Money, attitude towards, 8f., 47
Morality, 46, 79f., 108, 141, 158, 169, 179, 215
Moravianism, 12, 20ff., 31ff., 40ff., 53ff., 80, 83ff., 98f., 115, 129, 139, 160, 173, 186, 198ff., 204ff.
Mortification, 207
Mysteries of religion, 124, 179, 205, 217; Ambrose on, 155
Mysticism, 14, 53, 94, 99, 123ff., 144, 161, 198ff., 204ff., 210, 216

Natural Philosophy (Wesley's), 212
Nature, God's, 88, 91; divine within us, 92; human, 113, 116; 'the natural man', 117, 159; natural knowledge, 213, 217
Neighbourliness, 73, 122f.
New Birth, 125. (See Regeneration.)
New Commandment, 125
'New Doctrine.' (See Doctrine.)
'New faith', 43, 141.
'New Gospel.' (See Gospel.)
New Life, 11, 75, 77, 84, 100, 137, 141f. (See Renewal.)
New Testament, 27, 45, 106; Wesley's Notes on, 108; Assurance in. (See *Part Three*, 103ff.)
New Way, 183
Nicene Fathers, 149ff.

Night, legal, 87
'Noetic' quality, of mystic experience, 205, 210f.
Nonconformity, 172

OBEDIENCE, 63, 74, 123f., 127
Objectivity, 47f., 78, 136, 141, 161, 165, 175, 204, 210, 216
'Offensiveness', 5, 46f.
'Offices', church, 189f.
Old Testament, 106, 108, 124
Opinion, Plato, 124; various opinions, 169, 184
Opposition, 19, 24, 71
Ordinances, 199, 201, 204f.
Ordination. (See Charles and John Wesley.)
Orthodoxy, 166, 185ff.
Outward, testimony, 68, 123; marvels 141; signs 142; forms of religion, 173; works, 198, 201; ordinances of church, 205; fruit, 210
Oxford, 5, 7, 12, 17, 26, 39, 59, 61, 65, 105, 108, 141, 181, 194

PAPACY, 165f. (See Pope.)
Paraclete, 192
Pardon, 44, 65, 89, 91, 96, 100, 114, 130, 143, 155, 165f., 181
Passion of Christ, 46, 87, 93ff., 175
Passions, 114, 166, 181
Passivity, 205
Peace, 14, 16, 21, 24, 27, 32f., 34, 36, 41ff., 48, 58, 62, 64, 80, 88, 95, 98, 122, 129, 156, 169, 192, 201. (See Calm, Serenity.)
Penitence, 62, 88, 91, 159. (See Repentance.)
Pentecost, 11, 42, 139, 142, 144, 191
Perception, 64, 66, 68, 73, 77, 199, 208; *esse est percipi*, 213
Perfection, 5, 83, 86, 101, 107, 116, 123, 130, 132, 151, 190, 206
Permanency, of joy, 40, 64, 97; of assurance, 36, 62, 64, 137, 153; of witness, 92. (See Perseverance.)
Persecution, 46, 189
Perseverance, 13, 61, 77, 129, 130, 167
Personal nature of assurance, 47, 124, 131, 136f., 142, 163, 165, 189, 197; of salvation, 11, 33f., 41, 49, 58, 60, 88, 93, 115, 118, 141f., 145, 190, 206, 210; of religious experience, 96, 161, 163, 209, 211
Personal faith in Christ, 57, 60, 78, 115, 136; knowledge of God, 163f.
Personality of Christ, 136, 144f.; of Holy Spirit, 111, 116, 144, 189; human, 47, 204
Persuasion, 125, 129, 136, 151, 162, 165, 172, 181

Philosophy, 124, 157, 179, 185, 204, 210ff.
Pietism, 25, 29, 166, 207
Piety, 39, 205. (See Holiness.)
Pioneers, 47, 139
Plainness, 38, 205, 212, 214
Plerophory, 64, 70, 78, 128ff. (See Degrees.)
Politics, 171, 180
Pope, 160, 163, 165
Possession by Christ, 84f., 88; by God, 92; of God, by believer, 195
Power, 31ff., 36f., 49, 59, 74, 81, 83, 88f., 91, 100, 113, 122, 135, 137, 139, 141ff., 153, 161, 174, 182, 191, 193.
Practice, 53, 82, 86, 106, 123f., 161, 203
Praise, 71, 94, 154f., 190
Prayer, 6, 17, 22, 42, 45, 47f., 53, 62, 85f., 88, 112, 115, 129, 153, 186, 189, 194, 200f.
Prayer Book, 74, 187, 197
Preaching, 4, 9, 13, 17, 19f., 26, 30, 39, 43ff., 48, 55, 61, 65, 71ff., 75, 77, 105, 108, 118, 122, 141, 150, 181f., 186, 191, 194, 201
Predestination, 167
Presence, of Holy Spirit, 74, 193; of God, 98f., 107, 141, 155, 161, 174; of Christ, 141, 162, 175; 'a special', 182
Present nature of assurance, 58, 62, 77, 92, 130, 137, 150, 167, 169, 173, 175, 181, 186, 189
Presumption, 74, 76, 79, 181
Pride, 20, 24, 86, 181, 205
Priesthood, 40, 160, 194. (see clergy); of Christ, 131
Prison, 8, 26, 87, 100
Privilege, Christian, 61, 73, 77, 81, 95, 159, 169, 173, 181, 186
Promise, Divine, 12, 30, 70, 95, 137, 139, 151, 165, 172, 186, 192, 194f.
Proof, 16, 22, 24, 32, 68, 75, 100, 109, 113, 119, 122f., 126, 128, 136, 155, 167, 186, 206, 209f., 212, 217
Propitiation, 49
Protestantism, 161, 163, 166, 195
Psalms, 40, 82, 108
Psychology, 44, 48f., 80, 211, 216
Purgation, 101, 207
Puritanism, 172f., 180
Purity, 6, 67, 90, 101, 136, 150, 153, 159, 189, 201. (See Sanctification, Holiness.)

QUAKERISM, 173f.
Quest, for Assurance, 12, 37, 39, 41, 53, 57, 81, 129; for Holiness, 6; for Union with God, 151
Quickening, 116, 143, 191
Quietism, 80, 99, 198, 206. (See Stillness.)

INDEX OF SUBJECTS

RATIONALISM, 185, 188, 213
Reality, 25, 40, 74, 86, 131, 137, 141, 175, 188, 209, 213, 215, 217
Reason, 16, 64f., 68, 73, 76, 78, 80, 119, 123f., 153, 163, 172, 174, 179, 184, 209, 212, 215. (See Intellect, Rationalism.)
Receptivity, human, 79
Reconciliation, 28, 33f., 36, 62f., 65, 70, 76, 96, 130, 164, 194
Redemption, 46, 53f., 60, 63, 84, 95f., 100, 113, 129, 139, 154, 175, 206
Reformation, 105, 157, 160f., 163ff., 171, 187, 196
Regeneration, 12f., 28, 40, 63, 74, 77, 92, 95, 114, 123, 154, 190f., 193, 201
Rejoicing, in God, 63, 73f., 121; in comfort of Spirit, 190; in faith, 192. (See Joy.)
Relationship, with God, 153, 163. (See Fellowship, Communion.)
Reliance, on Christ's Blood, 60; upon God, 118
Religion, 6, 46, 63, 80, 82, 86, 101, 114, 124, 141f., 144, 154, 157, 161, 171, 173, 179, 184, 204ff., 210, 212, 215f., 218
Remission of sins, 34f., 37, 153, 171, 192, 195
Renewal, 84, 101, 139, 155, 189, 195, 199, 201
Repentance, 12, 63, 74, 151, 206
Rest, 14, 35f., 42, 46, 63, 84, 91, 129, 155, 167, 169. (Cf. Peace.)
Restlessness, 14, 35, 39, 49, 155
Resurrection, 60, 109, 137, 139, 142f., 150, 191
Revelation, 24, 27, 40, 65, 69, 90, 92, 106, 108, 130, 136, 140, 153, 158f., 162, 164, 165, 167, 179, 182, 190f., 194, 212
Reverence, 118, 204
Revised Version, 110f., 112, 116, 122, 125, 128, 130, 132
Revivals, 141, 207
Righteousness, 20, 28, 32, 65, 70f., 77, 81, 88, 123, 167, 192, 203 (See Holiness).
Rights of sonship, 112f.; of the individual, 162
Roman Catholicism, 54, 157ff., 163, 167

SACRAMENTS, 154, 157, 159, 198. (See separate headings.)
Sacrifice, in service, 47, 56, 142; of Christ. (See Galatians 2²⁰.)
Saintliness, 6f, 130
Saints, the 132, 161
Salvation, 9, 11, 12, 18, 21, 26, 32, 41, 46, 53, 56f., 59, 61f., 63, 65, 69f., 71, 78, 81, 88, 92, 95, 98, 101, 108, 115, 118, 124, 132, 136f., 141f., 143, 151f., 155, 157f., 165, 167, 169, 171, 181, 190, 192, 194, 197f., 201, 206, 209, 212, 216
Sanctification, 53, 89, 91, 116, 129, 191, 195
Satan, 74, 86, 160
Savannah, 22f., 40, 83, 198
Saviour, the, 21, 25, 39, 56, 58, 84f., 87f., 195
Scepticism, 215
Scholasticism, 160, 163, 166
Science, 157, 215, 217
Sea voyage (of Wesley), 20f., 23f., 54
Seal of the Spirit. (See Holy Spirit.)
Security, sense of, 80, 95, 109, 152, 166f., 181
Self-confidence, 166
Self-denial, 6, 8
Self-despair, 88
Self-distrust, 166
Self-effacement, 118
Self-examination, 24, 41
Self-knowledge, 22, 24f., 172
Sense (of certainty, pardon, etc.), 61, 65, 68, 72, 74, 77, 82f., 86, 91, 94, 96f., 114, 117, 124, 128, 134, 139, 141ff., 153, 155, 159, 162, 165, 172, 209, 215f. (See Feeling.)
Senses, the, 74, 98, 212, 214; spiritual, 77, 153, 211
Serenity, 44, 98, 129, 162
Seriousness, 20, 24, 32, 38, 40, 205
Sermons, 43, 59, 61f., 63, 72, 80, 194, 214
Service, 18, 20, 41, 47, 56, 71f., 95, 113, 142, 151, 154, 203, 205
Services (Church), 108, 183
'Sight' (spiritual) 63, 65, 72, 91, 100, 150, 152f.
Signs, 99, 112, 142, 168. (See Marks.)
Silence, 18, 99, 174, 199
Sin, 5f., 11f., 14f., 19, 21, 24, 28ff., 41ff., 54, 59ff., 67ff., 73f., 76, 84, 87, 94, 99ff., 107, 131, 151f., 154ff., 159, 168f., 171, 182, 186, 192ff., 198
Singing, 21, 40ff., 86f., 182
Son of God, 29f., 58, 63, 72f., 89, 93, 95, 113, 119, 130, 151, 153f., 162
Sorrow, 42, 49, 69ff., 84, 90, 159
Soul, the, 39, 43, 57f., 62, 67, 74f., 83, 88f., 92, 95, 107, 112, 115, 119, 123, 130, 151ff., 161ff., 166, 172ff., 196, 202f., 205ff., 211, 215
Spanish hymns, 82, 85
Speculative Thinking, 82, 86, 205, 211, 215
Speech, 38, 42, 84, 123, 126, 141, 153, 191, 193, 205. (See Tongues.)
Spirit. (For various aspects of God's Spirit and human spirit, see separate heads.)
Standards, Anglican, 187, 196, 210

Stillness, 99, 198ff., 204. (See quietism.)
Strength, 31, 43, 93, 142, 155, 190, 195
Subjectivity, 47, 99, 116, 119, 137, 163, 198, 205, 209, 216
Suffering, 47, 100, 138, 189
Supernatural, 63, 129, 143, 159, 164, 179, 185, 217
Surrender, 88, 101, 120

TEACHING, 9, 30, 46, 77ff., 91, 101, 109, 137, 143, 149, 153, 157ff., 163ff., 192, 200, 206, 209f., 213, 217
Temperament, 38, 62; the English, 180
Temple, 85, 92, 123, 151, 192. (See Church.)
Temptation, 61, 161
Terminology, 40, 60f., 65, 70, 74, 78, 83, 109, 128, 133, 137, 142ff., 149, 152, 161, 182, 186, 197, 201
Testament, Greek, 109f. (See Old and New.)
Testimony, 112f., 115f., 119f., 127, 131, 154, 162, 165, 168, 171, 173, 189, 195ff., 202, 209; divine, 74, 78, 93; of our own spirit, 73ff.; concurrent, 112, 134f.; of the early Methodists, 39ff., 90; of the ancient Fathers, 105, 149ff. (See Witness.)
Tests, 122, 125, 159, 173, 217
Theology, 4, 9f., 21, 26, 37, 40, 45, 53, 56, 82, 86, 91, 95, 101, 114, 155, 160, 164, 196, 214, 217. (See Doctrine.)
Theory, 53, 56, 212, 216. (See Speculative Thinking.)
Tongues, gift of, 141, 191. (See Speech.)
Translation, Biblical, 107, 111, 121ff., 133ff.; of hymns, 82f., 207
Trembling, 118, 181f.
Trinity, 154, 174
Trust, 11, 20, 28, 30, 57f., 60, 115, 131, 158, 194, 203
Truth, 26, 49, 55, 75, 86, 101, 106, 123, 125, 150ff., 157, 164f., 168, 189, 192, 209, 211, 215ff.

UNBELIEF, 9, 15f., 24, 26, 29f., 35ff., 41, 57, 90, 201
Uncertainty, 4, 32, 37, 41ff., 63f., 139, 155, 157ff., 166, 169

Understanding, 110, 123f., 131, 150, 155, 179, 191, 212, 214
Unhappiness, 28, 46
Union, mystic, 99, 124, 151, 153, 204, 207
Unity in Christ, 12, 143; of Faith, 27; Christian, 31; of Godhead, 35; between Moravians and Methodists, 203
University, 39, 59, 141, 171
Unseen, 69, 78, 128, 140, 212, 214
Utterance, 142, 191. (See Speech, Tongues.)

Virtue, 5f., 19
Visible world, the, 212, 214, 217
Visions, 42, 48, 140, 207
Voice of Christ, 42; of God, 83, 96, 99, 218; of the Spirit, 195; inward, 48, 68, 75, 79, 99, 156, 173

WAITING UPON GOD, 41, 58, 99, 115, 129, 174, 199
Weakness of faith, 31, 61, 88, 118, 201f.
Westminster Assembly, 172
Will of God, 107, 160; human, 160
Wisdom, 38, 107, 116, 121, 142, 153ff., 212
Witness, 27f., 31, 51; of the Church, 139
Word of God, 80, 107, 123, 142, 159, 165, 174, 191, 202. (See Bible.)
Words, inadequacy of, 73, 209
Work of God, 10, 28, 139, 165, 169, 174, 183; of Christ, 60, 137, 141, 175; of Early Church, 139; for God, 117, 118, 205. (See Witness.)
Works, 14, 20, 36, 41, 45, 53f., 56, 70f., 76, 81, 101, 117ff., 122ff., 160, 165, 181, 190, 192, 198, 200ff., 205, 210
World, the, 66f., 101, 116, 121, 125, 212, 217; Spiritual, 153, 211, 217
Worship, 21, 139, 154, 203, 216f.
Wrath of God, 67f., 111; child of, 87
'Wrestling Jacob' (hymn), 88, 91
Wroote, 7, 40

YOUTH, 49

ZEAL, 30, 80, 132, 191, 198

INDEX OF BIBLICAL REFERENCES

Genesis
32^{24-31}...88

Deuteronomy
$8^{2, 16}$...24

1 Kings
19^{12}...49

Psalms
39^{7}...42
40^{3}...42
74^{12}...108
84^{7}...31
104...82

Isaiah
8^{20}...27, 106
11^{9}...37
$40^{1, 2}$...42
42^{3}...22

Jeremiah
9^{24}...124
31^{34}...124

Habakkuk
2^{14}...37

Matthew
5^{6}...32
6^{44}...38
$7^{16, 20}$...69, 79, 122
8^{25}...24
9^{2}...48
12^{20}...22
$17^{1ff.}$...44
$25^{18, 25}$...30

Mark
2^{5}...48
$9^{2ff.}$...44
9^{24}...10, 29
16^{11}...139

Luke
1^{47}...40
4...109
5^{20}...48
6^{46}...125
6^{49}...24
7^{48}...48
8^{24}...24
$9^{28ff.}$...44
$14^{16ff.}$...98
22^{19}...201
24^{11}...139
24^{17}...139
24^{21}...139
$24^{26f.}$...143
24^{32}...140
$24^{45ff.}$...139, 143

John
General...125
$2^{24ff.}$...139
3^{16}...35
5^{36}...109
7^{17}...107
8^{38}...119
8^{47}...159
10^{25}...109
12^{13}...48
13^{10}...33
13^{34}...125
14^{1}...24
$14^{13f.}$...153
$14^{15ff.}$...125
14^{16}...145, 192f., 153
14^{17}...153
14^{26}...193
16...192
16^{7}...153
16^{12}...153
16^{13}...192f.
17^{3}...125
20^{22}...139

Acts
$1^{4f.}$...140
1^{8}...142f.
2...141
2^{3}...143
$2^{22-4, 32-9}$...143
2^{36}...143
2^{47}...143
3^{6}...42
3^{19}...73
4^{31}...142
5^{14}...143
5^{23}...109
9...138
10^{35}...71
12...87
14^{3}...109
14^{17}...109
17^{31}...109
$18^{24ff.}$...43

Romans
General...136
1^{16}...118
2^{15}...109
2^{29}...59
4^{7}...76
4^{21}...110
5...169
$5^{1ff.}$...60
5^{5}...14, 17, 32, 39, 63, 131, 200
6^{14}...33
8^{2}...60
8^{9}...152, 192
8^{11}...117
8^{12}...153
8^{14}...112, 122, 153
8^{15}...11, 44f., 63, 96, 111f., 116, 134, 152f., 193f.
8^{16}...11, 13, 17, 22, 28, 39, 43, 45f., 57, 63, 66, 68, 72, 75, 79, 91f., 95, 109, 111f., 116, 122f., 127, 134, 154, 162, 168, 172, 193ff.
$8^{26f.}$...193
8^{29}...153
$8^{38f.}$...137, 169
9^{1}...109
$13^{13f.}$...156
14^{5}...110
15^{5}...110
$15^{13, 19}$...142
17^{31}...109

1 Corinthians
2^{3}...118
2^{4}...142
$2^{9ff.}$...116ff., 153
3^{16}...192
4^{4}...117
4^{15}...122
8^{3}...164
$11^{24f.}$...201
13^{7}...65
15^{45}...144

2 Corinthians
1^{12}...121
1^{22}...137, 194
3^{17}...144
5^{4}...152
5^{5}...155
5^{19}...36, 63
7^{15}...118
9^{4}...128
11^{17}...128
$11^{23ff.}$...138
13...5, 63, 121

Galatians
General...56, 136, 203
1^{12}...65
2^{20}...42, 45, 49, 58ff., 63, 67, 73, 78, 115, 119, 128

4...95
4⁵...113
4⁶...45, 113, 152ff., 162, 168, 194
4⁷...113, 135, 154
4⁹...164
5²²...122, 125

Ephesians
1⁶...16
1¹²f....137, 194
1¹⁷f....153
2³...15
2⁸...55
3¹²...169
3¹⁶...142
4³⁰...137
4³²...63
5¹⁶...17
6⁵...118

Philippians
2⁵...54
2¹²...118

Colossians
2²...110, 131, 134
4⁵...17
4¹²...110

1 Thessalonians
1⁵...110
5³...109

1 Timothy
2²...24
3⁴...24

2 Timothy
1¹²...137, 196

Hebrews
General...131
3¹⁴...128
6¹¹...70, 110, 131, 134, 169
8¹⁰...63
10²²...16, 70, 110, 129, 131f., 134, 182
11¹...16, 78, 110, 128
11⁶...131, 168
11³⁶...110

James
1⁵...107
1⁶f....168
1²⁷...101

1 Peter
4¹⁴...192

2 Peter
1⁴...105

1 John
General...97, 119f., 123, 125, 136
2¹f....49
2³...123f.
2⁵...119, 123f.
2⁷ff....124
2²⁰...193
2²⁷...192f.
2²⁹...123f.
3⁴ff....124
3¹⁰...119
3¹⁴...123, 125
3¹⁶f....125
3¹⁸...123, 26
3¹⁹...119, 123, 125
3²⁰...125
3²⁴...119, 123, 127
4¹⁰...63
4¹³...123, 127
4¹⁷...119
4¹⁹...135
5¹...28
5²ff....119, 124
5¹⁰...28, 119
5¹⁸...28, 119, 124
5¹⁹...63, 124, 168
5²⁰...124, 168

www.ingramcontent.com/pod-product-compliance
Lightning Source LLC
Chambersburg PA
CBHW050438240426
43661CB00055B/2427